Beidh Tú Alright

About the Author/*Údar*

Joe McHugh is a Donegal man who started his career in education before entering politics in 1999. He has just completed 25 years as a full-time politician. He held six ministerial positions, culminating in his appointment as Minister for Education in 2018. Joe was at the helm during Covid-19 and was faced with difficult decisions around the 2020 Leaving Certificate. He was faced with many challenges during his time in political office, and none more so than the defective blocks issue in his home county. He took a stand on the issue and voted against his own government when legislation on the scheme was going through the Dáil.

Joe is an advocate for lifelong learning and a believer in the art of the possible. He has embraced the transition from politics by immersing himself in education once again. He is currently completing a MSc in Positive Health Coaching in the Royal College of Surgeons, and is pursuing a new career in coaching with a particular focus on group coaching. Joe's Irish language journey has given him the confidence to embrace a new life, and he hopes to become an advocate for change in people's lives. Learning Irish gave Joe a taste of three important principles: purpose, mastery and autonomy.

Joe lives in Dún Mór, Carraig Airt with his wife, Olwyn, and their three children, Darragh, Aedín agus Oisín. Spotty the cat also lives there, and they are down to two hens thanks to the madra rua!

Beidh Tú Alright

An Irish Language Journey

Joe McHugh

Published by
Red Stripe Press
Upper Floor, Unit B3
Hume Centre, Hume Avenue
Park West Industrial Estate
Dublin 12, Ireland

email: info@redstripepress.com
www.redstripepress.com

© Joe McHugh, 2025

Paperback ISBN 978-1-78605-198-1
ePub ISBN 978-1-78605-199-8

A catalogue record for this book is available from the British Library. All rights reserved. No part of this publication may be reproduced, stored in a retrieval system or transmitted in any form or by any means, electronic, mechanical, photocopying, recording or otherwise, without the prior, written permission of the publisher.

This book is sold subject to the condition that it shall not, by way of trade or otherwise, be lent, resold, hired out, or otherwise circulated without the publisher's prior consent in any form of binding or cover other than that in which it is published and without a similar condition including this condition being imposed on the subsequent purchaser.

Printed in Dublin by SPRINTBOOKS

To my wife, Olwyn, and my children, Darragh, Aedín & Oisín

Acknowledgements/ *Buíochas*

Olwyn, thank you for all your love and support no matter what the cause. You are on a busy project yourself now and I'm missing you. Absence does make the heart grow fonder. Darragh, thank you for the advice to stop making changes to the book. As you said yourself, 'ah sure look, you're going to have to stop sometime, aren't you?!' Aedín, thank you for helping me decide on the book cover. You can see this kind of stuff better than me. Oisín, thanks for reminding me to thank my editor for her patience in dealing with me. Thanks Eileen. And thank you Oisín for keeping my 'amygdala' in check during a very stressful time.

    A special thanks to Seán Ó Coisdealbha who kept me going when I was struggling with the book. GRMA a Sheáin for your help *agus comhluadar*! I have two Tír Eoghain men to thank. Thanks to Cathal Ó Manacháin who had the job of looking after the Gaeilge. You went above and beyond with your work, and I will always be grateful for the *cuidiú*. Secondly, thanks to Charles Dillon for keeping me right with the history behind the Irish names. Thank you Seosamh Ó Ceallaigh for giving me a steer on the deeper meaning behind the language. You also helped me develop my own thinking and connection with the language. GRMA a Sheosaimh. Thanks Ken Enright and Patricia McGuckin (big sis) for doing a final scan far too close to the deadline.

Apologies! Eimer Friel has kept me right on the Gaeilge front since 2014 so thanks Eimer for taking the time to read over the Gaeilge chapter. Thanks to An Brainse Logainmneacha sa Roinn Turasóireachta, Cultúir, Ealaíon, Gaeltachta, Spóirt agus Meán for their help with the Logainm entries – *go raibh míle maith agat*. To my eclectic array of readers at different times over the last four years, thank you for taking the time to read the book and I'm grateful for the feedback. These readers include Ofrit Liviatan, Greg Harkin, Mark O'Doherty, Ed Carty, Séamus Mac Giolla Chomhghaill, Micheál Ó hÉanaigh agus Liam Ó Cuinneagáin.

A special thanks to Michael Brennan and editor Eileen O'Brien from Red Stripe Press. Thanks also to Niamh Hatton, Deirdre Roberts and Gerry Kelly.

Thanks to everyone who helped me and supported me during my time in politics. Without that support I would never have got the phone call in July 2014. Thanks also to all the people who are helping me with my transition from politics to a new life. These include the 'Splash & Dashers' sea swimmers, my classmates at RCSI and the great and the good with whom I have been jogging, and who have kept me moving over the last decade or so. Thanks to all who have welcomed me into their world and encouraged me to try new things. Qi-gong, gym classes, yoga, cross-country running, adventure racing, stone wall building and learning to chill.

Thanks to my siblings, Patricia, Denise, James and Paul, for putting up with me over the years, and still do! A shout-out to all my wonderful nieces and nephews. You are all amazing. Thanks to all my sisters- and brothers-in-law. You are all amazing too! A special thanks to Tom and Rita for looking after me over the past 24 years. You have been good to me *gan dabht*.

Thanks Mum and Dad for keeping me on the straight and narrow, and investing so much of your life in me when I was younger. You supported me to be myself, always.

This book started out four years ago. It kept changing and evolving right up to the last edit. This is because I kept bumping into people who had something new to say. Thank you all for passing on your bits and bobs over the years. Thanks to Siobhán Ní Churraighín agus Liam Ó Cuinneagáin and all the team at Oideas Gael for opening their door and leaving it wide open for me. Thanks to all my teachers who imparted their knowledge both *istigh agus amuigh* the classroom. Thanks to Breandán Delap for leading a wonderful and memorable class/expedition traversing Sliabh Liag and ending in 'Port'. Thank you Enda for the start. My curiosity is '*beo*' with the sound of the Irish language.

Foreword/*Brollach*

Learning a new language is never an easy task. Relearning an old language is equally challenging, even more so when the learner is exposed to the full glare of public scrutiny in the Dáil chamber, in community engagements or in broadcast studios. That was Joe McHugh's fate when his promotion to the position of Minister of State in 2014 saw him take responsibility for Gaeltacht and Irish language issues which required him to reacquaint himself with our national language.

Cé gur rugadh agus gur tógadh é gar don Ghaeltacht admhaíonn sé féin gur beag cumas Gaeilge a bhí ann faoin am go bhfuair sé ardú céime ó Thaoiseach na linne sin, Enda Kenny. Bhí air dul ar 'aistear teanga' le go mbeadh sé in ann dualgais a cheapacháin a chomhlíonadh trí Ghaeilge.

I hope that Joe McHugh's account of his personal language odyssey will encourage others to undertake their own *aistear teanga* – language journey. I suspect that very many Irish people actually have far more understanding of Irish than they immediately realise and that while it may be buried somewhere in the recesses of the mind it may not prove too difficult to unlock. For many too, it may well be a matter of *muinín* – confidence – or an unrealistic fear of the embarrassment of making mistakes.

The discourse in relation to Irish has changed significantly over the past 20 or 30 years from an often negative perception of Irish as a 'dead language' to a much more tolerant and positive one as it moved effortlessly into the digital age, bringing with it a myriad of new opportunities.

The evidence is clear that our ancient native tongue is very much alive and kicking, forging new spaces for itself in our modern world. TG4 has played a significant part in changing hearts and minds and presenting the language in daily use with a creativity and vibrancy heretofore unimagined.

But we must not become complacent that our national language is safe and free from all threat. On the contrary, while the most recent census data published in May 2023 showed an increase in the number of people here who indicated they had Irish, the same data confirmed that the number of daily speakers of Irish in the Gaeltacht had fallen for the second successive census.

For many, this suggests an existential crisis for Irish as a community language. Keeping Irish as the dominant language in the Gaeltacht may in fact be much more difficult than previously conceived but it is a challenge from which we must not shy away. The second great challenge is to encourage a significant number of the 1.9 million people who indicated in the 2022 census that they have Irish to become active daily users of the language.

For those who set out on their own language journeys, I believe they will find nothing but wholehearted support and encouragement from all Irish speakers who are concerned for the future of the language. Beidh fáilte *mhór romhaibh mar chuid de phobal na teanga.*

Michael D. Higgins
Uachtarán na hÉireann
President of Ireland

Contents/*Clár*

About the Author/*Údar*. ii
Acknowledgements/*Buíochas* vi
Foreword/*Brollach*. ix
Focal Uaimse – A word from myself – An Ghaeilge xvii
Réamhrá. 1
    Oscail na fuinneoga agus na doirse
    The windows and the doors open
Caibidil 1 4
    Má theastaíonn uait aithne a chur orm, mair i mo theannta
    If you want to get to know me, live with me
Caibidil 2 10
    An rúd nach maraíonn thú déanann sé níos láidre thú
    The thing that doesn't kill you makes you stronger
Caibidil 3 17
    Mol an óige is tiocfaidh sí
    Praise the youth and they will flourish
Caibidil 4 22
    Ní mar sin a bheadh sé
    It was not to be
Caibidil 5 27
    Tús maith leath na hoibre
    A good start is half the work

Caibidil 6 33
    Éist le ceol na habhann agus gheobhair breac
    Listen to the music of the river and you'll catch a trout

Caibidil 7 43
    Bainis an ghortáin fataí agus scadáin
    The miser's wedding is potatoes and herrings

Caibidil 8 53
    Is fusa rud a rá ná a dhéanamh
    It is easier said than done

Caibidil 9 59
    Cé ná bíonn aon chnámh sa teanga, is minic a bhrís sí ceann duine
    Even though the tongue is not a bone, it can often break a person's head

Caibidil 10 67
    Is beag le rá an chuileog nó go dtéann sí sa tsúil
    A fly is a small thing until it gets in one's eye

Caibidil 11 75
    Ní bhíonn saoi gan locht
    Nobody's perfect

Caibidil 12 83
    Bíonn báisteach uafásach san fhásrach
    Rain is terrible in the desert

Caibidil 13 88
    Fásann níos mó i ngarraí ná a chuirtear ann
    More grows in a garden than is planted there

Caibidil 14 94
    Ná déan aon rud san oíche a mbeidh aiféala ort ar maidin faoi
    Don't do anything at night that you will regret in the morning

Caibidil 15 102
    Ar scáth a chéile a mhaireann na daoine
    We live in each other's shadows

Caibidil 16 108
   Bíonn dhá insint ar gach scéal
   There are two sides to every story

Caibidil 17 117
   Rotha Mór an tSaoil
   The Big Wheel of Life

Caibidil 18 124
   Aithníonn ciaróg ciaróg eile
   It takes one to know one

Caibidil 19 137
   Is fearr lúbadh ná briseadh
   It's better to bend than break

Caibidil 20 143
   Níl bua gan dua
   No pain, no gain

Caibidil 21 150
   Tír gan teanga, tír gan anam
   A country without a language is a country without a soul

Caibidil 22 155
   Téann focail le gaoth
   Words are like the wind

Caibidil 23 161
   Níl eagla ar an mac tíre roimh an ngadhar a bhíonn ag tafann
   The wolf does not fear the barking dog

Caibidil 24 166
   Nach tapa a imíonn an t-am nuair a bhíonn tú ag spraoi
   Time flies when you're having fun

Caibidil 25 173
   As an obair a fhaightear an fhoghlaim
   Learning is gotten through work – don't make your work a drudgery though!

Caibidil 26 181
    Briseann an dúchas trí shúile an chait
    Nature breaks through the eyes of the cat

Caibidil 27 189
    Ní neart go cur le chéile
    There is no strength without unity

Caibidil 28 196
    An t-eolas a mhúineadh do dhuine
    To show someone the way

Caibidil 29 200
    Is fearr go mall ná go díreach ag an am ceart
    You're better late than dead on time (Better late than never)

Caibidil 30 205
    Ní mar a shíltear a bhítear
    All is not what it seems

Caibidil 31 210
    Níl aon tinteán mar do thinteán féin
    There's no place like home (Or there's no hearth/fire like your own hearth/fire)

Caibidil 32 214
    Leanfaidh muid ar aghaidh le chéile
    We will follow each other forward together

Caibidil 33 221
    Fhad is a bheas an mhéar ag sileadh bíonn an teanga ag moladh
    While the hand is giving the tongue is praising

Cabidil 34 226
    Maireann croí éadrom i bhfad
    A light heart lives long

Caibidil 35 231
    An bairille a mbíonn an fíon ann fanann cuid de sna cláir
    The barrel that has the wine in it, some of it will remain in the boards

Caibidil 36 238
   Is maith an scéalaí an aimsir
   Time is a good storyteller

Caibidil 37 244
   Mair, a chapaill, agus gheobhaidh tú féar
   Live horse and you will get grass

Caibidil 38 249
   Teachtaireacht fá choinne an diaspóra
   Message for the diaspora

Caibidil 39 255
   Deir siad go bhfuil an fhírinne searbh, ní searbh atá sí, ach garbh!
   It is said that the truth is bitter, it's not bitter, but rough!

Caibidil 40 259
   Mol an lá um thráthnóna
   Praise the day in the evening

Seven Steps to Speaking Gaeilge Fluently **267**

Céim a haon – Step 1 269
   Céim ar chéim
   Step by step

Céim a dó – Step 2 273
   Tiocfaidh an fhírinne amach ar deireadh
   The truth comes out in the end

Céim a trí – Step 3 276
   An té a bhfuil builín aige gheobhaidh sé scian a ghearrfaidh é
   Whoever has a loaf will get a knife to cut it

Céim a ceathair – Step 4 278
   Is fanách an áit a bhaighfeá gliomach
   It's rare the place you'll find lobsters

Céim a cúig – Step 5 281
   Seachnaíonn súil ní nach bhfeiceann
   The eye avoids what it doesn't see

Céim a sé – Step 6 285
    Ní hé lá na báistí, lá na bpáistí
    The rainy day isn't the children's day
Céim a seacht – Step 7 288
    Bíonn súil leis an bhfarraige
    There's hope with the sea [Hope springs eternal]
General note regarding Logainm.ie 291
Appendix/*Aguisín* 293
    My 11-a-Side Football Team

Focal Uaimse – A word from myself – An Ghaeilge

Let me introduce myself

Is mise an Ghaeilge	*I am the Irish*
Is mise do theanga	*I am your language*
Is mise do chultúr	*I am your culture*
D'úsáid na filí mé	*The poets used me*
D'úsáid na huaisle mé	*The nobility used me*
D'úsáid na daoine mé	*The people used me*
D'úsáid na leanaí mé	*The children used me*
Nach iad a bhí bródúil	*How proud they were*
Mo réim a bhí ann	*It was my regime*
Ach tháinig an strainséir	*But the stranger came*
Chuir sé faoi <u>chois</u> mé	*Put me under the <u>cosh</u>*
Is rud ní ba mheasa	*The worst thing was*
Níor mhaith le mo chlann mé	*My family didn't like me*
Anois táim lag	*Now I am weak*
Anois táim tréith	*Now I am tired*
Ach fós táim libh	*But I am still with you*
Is mairfidh mé	*And I will survive*
Croch suas mo cheann	*Lift up my head*

Beidh Tú Alright: *Focal Uaimse – A word from myself – An Ghaeilge*

Cuir áthas ar mo chroí   *Make my heart happy*
Labhraígí mé   *Speak me*
Ó labhraígí mé   *Oh speak me*

(Author unknown: *Tá an t-amhrán á scaipeadh le ar a laghad 50 bliain gan ainm luaite leis. Á scaipeadh go forleathan i measc foghlaimeoirí, agus tírghráthróirí i Meiriceá go háirithe.*

The song has been circulating for at least 50 years without a name being attributed to it. It's been widely circulated among learners, and patriots in America in particular.)

Now that I've introduced myself, let me tell you a little more about me, the Gaeilge. I want to let you know how I feel about things and give you an insight into my hopes and where I see my place in the world. This story doesn't have an ending. That's where you come in. You oversee my destiny. You will decide my future. No pressure, eh! Where there is life there is hope and I will continue to live strong in both the Gaeilge and the English vernacular. Yes, I have had my battles. They tried changing me without my permission. I could be cross and upset about this and seek my revenge. Where would that get me though? There are enough battles going on in the world without me joining in the madness. All I ask of you, is to look at me with a sense of curiosity and fascination. And try not to look back in anger!

Réamhrá

Oscail na fuinneoga agus na doirse

The windows and the doors open

Following my appointment as a government minister to the Department of the Gaeltacht and the Islands in July 2014, I was immediately faced with many challenges. While it was undoubtedly a cause for celebration, it was nonetheless the hardest moment of my political career and at the time a difficult time personally. The then Taoiseach, Enda Kenny, had appointed me to a ministerial role with responsibility for the Gaeltacht, the Islands and the Irish language. An element within the Irish-speaking community smelt blood. '*Aire gan teanga, Aire gan clue*' – a minister without the language is a minister without a clue – they chanted outside Government Buildings. It was an understandable concern. However, balanced with my detractors were the many people who supported me and believed in my ability to to the challenge. Their support was critical in encouraging vating me to plough ahead on my journey. So, I invite

Beidh Tú Alright: *Oscail na fuinneoga agus na doirse*

into my world in those early hours, days, weeks, months, and years following my appointment. I went from a very dark and lonely place to embark on a journey of discovery that ultimately led to both a newfound love for the Irish language and an incredible opportunity to speak fluently in my native tongue. Now, as I reflect on the last ten years, two things come to mind. Where did those ten years go? And, secondly, if I was to do it all again, I wouldn't change a thing.

This personal journey – which started in the Gaeltacht Department and meandered to wonderful places like Milwaukee, Bere Island and Gleann Cholm Cille – is a reflection of and insight into language learning opportunities in various departments, which culminated in my appointment to a senior Cabinet role in Government as Minister for Education and Skills.

You may ask why I wrote this memoir. Something stirred within me and, putting it simply, I wanted to articulate and map my own journey. In doing this, I discovered it was more than that – it made me appreciate the value of the Irish language and how sharing that journey might inspire others to discover it. As a fluent Irish speaker now (who still struggles with the grammar, by the way), I want to impart the lessons I learned, which I hope can help other people trying to relearn Gaeilge and those learning for the first time. As the Kerryman said to the American tourist who asked for directions, '*I wouldn't start from here*'!

I delve into the main enablers which assisted my language journey. Place and history became key drivers in whetting my curiosity to learn more. W the English name of *Maam Cross* in Galway changed fr - Burnt House? Where is the 'big ring fort' that gave n townland of *Dún Mór* – Dunmore? The Irish g relevant to me for the first time. I learned too n just a communication tool. It is a gateway to t gave me a deeper understanding of people t a deeper understanding of my own place haps!

The opportunity to learn Irish properly for the first time changed my life. I want to tell my story in the hope that it will inspire more people to embark on a similar journey of discovery and enrichment. The Irish language is all around us and through broadcasting, social media and film it is becoming ever more visible and accessible. Colm Bairéad's *An Cailín Ciúin* (based on Claire Keegan's short story *Foster*), Seán Breathnach's *Foscadh* (based on Donal Ryan's novel *The Thing about December*) and *Arracht* (written and directed by Tomás Ó Súilleabháin) are but three examples of the recent revolution in Irish-language cinema. You can also add crime drama *Crá* to the list. And Belfast-based hip hop band Kneecap may be controversial, but their impact on the Irish language is undeniable. I want to challenge current policy makers so that they can look at new ways of making the Irish language journey more relevant and enjoyable.

'Sure, you were a senior policy maker yourself, Joe!', you may say. I was indeed, and I am confident that the Scéim Aitheantais Scoileanna Gaeltachta[1] policy initiative that I facilitated in the Department of Education in 2015 will provide a solid foundation for future policy initiatives. The fruits of the labour were evident at a public ceremony in Amharclann Gaoth Dobhair a few weeks back. The CLIL (Content and Language Integrated Learning) pilot that I initiated in 2019, which aims to teach Irish through PE, is another attempt to make the teaching of Irish both relevant and fun in the time ahead. The answer to the question 'How do you eat an elephant?' comes to mind here: *céim ar chéim* – bit by bit/step by step.

---

[1] Scéim Aitheantas Scoileanna Gaeltachta (Gaeltacht School Recognition Scheme) was launched by Richard Bruton TD in 2018. An Comhairle um Oideachas Gaeltachta agus Gaelscolaíochta (COGG) plays a key role in the development and implementation of this policy.

Caibidil 1

Má theastaíonn uait aithne a chur orm, mair i mo theannta

If you want to get to know me, live with me

Gathering empirical data on the intricacies of my development can be as clear as mud at times. My influence on the development of the English language in the United States is certainly worth some more consideration. Jazz music is something we associate with the United States. Did the word 'jazz' come from 'deas' – nice? Indeed, it did, which I know you won't contradict as there is always a great respect for our elders, especially if one is 4000 bliain d'aois – years of age. A lot of good research has been carried out in various Celtic Studies departments, including Notre Dame and Harvard Universities to name but two. However, attempts to test empirically the 'how' and the 'when' I may or may not have influenced or contributed to the development of the English language is, I believe, a road less travelled. There's no point standing still when there is gold at the end of the rainbow. If you get moving with me, I would be happy to accompany you.

>Ag teacht aníos liom – *coming up with me*
>Ag teacht anuas liom – *coming down with me*
>Ag teacht isteach liom – *coming in with me*
>Ag teacht amach liom – *coming out with me*
>Istigh liom – *inside with me*
>Amuigh liom – *outside with me*
>Ar mhuin na muice – *on the pig's back – on the move*
>Ar shiúl leis na síoga – *Away with the fairies – on the move*
>An té a bhíonn siúlach, bíonn sé scéalach – *He who travels will have stories to tell – on the move*

Keep moving with me. Our journey together to a destination unknown. It will be a journey of discovery. Agus, déanfaidh muid ár seacht ndícheall – *and we will do our very best – in fact our seven bests.* Sin gealltanas – *that's a promise!*

● ● ● ● ● ● ●

ONE OF THE GOOD GUYS

I met him in 'Feckers', also known as Roarty's – a larger-than-life character and one you'd like to share more than one pint with. He was sitting at the corner of the bar, arms folded, relaxed, happy, after a long day wrestling with scores of crossbred sheep. He had a smile on his face from ear to ear. '*Cad é mar atá tú, Paddy?*' I say. To which he replied, 'now Joe, if we're going to have the craic tonight, we'll stick to the *Béarla*, if that's alright with yourself?' That we did and a good night we had, followed by a few more in subsequent years. We covered a good bit of ground between football, politics, and farming. We talked about the Irish language too. It was obvious from our conversation that night, and from conversations with many other locals over the years, that Gleann Cholm Cille was rich in all the Gaeltacht cultural traditions. Paddy's natural ability to tell a story and create a picture that brings a story to life encapsulated the essence of Irish conversational skill and a masterclass in storytelling technique. Even though we were interacting through the medium of *Béarla*, our Irishness was alive and kicking, aided and abetted by the sheer presence and brilliance of an expert *seanchaí* – storyteller. Don't worry, Paddy, nobody will know that it's you that I'm talking about!

I needed the break from the Irish that night with Paddy. Enda Kenny had just sent me on a week's sabbatical to the Gleann Cholm Cille Gaeltacht – full immersion with fluent Irish speakers from Wales, Liverpool, Montreal and Moville. The plan for the summer holidays lay in ruins. My wife, Olwyn, was two hours up the road in Carraig Airt with Darragh, Aedín and Oisín – all under five years of age. Maybe the sympathy for me was misdirected!

My phone was on divert and, luckily enough, the mobile coverage and broadband in Gleann Cholm Cille was patchy at best. The Irish language enthusiasts were after me – their prize catch. A newly appointed Gaeltacht Minister with a poor command of the Irish – not even *measartha* – middling – at best. For an entire day, an unfortunate man from Port Láirge – Waterford – was fielding calls, as I had one digit wrong while I had the phone on divert. When I called to apologise, he felt sorry for me. Like me, he had spent the guts of sixteen years learning Irish and he had no clue what they were on about either.

Gleann Cholm Cille, or the anglicised Glencolumbkille, is the most beautiful and *draíochtúil* – magical – place in the world. I find it hard to describe adequately and do justice to a place that is more about a sensation or feeling than anything else – a good feeling at that. Margaret Rose Cunningham's ongoing photographic exhibition on LinkedIn portrays it in all its glory. I felt safe in the protection and surroundings of a valley that reminded me of a place near my mother's home called Gleann Bhairr/Glenvar and a lovely place in Inis Eoghain called

Ceathrú Meánach/Carrowmenagh. If you have the good fortune to be north of the peninsula, make sure to take in the glorious surroundings of two other incredibly named places nearby – Meenletterbale and Glennagiveny. Logainm.ie currently proposes the original Gaelic name Gleann Uí Dhuibheannaigh – the glen of Ó Duibheannaigh (Logainm.ie #15231) and research is ongoing for Meenletterbale (Logainm.ie #15232). Nonetheless, John O'Donovan suggested *Mín litir beul* – smooth letter of the mouth – in 1835. I don't have words to describe these places, I just find a great sense of *síocháin* – peace – when I'm there.

Shane McIntyre has done a brilliant job in the production of a guidebook celebrating the 1,500-year anniversary of the birth of Saint Colm Cille and raises awareness of an ancient pilgrimage, known as 'the Turas'. According to Shane:

> The people of Gleann Cholm Cille are extremely fortunate to live in such a rich archaeological heaven, with 5,000 years of Stone Age art located within this small community … which is steeped in thousands of years' worth of history and culture [that] deserves to be preserved and treasured.

We are grateful to the people of Gleann Cholm Cille who continue to open their doors and hearts to all of us who want to get a sense of a rich heritage and a pathway to our beautiful Irish language.

Ar scáth a chéile a mhaireann na daoine – through the shelter of each other, people survive, or just 'we live in each other's shadow'. I survived through the shelter of many good people from *An Gleann* to *An Port*,[2] *An Charraig* to *Teileann*, *Gleann Locha* to *Cróbh* go dtí *Mín an Aoire* to *Cill Charthaigh* – collectively known as 'in thru'. If

---

[2] Check out the band M'anam – a bunch of lads who are doing wonders for the language. I had the privilege to be in the company of Fergus Cahillane singing live in the rain at An Port (Port) i nGleann Cholmcille.

one wants to study a pace of life that seems to be going almost in reverse and stress-free, then get on your bike and head for 'in thru'. *The Road to Glenlough* by Christy Gillespie captures this general area very well: 'There is no road to Glenlough, not even a well-worn path. This valley, in the highlands of south-west Donegal, is as remote and monumental as it is enchantingly beautiful. It is a place that has attracted a number of notable visitors. These include American artist and illustrator Rockwell Kent, Welsh poet Dylan Thomas and, if strong local tradition is to be believed, Prince Charles Edward Stuart who sought refuge there as he waited for a French ship to bring him back to the safety of mainland Europe after his failed uprising in Britain.'

One of the things that I found difficult at the beginning of my language journey was figuring out where to start. Information was in abundance, bordering on overwhelming. What did help was biting off small chunks at a time. Learning one word per day or refamiliarising myself with words I learned a long time ago was a big help. This worked for me and is not necessarily a template for your learning journey. However, from the point of view of setting a goal, you might consider seven significant words you come across each week and list them in the column below. These words may already be in your vocabulary, but this could be a good opportunity to 'refresh' by using them in sentences and 'dabbling' with different tenses. I would suggest (should you decide to do this), to leave it for the second read (should you decide to do this!), as I don't want to stir up negative *obair bhaile* – homework – memories!

Dála an scéil – By the way

Brian Ó Conchubhair organised a conference at the University of Notre Dame which considered the study of Irish as an academic endeavour in an international context. The papers presented were published as a collection of essays, which he edited, under the title 'Why Irish?' – *Irish Language and Literature in Academia* (Arlen House, 2008).

Caibidil 1: If you want to get to know me, live with me

FOCAIL NA SEACHTAINE – WORDS OF THE WEEK

1. *Carraig* – rock
2. *Lag* – weak
3. *Scáth* – shadow
4. *Síocháin* – peace
5. *Measartha* – moderate/middling
6. *Seanchaí* – storyteller/custodian of tradition
7. *Draíochtúil* – magical

DO THURAS FÉIN – YOUR JOURNEY

1. _____
2. _____
3. _____
4. _____
5. _____
6. _____
7. _____

I found Teanglann.ie helpful for writing sentences. Type a word and numerous sentences are presented. As languages are about 'words', I will show some of the results from inputting 'words' in the search engine and give an example of some of these sentences at the end of each chapter. Here's the first:

> *Bhain tú as mo bhéal é* –
> You took the 'words' out of my mouth.

Caibidil 2

An rúd nach maraíonn thú déanann sé níos láidre thú

The thing that doesn't kill you makes you stronger

GAEILGE IS AINM DOM – MY NAME IS IRISH

I've been around a while. Speculation ranges somewhere between 3,000 and 4,000 years. According to 'Lebor Gabála Érenn' (11th century), I am a language created from all the confused languages from the Tower of Babel – fashioned by King Fénius Farsaid and named after his grandson Goidel. I do feel my age for sure, but the great thing about getting older is this: you gain respect and at times people turn a blind eye. People talk about me a lot, some good and some not so good. I get praised, I get ridiculed, I get debated – mostly as Béarla – and that's the way it is, was, will be and ever shall be world without end, AMEN. My much younger

Caibidil 2: *The thing that doesn't kill you makes you stronger*

friend, the Béarla, *who is still a relatively young 800+, gets a lot of bad press. Her youth leaves her vulnerable and open to criticism. Accusations vary and the main criticism is that English is only a 'makey-up' language comprising a bit of German, French, Latin et al and, of course, a good bit of my good self. I have been around the block, and, like any ageing process, there has been change. Remember, to change is to grow. It's been a long and intense four millennia. I'm still standing,* ag gluaiseacht – *moving – or* ag éirí ar nós eala – *taking off like a swan.*

● ● ● ● ● ● ●

Walking away from Government Buildings was a long, lonely walk that I wished was longer and less lonely. Did that just happen? Did I just accept the impossible? Elation to deflation in a matter of seconds. Did Enda Kenny say those words? How could such a joyous moment implode like this? As I sat in front of Enda, with the portrait of Michael Collins looking on, those first few minutes felt so good. It was me who broke the silence. I wondered whether I was there to give some advice on how to win All-Irelands. The answer was no. Then the real conversation started. The serious business of Government, when a Taoiseach wants to put the person in the job who will work day and night. The mood swivelled on two words – the Gaeltacht. Why did I not say *nil* – no? Why is the water *fliuch* – wet? Why is the sky *gorm* – blue? Why did I not listen more in school? All these questions. Answers nowhere to be found, with only one emerging fact. A brand-new Minister for the Gaeltacht.

'Two weeks in Gleann Cholm Cille', says Enda. My first phone call was to Olwyn. She knew I got the call up. She knew the drill. I was with Darragh earlier in the Merrion Park playground, and my phone was on seven per cent – *seacht* – a lucky number down through the millennia. I had given up hope of a new job, hence the phone not being charged. Olwyn asked, 'Well, what did you get?'

'Natural Resources, Inland Fisheries and Energy … and the Gaeltacht.'

Followed by 'Oh!'

Liam Ó Cuinneagáin ó Ghleann Cholm Cille – and of O*ideas Gael* fame – received my second cry for help. Liam spoke first: 'Well, did you get a job?'

'I did Liam, I'm in bother, I got the Gaeltacht.'

'*Beidh tú alright, a Sheosaimh*', says Liam. Even with my limited conversational ability I knew straight away that he was talking future tense: *beidh* – will be – (pronounced 'beg' down the country and 'bay' in Ulster). The present tense was my cross and trying to wrangle a way out was the crux. I was thinking more of survival, avoiding 'snipers' alley' and hoping this was all a bad dream.

To make matters more complicated, I was replacing Dinny McGinley, my constituency colleague in the Department. I knew that Dinny was always admired for his beautiful Irish, as commented on by many who heard him speak in the Dáil. Furthermore, my hard-working secretarial assistant, Pat McCarry, had to suddenly deal with queries as Gaeilge, which wasn't simple as she had spent her career up to then dealing with issues through the medium of English. Pat was also shrewd enough to know that the show must go on at a constituency level, with all the bread-and-butter work that keeps a politician in their job. Christine Reynolds, from Gaoth Dobhair, and Eimer Friel, from Fanad, came aboard and helped navigate things on the Gaeilge front, for which I will always be grateful.

I've been in far too many corners in my life. In my younger days I rotated between the red and the blue corner in dread, waiting for seconds out in a smoke-filled boxing ring. My coach (Dad) was always in my corner. He was there to encourage, warn of danger, pour cold water and, sometimes, wash away the blood. He also held the towel in case he had to throw it in. After the 'bouts' we ate fish and chips out of newspapers and nodded off on the bus. 'Stick with things', 'never give up' and 'see things through' were consistent messaging from my mother and father back in the 1970s and 1980s. My father had a special interest in this messaging, because the turf had to make its way to the shed somehow before the winter. This has never left me. When the dishes needed to be done, they were done. When the cow needed to be milked, that was done too. Or the turf needed to be *futted*, or the bales needed to be built, all this was done – no nonsense, all done. Roles based on gender were never up for discussion. There were no demarcation lines. And rightly so. Patricia and Denise (my two sisters) got their hands as dirty as the rest of us. James and Paul (my two brothers) were handy enough around the kitchen. Things just needed to be done and that was the long and the short of it. And when we all needed to give our beds to the guests and sleep in the annexe (our fancy word for the out-house) during the parades on the twelfth of July, we just got on with it. This wasn't hardship, those were good days for us. The people from the North will have a different account of their experiences. Driving from one B&B to the next at midnight on 12 July with small children in the back of the car was not easy. The uncertainty of lodgings due to the mass exodus of people mid-July was the norm. Thankfully it is no longer the norm.[3]

Back to reality, I was still dazed – a different sensation to my boxing days. Olwyn, Darragh and I had no cause for celebration. She felt my fear and was always better at predicting what happens next. She knew there would be trouble ahead. Darragh was just bored – he was *cúig* – five. This was a decision I had to make on my own. Do I take this job and run with it, or do I politely say *níl?* I had to own the decision and be prepared to explain it, no matter how, when or where the axe fell. Looking back, I now have a better sense of what was happening. It was a form of relapse. My Leaving Cert Irish class was back with a bang. The fear of rote learning and counting down the clock at the top of the class was back with a vengeance. 2014 was bringing back a torrential

---

[3] I find it difficult to explain to my children what things were like back in the days when 'booby trap' bombs featured regularly on the BBC and UTV news. However, this changed after watching Lisa McGee's *Derry Girls* with them. Lisa did a wonderful job in describing that period.

flood of memories, warts and all. I was returning to my Ordinary Level Grade B Irish 20-odd years later with the same feelings – of trepidation, knot in the *bolg*[4] – stomach – and *eagla* – fear. If I had a place to hide, I would have gone there, locked the *doras* – door – and thrown away the *eochair* – key.

Months later I came across a song by Antoin Ó Dochartaigh, '*Cad é sin don té sin?*' ('Oh what is it to that person it doesn't concern?') This song reflected exactly where I was in those early hours of my new job. I wanted to be on my own and for everyone to leave me on my own. There's a very apt line in the song which I could relate to – '*Má tá mise sásta i mo chónaí i gcró, o cad é sin don té sin nach mbaineann sin do*' ('If I am happy living in a shack on my own, what is it to that person it doesn't concern') – but I knew the appointment concerned people.

The phone was buzzing with texts. Even though WhatsApp had been around since 2009, I wasn't a user – maybe a good thing in hindsight as the satire through the memes would have been gloriously outrageous. 'Nidge vs Joe McHugh' could have been a taste of things that didn't come.[5] *Buíochas le Dia* – thank God. The bips kept bipping: '*Comhghairdeas*', '*Maith thú a stór*', '*ádh mór*' agus longer indecipherable messages as Gaeilge. Party members were preparing the homecoming celebrations. Their TD just got promoted, and the specific title was secondary. A banner was being prepared *as Gaeilge agus as Béarla* – in Irish and English – for *Droichead Leifir* – Lifford Bridge. A decision had to be made whether the celebration would be in Carrigart or Downings or, more appropriately now, *Carraig Airt nó Na Dúnaibh*.

The Fine Gael (Family of Gaels) organisation in Donegal North-East had a *deich bliain* – ten year – barren spell, with no Fine Gael TD

---

[4] *Bolg* – (pronounced 'bollig') – was a difficult word for me to remember so I paired it with the similar sounding '*tolg*' – couch. Word association was an important tool on my learning journey. Too much time on the *tolg* is not great for the *bolg*!

[5] 'Nidge vs Joe McHugh' – A skit from Tuairisc.ie worth checking out online. Nidge (of *Love/Hate* fame) is sent to Gleann Cholm Cille on probation and had a terse interaction with Minister Joe McHugh on the subject of *Gaeilge*.

from 1997 to 2007. There was momentum now and the organisation was eager to keep building. My mother was in hospital recovering from a serious illness, and I was missing my other two children, Aedín and Oisín. Incidentally, the Irish names were around before my appointment – Olwyn's forward planning, and predicting the future, again!

The next day was my birthday. I always looked forward to that date. I remember my seventh birthday clearly. If I could bottle happiness, that was the moment to capture. This one was going to be different though, and a decision had to be made. Decisions, decisions. Making your mind up time Joe, what will it be Joe? Talk to me Joe. Let's do this, let's go all in, seconds out, Round 1.

DÁLA AN SCÉIL – BY THE WAY

There's an important distinction between *'an'* (singular) and *'na'* (plural): *An Dún* – the fort; *Na Dúnaibh* – the forts. According to some local sources this is in reference to two forts. There is also a view that *Na Dúnaibh* is referring to the sand dunes – *dumhach*. Liam Mac Giolla Bhríde agus Liam Sweeney would be worth chatting to as they have been studying *Grammar of Ros Goill Irish Co. Donegal* by Leslie W. Lucas (Queen's University of Belfast, 1979).

FOCAIL NA SEACHTAINE – WORDS OF THE WEEK

1. *Láidir* – strong
2. *Maraigh* – kill
3. *Oideas* – prescription
4. *Bolg* – stomach
5. *Eagla* – fear
6. *Eochair* – key
7. *Droichead* – bridge

Beidh Tú Alright: *An rúd nach maraíonn thú déanann sé níos láidre thú*

Do thuras féin – Your journey

1. ___
2. ___
3. ___
4. ___
5. ___
6. ___
7. ___

> Teanglann.ie phrase:
> *I mbeagán focal* –
> In a few words

Caibidil 3

Mol an óige is tiocfaidh sí

Praise the youth and they will flourish

Some have tried battering me into people and some people had me battered out of them. This happened in rooms with turf-fires, rooms with central heating and rooms with no heating. This was the ultimate tragedy at the beginning of many learning journeys. You were not in control of your learning journey back then. Now you have a chance to take agency over your learning no matter what stage of life you are at. Re-acquainting yourself with me may be difficult in the beginning, however, once you take that step, you will discover that most of what you learn about me you already knew in the first place.

●●●●●●●

A lot of life is about choice: making a decision that can be the making or breaking of you. In making my decision I knew what was ahead of me. Lights, cameras, social media, barrels of ink and plenty of grief!

'*Aire gan teanga, aire gan clue*' they protested. A minister without a language is a minister without a clue. The stage was set. In saying that, while there were small pockets of people strongly opposed, there were others who were prepared to give me a chance. '*Náire*', the beautiful Irish word for shame, became an early entry in my bag of limited vocabulary. Furthermore, I learned the shame was on me, in me, around me and in my fingernails. *Bhí an náire orm*. At that point I learned that there was a very clear distinction between '*orm*' and '*agam*'. It wasn't at me (*agam*) – it was on me (*orm*). In the Irish language a deep additional understanding is expressed regarding emotions. They are 'on' you. *Tá brón orm/ Tá fearg orm*. Sadness is on me/anger is on me. The point is that if sadness comes 'on' you, you can also work to take it 'off' you. There's no doubt that in those few initial hours that I felt shame, I felt regret and I wished I wasn't ruining this very good moment for so many people, including myself. *Joe bocht* – poor Joe! The RTÉ *Six-One News* headline ran with 'Strong criticism of Joe McHugh's appointment.' Commentary within that news bulletin wasn't great for the ego. In general, politicians learn to deal with the 'ego' stuff. Developing a 'hard skin' is the general response. It's the physical stuff that's the hard part. That feeling in the pit of my stomach. A 'gut feeling', sending warning messages to my amygdala[6] in my brain. Fear ahead. Looking back, I can totally understand the genuine concerns that some people had. However, statements such as 'another insult to the Irish language' were a tad hard to take.

It was just like a car crash scene at the beginning of a movie – the difference being that we were all standing on the steps of Government Buildings: brand spanking new junior ministers on one side and the media on the other. Damien English and other colleagues were in a

---

[6] Britannica.com: although historically the amygdala was considered to be involved primarily in fear and other emotions related to aversive (unpleasant) stimuli, it is now known to be involved in positive emotions elicited by appetitive (rewarding) stimuli.

joyous state and rightly seizing the moment. Big Tom, the government press officer, leaned over and whispered in my ear, 'Minister, I've lined up an interview for you with TG4. It will be a great opportunity.'

'Cheers, big guy!' I thought to myself. After the official photo was taken, my eyes were fixed on slabs of well-worn granite paving in preparation for my interview with TG4. More significantly, I knew that when I started walking, I would have ten to twelve steps to decide, 'Should I stay or should I go?' It was not like the film *Heat*, where thirty seconds was the incredibly long threshold for coming to a decision.

Not even Seamus Heaney-inspired wisdom from one of his poems could help me – 'Whatever you say, say nothing'. I started walking. That's when I made my mind up. I was reminded of something my parents always said to me: 'When you're in a corner always tell the truth' (during a lecture following another porky pie, of course!).

I let the interviewer ask the question – as Gaeilge of course. Then it was my turn. I could have tried to wing it. I could have had a prepared statement learnt off, as that was something I was well schooled in from my rote-learning days. Suddenly everyone was listening. The mainstream media maelstrom was tuned in. TG4, Raidió na Gaeltachta and the print media – all one big happy family. It was their lucky day. A Gaeltacht Minister speaking *as Béarla* explaining that he couldn't speak *as Gaeilge*. In hindsight, there was something very liberating about that moment. I set out my stall and I knew that while the criticism would come, I would have plenty in my corner too. A good trait that most Irish people have is the love for the underdog. In this case I was the *tarc taircín* – runt of the litter. There was no turning back. The train had left the station. Call it *thranness* – stubbornness – or naivety, one thing was for sure – this was a step into the unknown. I could remember the French for à *gauche et* à *droite*, but for the life of me *ar chlé agus ar dheis* – on the left and on the right – just wouldn't come to me. Not a great start to the job, figuring out my left from my right!

This was different though. While fear presented itself in a very real way, I still managed to focus on what needed to be done. The threat of public humiliation didn't bother me. In fact, public humiliation was a necessary evil to make this work. The language part of the brain is a muscle, according to my wise mentor Liam Ó Cuinneagáin. My limited grasp of French and Arabic (I spent a year working in UAE) came to the fore – *'Je m'appelle Joe'*, *'Shukran habibi'*, agus *'an bhfuil cead agam dul go dtí an leithreas?'* There was a tug of war between a very limited vocabulary on all sides. But, as Liam said, get the muscle going and there's always enough space in there to expand. Like the boxing training, I had to get my stretches, skipping, and shadowboxing into motion. I had to become insanely preoccupied about the whole thing. My friends didn't want to be near me as I was annoying the hell out of them. I was like Dracula, on the hunt for Irish-speaking blood! However, after a while I realised I didn't have to chase it. It was all around me – it was always around me – and not just because of where I lived *ar imeall na Gaeltacht* – on the edge of the Gaeltacht. It was staring right at me, and I hadn't noticed till now. The pressure was still on though. The hunger was there, but while I'm reminded of my mother-in-law Rita's expression 'hunger is a good sauce', I still had to prove myself. The judges were watching closely and there was no medal ceremony in sight.

Dála an scéil – By the way

Gearr iog sa mhaide mhullaigh – to cut a notch in the chimney crossbeam. This was a way for young people to be recognised for doing something extraordinary. Recognition for an accomplishment was an important feature of Irish society. While they didn't have money for medals, trophies, and selection boxes, they still marked very significant events, accomplishments and magic moments with a notch.

Caibidil 3: *Praise the youth and they will flourish*

FOCAIL NA SEACHTAINE – WORDS OF THE WEEK

1. *Mol* – praise/suggest/approve
2. *Óige* – youth
3. *Imeall* – edge/fringe/margin/outskirts
4. *Cead* – permission
5. *Taircín* – runt of the litter
6. *Bocht* – poor
7. *Náire* – shame/embarrassment

DO THURAS FÉIN – YOUR JOURNEY

1.
2.
3.
4.
5.
6.
7.

Teanglann.ie phrase:
Briathra béil –
Spoken words

Caibidil 4

Ní mar sin a bheadh sé

It was not to be

Back in the thirteenth and fourteenth centuries, there was such an interest in me that even our visitors wanted to get in on the action. In the timeworn phrase, they became 'more Irish than the Irish themselves'.

The fact is that, from the very beginning, many of the settlers married into Gaelic families. From Gaelic mothers and cousins, they quickly picked up the Irish language, so that for many of them it became their first language. The De Angelos became Nagles. Mac Oistealbha became Ó Coistealbha (Costelloe). Mac Síordáin to Jordan and Mac Philip to Philips are other examples of name changes.

I've changed so much over the years that part of me has been reinvented. There wasn't much sign of leathanbhanda – broadband – in my early years. There wasn't much need for the fón póca – mobile phone – thousands of years ago. It took me a long time to accept change. When this happened, I embraced change and realised that, in order to grow and develop, change had to be central to my mission. Change is a good *thing. Interestingly though, the more things change, the more they stay the same.*

●●●●●●●

Ministers come and ministers go. Department officials stay, in the main. Incoming ministers get their official responses to oral parliamentary questions a day or two before they are due to be answered in the Dáil. On this occasion, 'Muggins' got his at 7 p.m., the evening before. Two hours later I was getting a comprehensive briefing from Michael Manley of the Department of Communications and Natural Resources on petroleum prospecting licences for offshore oil and gas. Belated apologies for being somewhat distracted that evening, Michael. Years later, when I was Minister for Education, I would have added to, edited and, where required, deleted some of the official responses. This was different though. I had to run with what I was being presented with and put all my trust in the Department officials. I had a job to do which involved familiarising myself with the words, the text and the policies. This wasn't simple, in fact it was head-wrecking. Béarla, when crafted in a technical manner, can be difficult to understand. Equally, in this instance I was given very technical Gaeilge – which had very little in common with the vocabulary I was familiar with from Séamus Ó Grianna's *Caisleáin Óir* back in my schooldays. In my imagination I was accompanying Séimí Phádraig Dubh in that story as he headed off to the Yukon in Alaska, stopping off for a few pints in Bethlehem, Pennsylvania with the lads and another catch-up in Bute, Montana. Alas, that was not to be. I was sitting at a table with a senior official in the Department of the Gaeltacht, my first day on the job, learning on the job. Máire Killoran was the personification of patience – a true professional, who guided me through a very challenging time. Other officials in the Department of the Gaeltacht were on hand too; mind you, they were in a state of shock as much as I was. I had honestly believed my far-from-halcyon days with the Irish language were behind me, and here I was right back in the tumble dryer. During those first few hours I could feel the tension amongst the Department officials and the mood music wasn't good. Nevertheless, the civil service code kicked in. The officials had a job to do; the new minister had arrived: let the games begin! Dr Aodhán Mc Cormaic and Bertie Ó hAinmhire were on hand around the clock to deal with all the trials and tribulations of a new (unusual) regime.

Summer was in the air and the city centre was buzzing with conversation, laughter and the clinking of glasses. My ministerial colleagues, who were celebrating less controversial appointments, asked me to join them – 'just the one Joe'. I had just said goodbye to Olwyn and Darragh, who were heading back to 'the hills'. I had work to do. *Obair bhaile* – Irish homework! Again! As tempting as the Michael McDowell-inspired outdoor café settings were, I knew that alcohol and craic wasn't conducive to rote learning. Oral questions as Gaeilge were at 9.30 a.m. the next morning. The tight time frame reminded me of my procrastination with my weekend homework back in the 1980s – the *Glenroe*[7] music on RTÉ at 8.30 p.m. on a Sunday was my cue for getting ALL my homework done. This is not advice by the way.

My fancy new title, Minister of State, gave me a new appreciation of the label. I was in a wild state. A state of despair. Walking past my colleagues, I politely refused their kind invitation, which was alien territory for me to be honest. I couldn't help but feel sorry for myself. That evening, I retreated to the bedroom early, leaving my phone with my sister-in-law. My appetite for answering congratulatory messages was minimal. 'I'm nearly down to 750 unanswered messages', I heard Ali shouting excitedly. Her closer proximity to the Leaving Certificate put her in good stead for responding to the messages as Gaeilge. Her ability to expand on my standard response of '*Go raibh maith agat*' was useful.

---

[7] I have happier memories of Glenroe in more recent years. Glenroe Community National School, Luimneach (*ag fás agus ag forbairt le chéile*) re-opened its doors on 27 August 2020 under the patronage of Limerick & Clare Education Board.

As the day galloped to a close, with midnight fast approaching, it was time to get some shut eye, *am dul a luí* – time to sleep. I slept soundly that first night, completely oblivious to what lay ahead and how the story would unfold the next day, 16 July 2014, my birthday.

So, I didn't get to celebrate my first ministerial post along with my colleagues that fateful night. *Ní mar sin a bheadh sé*. Ten years later I'm thinking of my late grandmother and her saying, 'what's for you won't pass you'. Or my other late grandmother: 'just keep smiling and all will be ok.' Every day I wake up, I am grateful, and I celebrate that I got the opportunity to go back and learn to speak my native tongue. A journey that continues to this very day.

DÁLA AN SCÉIL – BY THE WAY

It seems as if English, artistically speaking, is an altogether impossible medium for the lively, imaginative Irish who think in pictures. And it is that artistic language, the "word dress" [*orddrakt*] of the emotions that really is language.'[8]

FOCAIL NA SEACHTAINE – WORDS OF THE WEEK

1. *Caisleáin* – castles
2. *Ór* – gold
3. *Órga* – golden
4. *Am dul a luí* – time to sleep
5. *Obair bhaile* – homework
6. *Dáil* – legislative assembly
7. *Ní mar sin a bheadh sé* – it was not meant to be

---

[8] Séamas Ó Catháin (2014), *Gaelic Grace Notes: The musical expedition of Ole Mørk Sandvik to Ireland and Scotland.* The Institute for Comparative Research in Human Culture. Novus Press, Oslo.

Beidh Tú Alright: *Ní mar sin a bheadh sé*

DO THURAS FÉIN – YOUR JOURNEY

1. _____
2. _____
3. _____
4. _____
5. _____
6. _____
7. _____

‖ Teanglann.ie phrase:
Briathra móra, díomhaoine –
Boastful, idle, words ‖

Caibidil 5

Tús maith leath na hoibre

A good start is half the work

My friends across the water have a different story to tell – Tá siadsan faoi bhrú – *They are under pressure. Scots Gaidhlig, with its historical, cultural, and commercial connection to* Uladh – *Ulster* – *is in a fight for survival and is* seacht searbh sgíth – *seven times bitter tired. My good pal Manx, on the Isle of Man, has an uphill* streachailt – *struggle* – *too. As she might say,* ta mee skee whooinney – *I am tired, yessir! All in all, I'm in a good place. If my purpose was solely to be learned as a means of communication, then that would miss the point entirely. My genealogy is complex* – *my broad development encompasses Sanskrit, Old Irish, Middle Irish and Modern Irish* – *with a right bit of Hiberno-English thrown in for good measure. I am changing and evolving all the time* – *I stay away from the* éad – *jealousy* – *as I try to focus on* dóchas – *hope. I am acutely conscious not to mix the two as* éad *plus* dóchas *gives you* éadóchas – *despair!*

● ● ● ● ● ● ●

Beidh Tú Alright: *Tús maith leath na hoibre*

When then TD Gerry Adams stood up in Dáil Éireann to 'rare up' about my appointment as Minister for the Gaeltacht, he was speaking on behalf of a considerable cohort of people who felt it wasn't the greatest of moves. 'And here's the rub, when a delegation from the Gaeltacht comes in to meet with the minister, they will not be able to converse with the minister, and do a working meeting with the minister, in their own language.' The Taoiseach replied, 'I advised the Minister of State, Deputy McHugh, to go and take a refresher course in Oideas Gael in Gleann Cholm Cille, because he has the language inside him, but it is rusty.' (*Meirgeach* was a new word for me.) Micheál Martin got in on the action too: 'This is the most novel scheme for learning Irish I have ever heard. It is a great scheme: become a minister and learn Irish.' The Ceann Comhairle was busy trying to bring some order with deputies throwing in their tuppence worth. Mattie was flat out, and Michael Noonan wanted to know, 'where did Deputy Adams learn his Irish?' Gerry responded, '*Fuair mé an Ghaeilge fosta nuair a chaith mé tamall gairid sna Blocanna H* ... [I also learned Irish when I spent a short time in the H Blocks]'. Enda's suggestion of Gleann Cholm Cille was becoming ever more appealing! The Ceann Comhairle had to intervene a number of times, 'would the deputies please mind? While I know they are going on their summer break ...'. Darragh Calleary suggested 'we are all going to the Gaeltacht.' Other viewpoints were conveyed through RTÉ: 'If someone is appointed to a job, I can't understand how they would accept it if they haven't total fluency in the Irish language.' Criticism was coming fast and furious: 'It's another insult to the language and it shows how little ... those that are in control of the purse strings and those who are in control of the language nationally care.'

Part of me thought maybe people were right, and *amhras* – doubt – presented itself in a very real way. Up to a point though. What wasn't factored into the discussions on that morning of 16 July 2014 on the floor of Dáil Éireann was that I have a simple philosophy in life: hard work pays off. As a friend of mine used to say, the only place success comes before work is in the *foclóir* – dictionary – unless of course it's an Irish dictionary where *obair* does comes before *rath*!

Dúthracht oibre – work ethic – was essential to survival on our family farm in *na seachtóidí agus na hochtóidí* – the seventies and eighties. Good weather windows were there to be exploited. The early bird didn't always necessarily get the worm as Mother Nature tended to have a big say. While we had a glorious summer in 1995, throwing rotten hay on the back of a trailer to be dumped in the *'annus horribilis'* of 1985 is still a standout memory. My weather window was six weeks before the Dáil reconvened, and it could rain every day for all I cared. I was on a mission to brush up on the oul' Irish. *Tiocfaidh mo lá* – my day will come. *Tiocfaidh* is pronounced 'chuckee' and all you good folk reared with hens should remember a grandparent or two calling the hens for food with '*chuck, chuck, chuck, chuck*' – a play on the word '*tiocfaidh*' handed down from generations.

While the criticism mounted, I also had people on my side whom I had never met prepared to support me, publicly and privately. Without this encouragement I don't think I would be writing these words today. Seán Ó Coistealbha from Conamara was on Raidió na Gaeltachta giving me a dig out – at the time I hadn't a clue what he was saying! *Is fearr cara sa chúirt ná punt sa sparán* – a friend in court is better than a pound in your purse, or, in other words, a friend in need is a friend indeed. Sincere and belated apologies to *An tIar-Choimisinéir Teanga* – the former Irish Language Commissioner – Rónán Ó Domhnaill. *Chuala mé go raibh a fhón gnóthach an lá sin* – I heard that his phone was busy that day!

My first radio interview was a pre-record the morning after my appointment. Michelle Nic Grianna from RTÉ Raidió na Gaeltachta did a magical editing job on a gobbledygook attempt at speaking Irish. I will always be grateful for this. The entire team at Raidió na Gaeltachta in Gaoth Dobhair gave me exceptional support in those difficult early days, and nobody more so than the late, great Séamus Mac Géidigh. I think it reflected how native Irish speakers react when a person decides to take the plunge or throw a shape at learning Gaeilge. Edel Ní Chuireáin, Aodh Máirtín Ó Fearraigh, Mairéad Nic Seaghain, Frances Nic Geidigh, Colm Ó Dúlacháin and Áine Ní Churráin were all professional in the jobs they had to do but were also encouraging and supportive on my journey. TG4's Máire Treasa Ní Cheallaigh had a novel plan. She had a keen eye for a story and was eager to turn this into a yearlong expedition. She politely asked me a few times to allow her to shadow me. I eventually gave in and, between the jigs and the reels, herself and Sarah Blake produced the documentary *'Fine Gaeilgeoir'* for RTÉ's *Documentary on One*. Máire Treasa put her cards on the table. She wasn't enthused with my appointment, but she was willing to give me the benefit of the doubt and give me a chance. In hindsight, her passion for the language was contagious and her humour and *comhluadar* – company – helped shorten the journey to no end. *Giorraíonn beirt bóthar* – good company shortens the journey. A few years later, Máire Treasa branched into medicine and is now *an Dochtúir* Máire Treasa. Her native Irish-speaking patients will be delighted to have the opportunity to discuss their health concerns as Gaeilge no doubt.

The floor of the Dáil was the correct forum to address the people in *Dún na nGall* who I represented as a *Teachta Dála* – messenger of the people. It was also my opportunity to speak directly to the organisations and people with whom I would be working closely in my new ministry. I was under pressure, for sure – probably as much pressure as I've ever been under. I said in Dáil Éireann in July 2014, 'I'm prepared to put in the work in this job, like any job. I've already stated that I've to do a refresher course.' That was my 'hands up moment' and, while the satirists were busy sharpening the *pinn luaidhe* – pencils – and colouring crayons, I felt the pressure easing somewhat, even though I had other briefs to read into in another department. There is something empowering about showing vulnerability – not that I would have agreed with this back then. It was certainly a good political lesson for me as I could sense a mood change. The shift moved in my direction as I was asking for help. People like to be asked.

Caibidil 5: *A good start is half the work*

As a Donegal man, I was acutely aware of my county's form when it came to referenda. A tendency to side with the 'no'! This was the instinctive response to being given an instruction rather than the ask. A fella said to me one time, when the option of 'no' is on the ballot, he will vote 'no' every single time. A tongue-in-cheek survey a few years back about Donegal people highlighted these two maxims: never interrupt someone who is listening to the obituaries, and always say 'no'. Donegal people don't like being preached to! Maybe that's the same the world over and not just a regional or provincial thing. Could that be the same with *an teanga Gaeilge*? Maybe people don't like being told what to do. My ask was clear, and my audience was targeted. I wanted help and I was asking everyone and anyone with Gaeilge, no matter how proficient, to speak to me. Furthermore, I asked people to join me on my journey. I always struggled being on my own, so this worked for me. I maximised every minute of every day and I knew I was being monitored very closely by a significant and attentive audience. The pressure would be intense, but I was up for it. There were light moments too. I got a morale-boosting call from my friend Kevin Honan, a state legislator from Boston. He said the best speeches are the shortest speeches, so no need to panic!

Dála an scéil — By the way

Liam Ó Cuinneagáin has been the inspiration behind Oideas Gael since 1984 along with his co-founder Dr Seosamh Watson. Siobhán Ní Churraighin, Gearóidín Nic Ghongail and course manager Rónán Ó Dochartaigh lead a formidable team of educators who teach Gaeilge to students from all over the world. Anna Ní Chuinneagáin was one of my teachers in Oideas Gael. She taught me '*Go ndéana a mhaith duit*' as the Donegal equivalent for '*go raibh maith agat*' and I've been using it ever since. I am grateful for the *fáilte* I received in Oideas Gael – my second home.

Beidh Tú Alright: *Tús maith leath na hoibre*

FOCAIL NA SEACHTAINE – WORDS OF THE WEEK

1. *Teanga* – language/tongue
2. *Tiocfaidh mo lá* – my day will come
3. *Amhras* – doubt
4. *Dúthracht* – work ethic/tenacity
5. *Tús maith* – *a good start*
6. *Peann luaidhe* – pencil (plural – *pinn luaidhe*)
7. *Gnóthach*[9] – busy (pronounced '*Greeha*' in Ulster Irish)

DO THURAS FÉIN – YOUR JOURNEY

1. _____
2. _____
3. _____
4. _____
5. _____
6. _____
7. _____

> Teanglann.ie phrase:
> *Ní bheathaíonn, ní chothaíonn na briathra na bráithre* –
> fine words butter no parsnips

---

[9] Dún na nGall/Uladh dialect changes 'n' to 'r', e.g *gnó* – business – is '*gró*' and *cnoc* – hill – is '*croc*'. Check out the *fuaimeanna* – sounds – on Foclóir.ie.

Caibidil 6

Éist le ceol na habhann agus gheobhair breac

Listen to the music of the river and you'll catch a trout

In my formative and formidable years, I was so many variations of the same. I differed from parish to parish. Today, a lazy analysis comprises three component parts: Conamara, Munster, and Donegal Irish. The linguistic study of Ireland is never complete without a trip to the Kingdom. Lámha suas – hands up – anyone who has struggled with the Kerry accent going at a phenomenal speed, as Béarla? Gaeilge is spoken at a phenomenal speed there too, and that has been the way for centuries. The debate can be infuriating.

● ● ● ● ● ● ●

Some up the country say, 'I don't understand Munster Irish, and the Conamara Irish is wild hard to understand.' As for the Donegal/Ulster

Beidh Tú Alright: *Éist le ceol na habhann agus gheobhair breac*

Irish, some down the country say, 'I've no idea what those fadudas[10] *are saying.' Time to take a step back. The* Béarla *dialect challenges are no different. And those* Béarla *dialects come from the* Gaeilge *dialects. The Munster Irish, not unlike the* Béarla, *is a rather hard dialect:* conas atá tú? *– how's it going, boyeee? The Conamara* Gaeilge, *like the* Béarla, *is more gutteral:* cén chaoi a bhfuil tú? *You're talking from the* sceadamán *or the* scornach *– throat. Then there's the Donegal* Gaeilge, *which is not entirely the proper categorisation – it's Ulster Irish and it has its own distinct nuances. And it has a more musical ring to it – the Daniel O'Donnell effect:* Cad é mar atá tú? *– how are you? Get into the car and go on a wee trip through Ulster and you'll soon get a gist of the unique differences. The accents, expressions and local dialects in rural parts of Monaghan county will differ to those in Monaghan town. Distinctions are not just on a county-by-county basis: the dialect and expressions in Ballyshannon are as different to those of Culdaff as those in Ballymoney are from those in Ballymena. Even on Toraigh Island itself there are dialect differences on either side of the island. Explore the words and try to explore the beauty of their existence. Navigate with curiosity. In some instances, there won't be answers and the empirical data will not always be there. Don't shy away from coming up with your own conclusions and observations. Listening closely to different dialects will help you in your own language learning development. Don't hold back and don't let anyone else hold you back either. Bring on the different* canúintí *– dialects. There is a beauty to identifying an accent with a geographical region. Some people can identify people from a certain part of a county. I hope this continues into the future; however, I do have my concerns. You will hear plenty American accents (not Americans) on Dublin buses, who live closer to home!*

The Cavan dialect – whatever the language – differs from the Carlow dialect. Nobody, and I mean nobody can get their tongue around

---

[10] People with the Donegal dialect were labelled 'the fadudas' as *faduda* is used instead of *faoi*, which means about.

Bailieborough[11] as expertly as the Cavan native. The soft south Donegal/ west Fermanagh/Ballyshannon accent differs from the very distinctive Fanad accent. Elsewhere in Ulster, take a wee trip to Ballymoney and you will encounter a completely different dialect, guaranteed. The Ballymoney dialect is way off the grid. A former resident of Ballymoney in Antrim, the late Joey Dunlop, who frequented the Olde Glen Bar, was a joy to listen to in his unique Ballymoney accent. Logainm.ie lists nineteen entries for Ballymoney stretching from Doire go Dún; Dún na nGall go Loch Garman; Cill Mhantáin go Corcaigh. They all have their own Ballymoneys. Most of the *Béarla* entries have the standardised/anglicised spelling 'Ballymoney' – settled by the Ordnance Survey in the 1840s. The Gaeilge brings more depth, understanding, colour and meaning. The range is as follows: 'Baile Uí Mhoinigh', 'Baile Monaidh', 'Baile Móna', 'Baile an Mhuine', 'Baile Na Moinge' agus 'Baile Muine'. The places are different, the names are different, and the dialects are different.

Údarás na Gaeltachta, a regional state agency with responsibility for Gaeltacht areas in different parts of the country, deals with dialect challenges daily. Former Údarás CEO Mike Ó hÉanaigh, who was born in South Boston, attended primary school in the States and returned to Carna in Galway. He has a passion for the Irish language and never struggled with the Donegal dialect while working in a previous position at Donegal County Council. *Coinnigh á gabháil* – Keep going. *Agus ná déan déarmad* – and don't forget – the native Irish speaker goes at the speed of light. Don't be put off by that. Treat the language like a car with different speeds and, as many a wise person said, don't be rushing – you'll get there just as quick.

The Irish and British journeys are intrinsically linked. Irish football participation and Irish support for the great Arsenal, Manchester United and City, Aston Villa, Liverpool and Leeds United teams of the past and present is an obvious connection through sport. Other

---

[11] Pre-anglicisation it was *Coill an Chollaigh* – the Wood of the Boar – (Logainm.ie #3623) and not to be mistaken with *coileach* – rooster.

examples included the Irish men (shifters or navvies[12]) who built the British roads and the Irish *banaltraí* – nurses – who built the NHS.

Uachtarán na hÉireann President Higgins' first state visit by any head of the Irish state to Great Britain in 2014 was an opportunity to acknowledge and celebrate the current strength of that relationship. This visit was preceded by President Mary Robinson, who was the first Irish President to meet with a British monarch in 1993. These two rocky islands, *agus na hoileáin bheaga éagsúla fosta* – and the various small islands also – have interwoven connections through time, controversy, conflict, friendship, and history. Over time, the two languages kept bumping into each other, challenging, influencing, and changing. Manifesting itself in Gaeilge as '*Chuaigh mé go dtí an siopa ar my bhycicle*', or in Ulster Scots as '*I'm afeared – This is a quare hanlin' – we're all scundered*', or '*The buck o'er yonder made some haems of that, the clouster.*' Language development is a continuous process, and this will continue to change over time. People writing the history of any language must be circumspect, methodical and evidence-based, in so far as possible. Historians will point to the reasons for *meath na teanga* – language decline – to help us better understand why we have a first language in the Constitution[13] and it's not the main day-to-day spoken word. This is important work, and the facts are stark in relation to British influence in our own curriculum down the centuries. This is a piece of work for the *saineolaithe* – experts – for sure.

Neamh/Na Flaithis – Heaven

As I lay on my *leaba* – bed – in Caitlín's house[14] studying my irregular verbs, I did question what I was at. Could I learn a language properly

---

[12] Living conditions weren't always ideal for the Irish workers, with some living in *rupálaithe puitigh* – muck shelters.
[13] According to Article 8 of the Constitution, the Irish language is the first official language, while the English language is recognised as the second official language.
[14] Caitlín Nic Nairn's house was my lodgings when I stayed in Gleann Cholm Cille – a great welcome, great breakfasts, and many great chats.

in a matter of weeks? Sure, I had the basics, didn't I? This isn't impossible, is it? I was useless at languages, wasn't I? French up to Inter Cert and Ordinary Level Irish to Leaving Certificate. I was no good on my own at this craic, as was the case when studying in secondary school and university. That's when I decided I wasn't going to do this on my own. This wasn't going to be a lonely, solitary and *mé féin* – me, myself – learning journey. A 5.30 a.m. start in Teelin, and a five-hour trek over Sliabh Liag ending in Málainn Bhig along with five locals was just the tonic. Mark, Yvonne, Siobhán, Gráinne and Pat introduced me to the wonderful Gaeilge vocabulary along the way. One Man's Pass – *Cosán an Aon Duine* – was surmounted with the following logic: if I can face the fear of climbing this difficult terrain, I can surely face the challenge of learning Irish.

Fatigue set in after the trek and I was looking forward to an early night when the local garda arrived. Dismounting from his *bhycicle*, Odie McBride informed me that he was making an *iarracht* – effort – with the Irish. And where better to practise than John Eoinín's *Teach Tábhairne* – pub – over a few scoops (off duty of course). The locals would join in and within a short time we had figured out all the failings of the language, where it all went wrong, and what needed to be done. *As Béarla* of course! We had to start somewhere I suppose. The current ambassador at the Embassy of Ireland in France, Niall Burgess, joined us a couple of years later to brush up on his Gaeilge. He was Secretary General in the Department of Foreign Affairs at the time and his presence in Oideas Gael reflected the importance the Department of Foreign Affairs attached to the Irish language on the international stage.

The main religion in Gleann Cholm Cille and other parts of 'in thru'[15] is football. McShane, Cannon, O'Donnell, Gillespie, Hegarty,

---

[15] 'In thru' is a special geographical area that can be accessed by land through Gleann Gheis, Fintra bridge, or by air or sea. There is a scenic route too, thr~ two white pillars near Ard an Rátha.

Doherty, McHugh, McBrearty, McGinley, McClean, Carr, Gavigan, Byrne, Cunningham, Mc Intyre, Browne and Molloy are a selection of football names who have represented the county in the last few decades. Please forgive me if I've left surnames out as I enter the realm of 'begging for forgiveness later'! The individual players I spoke to had my back. They were willing to help and wanted me to succeed. This was a big help. Now that I had the GAA greats and the local Garda behind me, all I needed was the Church. Kilcar's local parish priest, an t-athair Eddie Ó Gallachóir, was just the man. We met in the parish hall with Margaret Ní Bhradaigh in the village of *Cill Charthaigh*. They spoke at 100 miles per hour, which was a joy to listen to but impossible to comprehend. For the record, this was the point where I dispensed with the widely used excuse – 'I can understand it but can't speak it.' At different junctures, Father Eddie would ask *'an dtuigeann tú?'* – do you understand? – to which I replied, as Gaeilge, *'tuigim'* – I understand – a blatant lie in the presence of a man of the cloth. *Tá brón orm*, Father Eddie – the sorrow is on me/I'm sorry. However, for me to learn I needed to listen and, while I didn't understand it all, I was listening – for a change. Two hours later (yes two hours), I emerged from that parish hall no further forward. That's what I thought. Father Eddie stopped at the door on the way out and started writing a note: *'An Ghaeilge: an chloch is mó ar a phaidrín'* – Irish: the most important stone on the rosary beads. From that moment I realised that this strategic intervention by an t-Athair Eddie was going to be my strategy for learning the language: *mo bhunchloch* – my foundation stone. I would remember a word, sentence or saying from the specific context and would never ever forget it. Those two hours were a big-time commitment for one sentence you may say. To this day I am grateful that Father Eddie and Margaret were so generous with their time. My parish priest, Charlie Byrne, is a Kilcar man, who says Mass as Gaeilge every Sunday in the Gaeltacht part of my own parish in Stella Maris, *Na Dúnaibh*. I know, I know, I should have gone to Mass more often. *Brón orm fosta Charlie!*

Caibidil 6: Listen to the music of the river and you'll catch a trout

Ultimately, being aware of the context in advance means I will never forget the word or the sentence. Similarly, I will always associate *Árainn Mhór* with '*seacht ndícheall*' – a kind lady from the island said to me, 'you're doing your *seacht ndícheall* – seven bests – and that's all that matters.' There's the number seven again!

Context was important for my learning. Irish speakers were eager to introduce new vocabulary. Associating the word with that person, in a particular location, would help me to remember the word. On your own language journey, should you decide to go down that road, build your vocabulary around your interaction with people and places. While the classroom will always have its place for the more technical parts of the language, nothing beats the great outdoors. That's where I learned *fraoch corcra* – purple heather – *nóiníní* – daisies – and *duilleoga* – leaves, as in plural of leaf. Peter Cunningham, from RTÉ, enlightened me recently on the beautiful sea-pink flower that dots our coastline from the month of May. As Gaeilge it is *Caoróg Mhara*. During my first visit to the Gaeltacht Department office in Gaoth Dobhair, I heard the following from one of the officials: '*D'ith damh dubh ubh amh ar neamh inniu*' – a black ox ate a raw egg in heaven today. While making no sense whatsoever, that wasn't the learning purpose. I learned two new Irish words, *damh* agus *amh*. Context, association and never forget.

I took criticism on the chin and used it as a motivational tool. I met a man who was keen to let me know that my appointment was a *scannal* – scandal. According to *Merriam-Webster.com*, 'scandal' is an old word, with attested use dating back to the beginning of the thirteenth century, and comes to English from the Latin word *scandalum*, which means 'stumbling block' or 'offense'. Motivation comes from the strangest of places! With no offence taken, I proceeded to add another word to my ever-increasing vocabulary. I loved these handy ones, like *speisialta, plámás, onóir, bródúil, smidiríní, closáilte*, which either sound like the English or have been imported into Hiberno-English or started out as Irish the first day.

Regarding 'smithereens', according to Merriam-Webster, 'although no one is entirely positive about its precise origins, scholars think that smithereens likely developed from the Irish word "*smidiríní*" which means "little bits".' That Irish word is the diminutive of *smiodar*, meaning 'fragment'. My nephew Sam, ó *Uíbh Fhailí*,[16] started chatting in the back of the car about the *smugairle róin* – jellyfish, but literally snot of the seal. His way of remembering the word is to think of Toblerone. Snot and chocolate would have little common ground, but the sounds certainly would. It's amazing what you forget, well maybe not all of us! Sitting at Caitlín's breakfast table, I was struggling to find the Irish for butter and honey. *Bainne agus arán* – milk and bread – is like riding a bike and up there with *madra agus milseán* – dog and sweets – as some of the first words as Gaeilge I learned in primary school. I'd no bother eating the produce, but finding the Irish word was a challenge. Luckily, other learners shared the breakfast table and when you have someone from Wales who can speak up to nine different languages – including Gaeilge – help is never far away.

Getting translations for butter and honey via Foclóir.ie is a piece of cake. Sorry, couldn't resist that! Butter is *im* and honey is *mil*. Interestingly, if you break up *milseán* you could argue it's 'old honey' but you'll find that *sean* (without the fada) is the Gaeilge for 'old' so hence we move on to Seán's honey or Shaun's sweets – or something to that effect. By moving the fada to make the word 'séan', we get deny or reject. If only to reject sweets was that easy. Exploring words whetted my curiosity no end and I was never afraid to draw my own conclusions.

Three years later, Peter Weil – who set up the first North–South Politics in Action[17] programme – sat at that very same breakfast table with me. From Belfast, Peter came to Gleann Cholm Cille to develop a

---

[16] There is an extended explanatory note on *Uíbh Fhailí* by Nollaig Ó Muraíle on Logainm.ie (#100031) which is well worth a read.

[17] Loreto Milford and Portadown College are two of the partner schools involved in the Politics in Action programme. They have just concluded the initial phase of 'Poreto'.

Caibidil 6: *Listen to the music of the river and you'll catch a trout*

better understanding of the Irish language. Triggered by the withdrawal of funding from the Northern Ireland Assembly's budget for Gaeilge support, Peter wanted to inform himself as to what the commotion was all about. As a way of conversation, he proceeded to tell me about this Gaeltacht Minister with no Irish who had been appointed three years earlier by Enda Kenny. Playing along, I let Peter continue for another few minutes. I was enjoying it no end. When I introduced myself as that guy, Peter nearly fell off the chair. Still though, that circumstance brought us together and Peter's cross-border education programme had its inaugural session in the Department of Education during my tenure as Education Minister in 2019. Never underestimate the power of new circumstances leading to new connections and leading to new opportunities. If you're into networking and want to brush up on your Irish, check out the Donegal Dublin Business Network (DDBN) up in the 'big smoke'. There's no shortage of Irish speakers who might give you your first business lead through Irish!

De réir a chéile a thógtár na caisleáin – gradually, castles are built. Liam Ó Cuinneagáin from Oideas Gael used this expression during our first call following my appointment. Liam was asked by Máire Treasa Ní Cheallaigh for her documentary, *Fine Gaeilgeoir*, 'how long would it take for me to become *líofa* – fluent – in Irish? Liam's honest assessment was that he 'wouldn't like to put a timeline on it, as learning a language is a lifelong project and you never stop learning.' Bit by bit. *Céim ar chéim* – step by step. *De réir a chéile* – gradually.

Dála an scéil – By the way

Online etymology has a comprehensive listing for the English word 'rink' (as in ice rink): 'Measured ground for a combat, joust; Scottish source; Probably from old French *renc, reng*, row, line; Germanic source from Proto-Germanic 'hringaz'.' I want to throw this into the mix for consideration: *Ag rince* – dancing – *rinc oighir* – dancing on ice!

Beidh Tú Alright: *Éist le ceol na habhann agus gheobhair breac*

FOCAIL NA SEACHTAINE — WORDS OF THE WEEK

1. *Éist le ceol* – listen to the music
2. *An dtuigeann tú?* – Do you understand?
3. *De réir a chéile* – gradually
4. *Neamh* – heaven
5. *Amh* – raw
6. *Smugairle róin* – jellyfish, literally snot of the seal
7. *Céim ar chéim* – bit by bit

DO THURAS FÉIN — YOUR JOURNEY

1. _____
2. _____
3. _____
4. _____
5. _____
6. _____
7. _____

> Teanglann.ie phrase:
> *Ní briathra a dhearbhaíos ach gníomh* –
> actions speak louder than words.

Caibidil 7

Bainis an ghortáin fataí agus scadáin

The miser's wedding is potatoes and herrings

To get to know me, you've got to live with me, be with me and understand me. That being said, we are playing catch up and things are a little meirgeach – *rusty* – so we need to walk before we run again. Céim ar chéim – *step by step* – take a deep breath, exhale and slow down. To my friends, my colleagues, my Gaeilge ambassadors, my leaders, and my role models, I make this plea. My glór – *voice* – needs to be heard. It needs to be heard everywhere and anywhere and as much as possible. Give me some space and time will sort the rest.

● ● ● ● ● ● ● ●

Our historical relationship with the potato has been well documented, and no doubt this will continue apace as we approach the 200-year commemoration of the *Gorta Mór* – Great Famine.

The *Revue Francaise de Civilisation Britannique (French Journal of British Studies)* notes:

> It is generally considered that very few songs from the Famine era have survived: it is indeed testimony to the power and importance of traditional music and songs, and remarkably so in Ireland, that illiterate people on the threshold of exile or death could find the strength to express their misfortunes in such a poetic and elaborate form, as in this *caoineadh* (i.e. keen or lament) by Peatsaí Ó Callanáin, a small tenant farmer from County Galway, in 1846:
>
> *Míle bliain agus ocht de chéadta,*
> *Dhá fhichead gan bhréig is sé ina cheann*
> *Ó thuirling an Slánaitheoir i gcolainn daonna.*
> *Go dtáinig léirscrios ar phataí an Domhain*
>
> One thousand years first and these eight hundred,
> Two score most truly and six besides,
> Since the Saviour took on him our human nature,
> 'Till the potatoes through the world died.
>
> *Sin é an dáta, is ní fath gan abhár*
> *A mbeidh cuimhne is trácht air i gcaitheamh an tsaoil*
> *Mar níor tháinig an uireasa dhá mhéad ar a cháilíocht*
> *Is mó na ganntan is easpa an bhídh*
>
> That is the date and we'll long remember,
> For 'twill be talked of for many a day,
> For no disaster before was heard of,
> Which took like that all our food away.

Caibidil 7: *The miser's wedding is potatoes and herrings*

The journal also includes the following comment:

> One song in Irish which has been carefully passed on since the mid-nineteenth century, is called '*Amhrán na bPrátaí Dubha*' – 'The song of the black potatoes' – and was probably composed during the great famine, by Máire Ní Dhroma, who lived near Dungarvan ... it features ten verses and stands out a strongly discordant voice, with a tone of social and political protest summed up in one line of the song, where faith gives way to passionate objection: *Ní hé Dia a cheap riamh an obair seo, daoine bochta a chur le fuacht is le fán* – it wasn't God's work sending out poor people to cold and wandering.

Dúchan na bprátaí – potato blight – will forever feature in *ár n-oidhreacht* – our heritage – *agus in ár stair* – and in our history.

In more recent decades, Donegal prides itself on its positive relationship with the humble spud or potato. Many farms, including my father's farm, produced seed potato for export in the 1970s. *Tá mo dhroim nimhneach ón lá sin* – my back is sore from that day. Speaking of *nimhneach* (sore or poisoned), 'The Poisoned Glen' in Donegal stands out in this regard. Apparently, it started out as the 'Heavenly Glen' – *An Gleann Neimhe*. Logainm.ie (#111318) now goes with *Cró Nimhe* – Poisoned Glen. The words 'heavenly' and 'poisoned' or 'poisonous' as *Gaeilge* are quite similar phonetically. *Nathair nimhe* (poisonous snake) and *úll nimhe* (poisoned apple). This is one theory, and no doubt legend will have alternative versions, but irrespective of the *ceart agus micheart* (right and wrong), just like politics, 'it is better to have people talking about you rather than not talking about you at all.' Down the country you will hear *scornach tinn* for sore throat whereas up the road it is *sceadamán nimhneach* – effectively saying your throat is poisoned! An appropriate description for sure. Lastly, it is important to point out that The Poisoned Glen takes in *Dún Lúiche* – Dunlewy (Logainm.ie #1166990). In folklore Lugh was a king and warrior and possibly had a fort here in his name, *Dún Lúiche*. Lastly, if you ever wondered where London came from there's a school of thought that *Lugh Dún* was its genesis. I'll just throw it out there for debate!

The Famine song 'The Praties They Grow Small' includes a play on the Irish word for potatoes, *prátaí*, which is commonly used in parts of Ireland. There is a more light-hearted American version, which mentions Kansas rather than Donegal.

> Oh the praties they grow small, over here
> Oh the praties they grow small
> And way up in Donegal
> We eat them skins and all, over here, over here,
> We eat them skins and all, over here.

Across the way in rural Derry, Seamus Heaney penned a poem about peeling potatoes with his mother, 'When all the others were away at Mass'. Patrick Kavanagh also recorded a famous poem, 'Spraying the Potatoes'. All these years since the Leaving Certificate, I can now feel a degree of sympathy for him spending all that time *ag bailiú* – gathering – spuds in the 'stony, grey soil of *Muineacháin* – Monaghan.'

On 21 May 2023, President Michael D. Higgins spoke in Milford, Co. Donegal at the National Famine Commemoration. He opened his speech as Gaeilge:

> *Is cúis mhór onóra dom, mar Uachtarán na hÉireann, a bheith i gcómhar le muintir mo thíre féin, cibé áit ina bhfuil siad, is cuma cén cúinsí atá orthu, agus muid ag comóradh eachtraí tubaisteacha ár staire, agus ach go h-áirithe nuair atá muid ag tabhairt chun cuimhne saolta, básanna, agus streachailt na ndaoine a cailleadh i rith na tréimhse tragóidí a leagadh ar mhuintir na hÉireann ar a chuirtear an teideal An Gorta Mór.*

Caibidil 7: The miser's wedding is potatoes and herrings

(It is my honour and privilege, as President of Ireland, to join with fellow Irish people, wherever they may be, and in whatever circumstances, as we mark the cataclysmic events from our past, and in particular as we recall the lives, deaths and suffering of all of those individuals who perished during that tragic event imposed on Irish people that we refer to as An Gorta Mór, the Great Hunger, the Irish Famine).

While I started out talking about the potato, my mission is to show that the Irish language and our history go hand in glove. Just choosing random words to learn off by heart diminishes the status of our linguistic heritage. By connecting to our past, the language learning journey takes on a new relevance. And no better person than our president to articulate this.

Hanging on the wall on Price's Lane, off Fleet Street, as part of the Icon Walk/*Siúlóid na nÍocón* in Dublin city centre, is a plaque with the following text:

> It is said of Maria Edgeworth that she invented the form for the modern novel, the genre of the regional novel, when she wrote *Castle Rackrent*, based on her experience helping her landlord father run his estate in Longford. ... She died saddened during the Famine being one of a few trying to bring relief to tenants out of her own pocket.

Every day is a doubting day, *gan dabht* – without doubt. The whole thing was a disaster for the first few weeks following my ministerial appointment. Travelling around in a car with no air conditioning didn't help. And when I say travelling, I mean travelling through the night and with early, early morning starts. Having responsibility for the Gaeltacht and the Islands, all the rivers, fracking,[18] all the onshore mineral licenses and all the offshore potential oil and gas licenses brought travelling to a new level indeed. Every morning, I tuned into Raidió na Gaeltachta and every morning I was guaranteed trouble. If Joe McHugh wasn't mentioned in the *Nuacht an Tuaiscirt* – Northern News – or the *Nuacht an Deiscirt* – Southern News – then there was going to be a mention on the *Nuacht an Iarthair* – Western News. Leaving the learning of the language aside, I still had my day job and all the delights that went with being a minister. I had to dig deep. Two departments with such a broad policy range – trying to put a stop to fracking in one and trying to restart funding for capital investment in the other.

Hold on. Let's pull back a little. Isn't this what I always wanted? On 11 June 1999, I was perched on top of several shoulders celebrating my first election to Donegal County Council. After a 13-week campaign, the electorate decided to 'Go With the Flow and Vote Young Joe'. I dropped the 'young' in my last few elections, but I hoped I still had the same flow! It was very much a case of giving it a lash and seeing how it went. Never in a million years was this political journey planned. Prior to the local election, my bags were on standby for a return to the States, or anywhere else in the world for that matter. So, there I was resting on the shoulders of my campaign team wondering what the hell would happen next. Then, almost immediately, my instructions for the next quarter of a century were belted out. 'Next stop Dublin, McHugh.' And that was that. My whole career/life mapped out in front of me while my feet were off the ground. Echoes of good advice, 'keep your feet on the ground', came to mind. There was a chronological sequence of stepping-stones: county councillor, senator, TD, committee chair, minister of state, chief whip – and finally – senior

---

[18] *Ag fraiceáil* – fracking – was an early day's word for my vocabulary as there was a strong campaign to ban it outright. Eddie Mitchel led a Sligo/Leitrim-based campaign which culminated in former TD Tony McLaughlin submitting a private members motion to ban fracking outright. Fracking was banned in 2017.

minister at Cabinet. Back then I couldn't see as far as the following Tuesday, never mind the next twenty-five years.

So that was the start of it I suppose. The start of a series of new beginnings that would bring their own challenges. Challenges that needed to be faced head-on with all the slings and arrows of outrageous fortune thrown in. What doesn't kill you makes you stronger, they say. I wonder! Too many corners, too many headlights, too many knots in the stomach. Far too many hours unintentionally fasting, not enough sleep and without doubt too much stress. So why do it? Why not call it a day then Joe? I stood for Dáil Éireann four times, once for Donegal County Council and once for Seanad Éireann. In politics – unlike my boxing career – I remain undefeated! Once elected, I was always fully committed, *agus níl aon aiféala orm, beag ná mór* – I have no regrets, small or big.

Looking back and thinking about all the tight corners and pressure cookers I found myself in, the end game was always in sight – the decision to call it a day on my political journey. The end of the madness, flux and chaos and the beginning of that normality that I had always shied away from. A normality that so many people get at an earlier stage in their life. My new aspiration is for a quieter life, less notoriety, and some calm. In saying that, I would still advise people to run for political office. However, do not use me as an example of how to go about it. Rural constituencies can place very high demands because of geography alone. My style of politics included drinking lots of cups of tea (which I will always be thankful for) and spending a lot of time on the ground. The world has changed since I entered politics 25 years ago. Advanced communication systems and virtual meetings will help to bring more balance to the role of a politician. Getting the balance will be key, as the electorate will always demand visibility at a grass roots level. This is important. My father-in-law and former TD, Tom Enright, placed a strong emphasis on meeting people regularly in his constituency. He never took the direct route on his way to the Dáil or on his way home. He always had people to see and things to do.

The chance opportunity to speak as Gaeilge – properly this time – assisted my rite of passage out of politics. It helped me identify the pulse of Gaeltacht communities. I gained a deeper understanding of the history of my own parish, county, province and country, and of Ireland's place in the world. Through this process a lovely calm descended. That nervousness before public speaking events disappeared. A new-found confidence in myself brought me to a new place. I remember attending an event in Buncrana where an American guest asked the question, 'Why are some of the speakers sweating during their speeches and why is it when you move from Irish to English you don't show any signs of panic?' I replied by saying that I was that soldier once upon a time, until I started speaking as Gaeilge more frequently and confidently. I can't explain this, but it might be something to do with the Gaeilge DNA in my system – in all our systems.

So what is it with public speaking for most of us? Was it a lack of preparation for public speaking in my primary and secondary education or was it just the times we lived in? Whatever the reason, public speaking was always a grind and that included my time as a secondary teacher. Ironically, I remember filling in for an Irish teacher, Martina English, for a week back in the nineties. Sadly – for me, not the students – they had a free study period for a week due to my shortcomings on the Gaeilge front. Moments like those always prompted the question 'should I do something about speaking Irish?' And I knew I wasn't on my own in this questioning. I did spend a week in Gleann Cholm Cille back in the 1990s but when I say I have very little recollection of the learning that week, it shows my hand as to what I was up to for the week. Let's just say the craic came before the Irish under the *ceannaireacht* – leadership – of *mo chara* – my friend – Louis. *Go raibh maith aige* – my thanks to him!

Delving further into the tired old debate identifying the trouble with the language hasn't achieved much. Some people say, 'look at Wales'. Others say, 'it's the way it's taught.' And if there's anybody left, they'll probably say, 'it's a dead language.' With no authority, wisdom,

Caibidil 7: The miser's wedding is potatoes and herrings

or significant insight, I can safely say 'all is not lost'. To give you an example: for the best part of four decades, I have been coming to my local village in Carraig Airt (as I affectionately call it now) and communicating entirely through English. Whereas in the last ten years I have engaged with at least one person as Gaeilge on every occasion I've been there. The local pharmacist, Aidan, and some of the staff in Boyce's shop will always engage. That's not to mention the customers. There's always someone willing, ready, and able to have that chat. I met Declan McFadden for breakfast over the summer – even though he spent a lot of his life in Singapore he has kept his Irish alive. When we recognised Róise Ní hOireachtaigh across the Galley restaurant we continued with a three-way conversation as Gaeilge. It's a nice feeling, being part of this. That's the litmus test of any language: daily usage. *Beatha teanga í a labhairt* – a language is alive when she is spoken. Our great language is alive and whether people have a little, or less than a little, or even with a bit of *Béarla* thrown in, that will do too. *Bheinn thar a bheith impressed le sin* – I would be more than impressed with that! *Úsaid í nó caill í* – use it or lose it – that's the key. I started this chapter with a focus on the Famine. My reason for doing this was to shed a light on my love for history. Equally, as I travelled through my Irish language journey, I was able to piggyback on my love for history and combine the learning of Irish. Treating the learning of Irish in a non-compartmentalised (single subject) manner has been a godsend.

DÁLA AN SCÉIL – BY THE WAY

Prátaí brúite – mashed potatoes – were an integral part of the Irish staple diet. *As Béarla* we had 'mash', 'poundies' and 'champ'. Poundies with scallions, hot milk and butter kept the *bolg* – stomach – *lán* – full – back in the day. When the stomach was *folamh* – empty – edginess could creep in leading to a state of *prátaí brúite tiubh* – thick as poundies. Check out Foclóir.ie for the difference in pronunciation of the word *práta* – potato. Ulster and Munster go with what it says on

Beidh Tú Alright: *Bainis an ghortáin fataí agus scadáin*

the tin, while in Conamara you will hear a lovely way of pronouncing *práta*: 'fata', short and sweet! If you are looking for early spuds, put Manor Cunningham in your satnav and you will be sure to find a sign that says 'Pirties for Sale'.

FOCAIL NA SEACHTAINE – WORDS OF THE WEEK

1. *An Gorta Mór* – the Great Famine
2. *Gan dabht* – without doubt
3. *Go dtí an lá inniu* – to this day
4. *Ag bailiú* – gathering
5. *An Tuaiscirt* – (of) the North
6. *An Deiscirt* – (of) the South
7. *An Iarthair* – (of) the West

DO THURAS FÉIN – YOUR JOURNEY

1. _____
2. _____
3. _____
4. _____
5. _____
6. _____
7. _____

Teanglann.ie phrase:
Le beagán cainte – In a few words

Caibidil 8

Is fusa rud a rá ná a dhéanamh

It is easier said than done

We can still have our fun too. Like the Donegal man ordering two cups of hot soup in Kerry at 211 kph – 'Ya hoo heh doo hai'. You try it! In written form it goes like this – Dhá shú thé domh, haigh – Two hot soups, haigh – compliments of Ray Mac Mánais ó Bhéal Feirste. Who knows what lies ahead or what the future holds. That's the great thing about life, you just never can tell. Even for myself with the advantage of a few thousand years on the planet, I still get surprised. I love surprises. I'm also an eternal optimist, and I look forward to the day when we won't be having this conversation. The day when it is normal to chat in the bar, barbershop, hairdresser, waiting room, cafeteria, mart, cooperative store, local shop, church, etc. as Gaeilge. That will be a very good day.

● ● ● ● ● ● ●

I never intentionally went out of my way to be different or do things differently. Most of the time it just happened naturally. As a young lad I dabbled with the notion of priesthood. As time wore on, and as I was enjoying the work on the farm I came to a crossroads, where I ingested my very first tonic of compromise. A farmer-priest was going to be my vocation. I corresponded regularly through the Society of African Missions (SMA) with the SMA fathers in Dromantine in the Diocese of Down and Connor at night and shovelled the dung out of byres at the weekend.

Secondary school put an end to all of that. I became a Loreto boy in a mixed convent in Milford in 1983. A new world opened up to me, all of twelve kilometres up the road. Not that I was backward or anything like that as my forward-planning parents had invested in the *Childcraft* and the *World Book Encyclopaedias* – the then equivalent of the internet. I was ready to take on the world! However, there were certain things that had me at a disadvantage. For example, I didn't 'have' a football team. Most of my peers had two, one in England and one in Scotland. Liverpool sounded like a good option for me, while I generously presented Wolverhampton Wanderers and West Ham United to James and Paul, my two little brothers. That didn't last long as they arranged two free transfers to Liverpool within a matter of days!

The Scottish end of things was a different ball game altogether. There were two major teams, Celtic (a club formed by Donegal men) or Rangers. That one seemed a no-brainer.

However, there was a catch. My classmate was a fanatical Celtic supporter to such an extent that science class became a 'history-of-Celtic class' – and his specialist subject was the year 1967. It was exhausting; I wasn't being awkward, or as a former teacher of mine used to say, 'obtuse', but just like that, I became an Aberdeen supporter. Like many voters in elections, I backed a winning horse. European Cup Winners' Cup champions in May 1983, they seemed like a good bet. Overnight I had to get to know my team, managed by Alex Ferguson. Players like

Strachan, Black, Hewitt, Miller, Leighton, McLeish et al. I didn't intend to be different, it just happened. I had posters of the entire team on the wall, and I never got a chance to watch them once on the television. Blind loyalty at its best. Apart from *Midweek Sports Special* and *Match of the Day*, the only other live sport that I watched was snooker. Many the argument I had with my father in deciding whether the ball being aimed at was blue, black or brown on our black-and-white television. On the music front, I steered away from U2, AC/DC and Megadeth and my school bag was the only green army bag with 'The Alarm' in block letters. Tracy Chapman, Annie Lennox, Elvis Costello, Billy Idol and Simple Minds featured strongly too.

Playing football around the clock in secondary school, culminating in an All-Ireland senior football final in 1989, wasn't conducive to good outcomes in the points race. We came second! My CAO form had a final and tenth entry for Maynooth University. They were good days. Maynooth came and went, and I ended up at the top of a classroom, teaching for a couple of years, and that's when my emphasis on change went into overdrive. I changed countries in 1995 for a stint in the UAE. A few of us saw a gap in the market in Dubai and teamed up with a group of Irish lads and an English man to form Dubai Celts CLG. Just recently a new Donegal Dubai GAA club has been set up. I'll have torn loyalties! I played *sacar* with Dubai Creek with a group of Scottish and English men, and I departed from teaching in 1996 to return to Donegal. I became a community youth worker that same year, and after that I entered the world of group facilitation, leadership and communication in 1998.

With change being a constant in my life, my baby steps into politics arrived in 1999. My Dad wasn't a Fine Gael supporter, but my Mum was, which was good enough for me, and the rest is history. At a personal level, that decision was probably the most important decision of my life. Sorry, let me rephrase that. That decision was *the* most important decision in my life. Olwyn has repeatedly and consistently said she would never have gone on that first date (on my birthday) if

I wasn't a Fine Gaeler! I'll always argue the toss with her on that one but between me and you I'd say she was serious enough.

The point of all of this is the following: I was well used to change, adapting to change, and facing new challenges head-on, and no matter what was thrown at me I would manage, somehow. My account of what happened in the Oifig an Taoisigh with Enda that July evening has been well documented at this stage. What I haven't said is this: while I was absolutely petrified about what was ahead of me, I was also strong in my conviction that with serious effort I could make it work. This new job offer changed everything for me. In hindsight, it was a gift and not a hospital pass. Shane Ross coined the phrase 'the Joe McHugh moment', which resonated with me strongly. This was my moment. This was the moment when I was given the chance to fully understand the beauty and importance of our language. This was the moment to dispense with the negative baggage of past experiences. This was the moment to say, this can be done. Time to face this head on, *céim ar chéim* – step by step – and that is what I set out to do.

Is féidir liom – Yes I can.
Is féidir linn – Yes we can.
Is féidir libh – Yes you can! (Not just you singular but *all* of you.)

DÁLA AN SCÉIL – BY THE WAY

My *seanmháthair* (*nó mathair mhór* in Donegal) introduced me to *carraigín* moss when I stayed with her during the summer. While it was *iontach blasta* – very tasty – I didn't realise at the time it was referring to the moss of the 'little rocks'. Many believed that the *carraigín* held a cure for the flu and congestion and a cure for sick calves. *Leigheas* is the Gaeilge for cure. Down the country pronounced 'lice' and up the road a bit like 'lace'.

Caibidil 8: *It is easier said than done*

***Focail na Seachtaine* – Words of the week**

1. *Comhthéacs* – Context
2. *Déan/Déanta/Rinne* – To do/done/did[19]
3. *Carraigeacha* – Rocks
4. *Forbairt* – Develop
5. *Gaeilge agus stair fite fuaite le chéile* – Irish and history interwoven with each other
6. *Is fusa rud a rá ná a dhéanamh* – easier said than done
7. *Deirim* – I say

***Do thuras féin* – Your journey**

1. _____
2. _____
3. _____
4. _____
5. _____
6. _____
7. _____

---

[19] The Irish language is clear when differentiating between 'done' and 'did'. *Tá m'obair bhaile déanta/Rinne mé m'obair bhaile* – my homework is done/I did my homework. Moving from Irish to English is not as clear cut. I 'done' my homework can be heard quite frequently. Listen out for it and you will be surprised how often you hear 'done' instead of 'did'. Maybe there was confusion during the transition from Gaeilge to Béarla!

Beidh Tú Alright: *Is fusa rud a rá ná a dhéanamh*

> Teanglann.ie phrase:
> *Níl cáin sa bhuille nach mbuailtear* –
> Hard words break no bones

Caibidil 9

Cé ná bíonn aon chnámh sa teanga, is minic a bhrís sí ceann duine

Even though the tongue is not a bone, it can often break a person's head

My Indo-Eurasian ancestors contributed to much more depth and feeling in my expression in comparison to the Béarla. Donegal men would have used 'gasta', the Gaeilge word for 'quick' or 'fast' on the building sites in Cricklewood. The Conamara man would have used sciobtha *(pronounced 'scioppie'). My Arabic cousins also used 'gasta' while building the pyramids in Egypt, and with a lot more gusto too. Gasta, gasta, gasta! My guttural strengths can be heard throughout Conamara. Cén chaoi a bhfuil tú – How are you? You need to dig deep for that guttural effect. And back up the road in Donegal you'll hear parents instructing their 'wains' to 'hurry up' – gutcha, gutcha'.*

● ● ● ● ● ● ●

Beidh Tú Alright: *Cé ná bíonn aon chnámh sa teanga, is minic a bhrís sí ceann duine*

Is fada an bóthar nach bhfuil aon chasadh ann – It's a long road that has no turning

I came across a book recently by Jane Harper – *The Lost Man*. A title I could relate to when I think back to difficult periods in my own life. Something captivated my attention at the start of the book. A place called Balamara. The author emphasised the peripherality of Balamara by cleverly sketching the town's lowly populated scattered settlement, one road in and out of the place and the 1,500 km road to the sea. A quick internet search showed that there is a place in New South Wales called Balamara. I wonder if the author was aware of the meaning behind the place name Balamara? Breaking up the word phonetically it gives us either *Baile Mara* or *Bealach Mara*. In Dublin we have the townlands *Baile na Mara Thiar*/Seatown West and *Baile na Mara Thoir*/Seatown East but these official forms are translations (see 'le seiton (1326), Logainm.ie #17053). In my own parish we have a housing estate called *Radharc na Mara* – View of the Sea. Is it possible that Balamara made the trip down under and lost '*na*' en route? This can happen and has happened. It happened to rugby legend Dave Gallaher (who lost the 'g' in the middle), who left Ramelton, *Dún na nGall*, for Auckland, New Zealand with his family at a young age. A national hero on the pitch, the first All Blacks rugby captain and a brave soldier, he lost his life on the battle fields of Passchendaele, Belgium, in 1917. I've also searched for '*bealachmara*' and *bealach na mara* in Logainm.ie but no joy. I did come across Bealach an Mhéara (Logainm.ie #11532) in Port Lairge – Mayor's Walk. Logically, this place in New South Wales, which is 1500 kilometres from the sea, could hardly be a sea town? However, I have a sense that *Bealach na Mara* – way to the sea – might be the perfect description. If you read the book, you will get a sense from the author's description of the location that is Balamara, with only one road in and one road out and the only way to escape the isolation is the road to the sea.

Caibidil 9: *Even though the tongue is not a bone, it can often break a person's head*

My reason for sharing this story is twofold. Firstly, there are many anglicised place names, and not only in Ireland. Secondly, trying to research the origin of these words is a joy, and while doing this research you will open new windows on your language journey.

I received many messages of support and encouragement in the early days of my *turas teanga* – language journey. One that stood out was from a Donegal man, John Wilson, living 'Down Under' in Victoria, Australia. He contacted me to wish me well on my journey as he was on a similar journey which he had just started. *Thosaigh John ag athfoghlaim nuair a bhí sé ceithre scór bliain d'aois* – John started relearning when he was 80 years of age. It's never too late.

DÚN NA SÉAD – BALTIMORE

Logainm.ie records two suggested derivations made by O'Donovan in 1841 for Baltimore in West Cork:

- *Baile an Tighe Mhóir* – Town of the Great House
- *Bealach an Tighe Mhóir* – Road of the Great House

Notably, there is another 1841 entry for Baltimore:

- *Dún na Séad* – Fort of the Jewels – The old Irish name for this place. This latter name, which local Irish speakers continued to use, is the official modern Irish version (see Logainm.ie #13321).

A visit to Baltimore is well worth the time to gain some insight into the history of the name. I spent some time there prior to my trip (on the invitation of John Walsh) to *An tOileán Mór* – the Big/Great Island – Bere Island (#8697). Logainm.ie records an interesting 1841 note by O'Donovan – *Inis Béirre* – 'Beara's island'. 'Beara is said to have been the Mother of *Oilioll Olum*, King of Munster.'

During my many visits to the islands off the *tír mór* or *mórthír* – mainland (depending on what part of the country you're from) – you get a sense of the challenges of island life and, of course, the rewards of tranquillity and peace. With the day job and important responsibilities that went with that, I didn't give those visits the time needed to explore the unique history of each of those islands. Bere Island[20] was certainly one of those special places which will get a return visit another time, *le cuidiú Dé* – with the help of God.[21]

While I was investigating the meaning behind the name of Baltimore in West Cork, I decided to see what other Baltimores there are around the world, starting with the US city in the state of Maryland. According to Britannica, 'Baltimore was established in 1729 and named for the Irish barony of Baltimore (seat of the Calvert family, proprietors of the colony of Maryland, USA). It was created as a port for shipping tobacco and grain, and soon local waterways were being harnessed for flour milling.'

According to Mapcarta, Baltimore is a homestead in New South Wales. Baltimore is situated near Mandoe, and west of Morell Creek.

Google tells us there is a village called Baltimore located in the southeast portion of Hamilton Township in Northumberland County in central Ontario, Canada. It is just north of the town of Cobourg, located at the intersection of County Road 45 and County Road 74.

There is also a small township called Baltimore situated on the N11 Highway in the Limpopo province of South Africa. It is a main stopover for the Groblersbrug Border Post with Botswana.

And one more: New Baltimore is a town in the north-eastern part of Greene County, New York, United States. The population was 3,370 at the 2010 census.

---

[20] Logainm.ie has the island as '*An tOileán Mór*/Bear Island', but it's more commonly known in Cork as Bere Island.

[21] '*Le Cuidiú Dé*' is a beautiful song by Daniel O'Donnell *as Gaeilge* which I would strongly recommend listening to, and if you're in that relaxation mode check out '*An Tráthnóna sin Fadó*' by Aodh Ó Duibheannaigh ó *Rann na Feirste*.

Caibidil 9: Even though the tongue is not a bone, it can often break a person's head

So, whether it's the Town of the Great House or the Way/Road of the Great House and if you're from Baltimore in Cork, Maryland, Ontario or South Africa, there is a historical connection to the place name in the form of *Dún na Séad* – fort of the jewels. I would go into a tell-all, warts-and-all analysis of the common-thread-of-colonisation factor here, but for the want of space and time. Another day's work perhaps!

Castar na daoine ar a chéile ach ní chastar na cnoic nó na sléibhte

The *clachán* – a cluster of houses where three generations lived in one commune – won't be coming back anytime soon; however, there is an emerging consensus that the virtual *clachán* will create a mechanism for people to meet irrespective of *tíreolaíocht* – geography, literally science of the land – and communicate in a language of choice. A group in Ontario, Canada, came up with the virtual *Gaeltacht* a few years back. The arrival of people from Ireland to places like St John's in Newfoundland meant that Gaeilge was spoken right up to the middle part of the nineteenth century in that part of Canada. They still speak with a strong Irish lilt in the coves above St John's to this day. Similarly, on Beaver Island in Lake Michigan, the O'Donnell, Gallagher and Boyle clans who emigrated from Árainn Mhór island were speaking Gaeilge right up to *na caogaidí* – the fifties. Fast forward to the present day, we have the wonderful example in Boston where the Catholic Memorial High School has Gaeilge on their high school curriculum. Máire Concannon ó Chonamara has been the driving force behind this wonderful project. She was brought up in Norwood, Massachusetts, where it is very common to hear Irish in the Irish Heaven, the Shamrock or Napper Tandy's in downtown Norwood. There will be other pubs too, so watch where you speak and what you speak as there is always a Gaeilgeoir nearby. The common thread through all those encounters was the love for the language and culture and the sense of a duty to preserve it. Máire is a great advocate of the following *seanfhocal gálanta* – beautiful old saying:

Castar na daoine ar a chéile ach ní chastar na cnoic nó na sléibhte – the people meet, but the hills and the mountains do not.

On the face of it, this is a self-explanatory and logical thing to say. However, when you think about it further, it emphasises the real importance of people meeting *gualainn ar ghualainn* – shoulder to shoulder. The *Covid naoi déag* – nineteen – experience has certainly reminded us of the *bearna* – gap – that exists when we are *sáinnithe* – stuck – between the hills and the mountains. Máire also introduced me to the expression '*go leor*' – lots, anglicised as 'galore'. *Ráfla* – rumour – has it that Máire is connected to the Concannon family of wine fame in California – she neither confirmed nor denied!

All in all, somebody somewhere is advocating in their own unique way for our language. As the Irish language is now officially recognised in the EU, other European countries are beginning to acknowledge this significance. The French embassy in Dublin sent me a Christmas card in French, *Béarla agus Gaeilge*.

> *Guíonn an tAmbasadóir Vincent Guérend agus foireann iomlán Ambasáid na Fraince in Éirinn Nollaig Shona <u>daoibh</u> agus gach rath <u>oraibh</u> do 2024. Feicimid <u>sibh</u> i bPáras do na Cluichí Oilimpeacha agus Parailimpeacha.*

I didn't make it to Paris, but I was still grateful for the Christmas message as Gaeilge. *Merci*, Vincent. Outside the EU, I got a nice letter from the ambassador of Australia to Ireland, Gary Gray, after I announced I was standing down from politics. His contact details included the following: *Ambasáid na hAstráile in Éireann*. Thanks for the note and your friendship during your time in Ireland, Gary.

I've just spotted a postage stamp on my desk with '*coirceog airgid* (silver cone), mid-tenth century'. This is the very first time I've come across the word *coirceog*. Another quick win for the language thanks to

Caibidil 9: *Even though the tongue is not a bone, it can often break a person's head*

An Post. We all have a role. We all have a duty. *Tá an freagracht orainn uilig* – the responsibility is on us all.

Dála an scéil – By the way

Tip of the day: try to avoid learning pronouns by rote. I found it better learning them in a particular context. See *'orainn'* above in last sentence and *'daoibh'*, *'oraibh'* agus *'sibh'* in the French ambassador's *teachtaireacht* – message.

Focail na seachtaine – Words of the week

1. *Ráfla* – rumour
2. *Coirceog* – cone
3. *Sáinnithe* – stuck
4. *Fosta/freisin/chomh maith* – also
5. *An tÓileán Mór* – the Great Island
6. *Tír mór/mórthír* – mainland
7. *Cionn Mhálanna*[22] – Malin Head

Do thuras féin – Your journey

1. _____
2. _____
3. _____

---

[22] In the complete opposite direction, we have Banba's Crown in Malin Head (also known as Ireland's crown). This location was named after the mythological patron goddess of Ireland and a lookout tower was built there by the British in 1805. Banba had two sisters named Eriu and Fodla. Éire or Ireland came from Eriu. The Romans referred to Éire as Hibernia (A native or inhabitant of Ireland). *Hibernus* meaning wintry, of or pertaining to winter. ("Hibernian" Merriam-Webster.com Dictionary, https://www.merriam-webster.com/dictionary/Hibernian.)

Beidh Tú Alright: *Cé ná bíonn aon chnámh sa teanga, is minic a bhrís sí ceann duine*

4. _____
5. _____
6. _____
7. _____

> Teanglann.ie phrase:
> *Sin mar a chuir sí uirthi* –
> those were her very words

Caibidil 10

Is beag le rá an chuileog nó go dtéann sí sa tsúil

A fly is a small thing until it gets in one's eye

I am a language that needs a kiss of life, and I don't want to be excluded. Whether that's on the Newtownards Road in East Belfast or the streets of London or New York. I need all the help I can get, to breathe new life into me again. Séideog – a breath of wind. Lest we forget, I am alive today because so many people on an individual, family and community basis continued to speak as Gaeilge and continued to converse in their mother tongue. In the meantime, the díospóireacht – debate – will rage. This was wrong. That was wrong. And it's still wrong. In the meantime, I will struggle. The glór – voice – will rage as Béarla. Join with me. Celebrate with me. Cry with me. Laugh with me. Remember, I am you.

● ● ● ● ● ● ●

Beidh Tú Alright: *Is beag le rá an chuileog nó go dtéann sí sa tsúil*

THE FADA – FADÓ, FADÓ

Fado is a Portuguese folk song typically of doleful or fatalistic character and usually accompanied on the guitar. Throw a fada on it and you get *fadó*. According to Teanglann.ie:

- *Na laethanta fadó* – the days long ago
- *In Éirinn fadó* – in Ireland long ago
- *Bhí rí ann fadó* – once upon a time there was a king
- *Lá fada samhraidh* – a long summer's day

Getting to grips with the fada was critical for proper pronunciation. *Mala tiubh* is thick eyebrow while *mála* is what you bring your books to school in. *Lon* is a blackbird and *lón* is what you eat in the middle of the day. *Cás* is case and *cas* is turn. *Sólás* is consolation and *solas* is light – you need one when you are in the dark metaphorically and the other when you are in the dark literally. *Leamh* is lacklustre or dull and *léamh* is what you are doing right now.

The Gaeilge word *fada* – meaning long – is a great opportunity to illustrate the difference between feminine and masculine. Don't worry, I'm not going to scare you into this space. *Éist liom* – listen to me.

BAININSCNEAMH – FEMININE

- *Gruaig fhada* – long hair
- *Oíche fhada* – long night
- *Rud a chur ar an mhéar fhada* – to put something on the long finger, the place where I had the language on for too long!

FIRINSCNEAMH – MASCULINE

- *Tamall fada* – long while

- *Saol fada* – long life
- *Muineál fada* – long neck

Basically, I had to learn the distinction between feminine and masculine words. I did not do this by rote. I did it by listening to Irish speakers and knowing what sounded right and what didn't. Tuning into Raidió na Gaeltachta is a good opportunity for this or a visit to the Gaeltacht. *Oíche* is feminine and therefore the adjective has an 'h', *oíche fhada* while *lá* is masculine and gets *lá fada*, with no 'h'. That's the formal distinction, however I focused on the sounds rather than the rules and while I can now digest the formal construction of the language, I couldn't back in 2014 – *fadó, fadó*. Bitesize Irish is a good reference point for differentiating between masculine and feminine: www.bitesize.irish.

Back to the *fada*.[23] This little mark is an important part of the Irish language. Handle this one with care. Think of the importance of quavers and semiquavers to musicians. Reflecting on my primary and secondary school days, I feel that my teachers were fighting a losing battle. They had one hand tied behind their back. The classroom duties were being complied with for sure; however, outside the class, in the playground or detention, no name club, school tours, the bus or the football pitch, *Béarla* took over. Opportunities to listen to and immerse in the Irish language were few and far between.

The cart was before the horse. It was akin to learning to play football without the football. Where was the love? The relationship was doomed from the start. A lot of water has passed under the bridge since 2014. It has been ten years since my appointment, longer than the

---

[23] Interestingly, when you key 'Longford' into Logainm.ie search engine, the name appears in a number of counties, including County Longford itself. *An t-Áth Fada/Longford* (Logainm.ie #49029) appears in *Tiobraid Árann*. More appear in Galway, Laois, Limerick, Mayo, Meath, Offaly and Roscommon. Longford Terrace and Longford Villas appear in Dublin.

time I spent in primary school. Ten years of full and partial immersion. Hours and hours of conversation. Repeating words and sentences over and over again. It wasn't always a barrel of laughs but in the main I wanted to do this. I owned it. When I hear economic discussions about the 'double Irish' (in connection with the taxation of large corporations), I can't help but think back to sitting through a double Irish class. It was a tough ordeal *go deimhin* – indeed. One of the biggest challenges I faced was making the simple connections once I started moving. It became glaringly obvious in the car. Simple instructions like *díreach ar aghaidh* – straight ahead – or *tóg an chéad chasadh eile ar chlé* – take the next left turn – wasn't something I could draw on from my 'limited' vocabulary. Asking for help is a must and the websites Foclóir.ie (Foras na Gaeilge's English–Irish Dictionary), Teanglann.ie (online dictionary and language library), Téarma.ie (a lexical database for terminology in the Irish language) and Abair.ie (a pronunciation guide) are excellent resources.

A child learning a language will get to grips with all the important commands. Where's my food? It's on your left. Where's my Mammy? She's straight ahead. We learned the Gaeilge for going to the shop on our bicycle and at times we didn't even have a bike, never mind knowing where the shop was. It goes back to relevance again. I needed to get to places in the car as part of my job. Responsibility for Islands and Gaeltacht areas – stretching from Bere Island in Cork to *Gleann Bhairr* (the top of the glen) in Donegal; from *Rath Cairn* in Meath to *Inis Oírr* in Galway – required good communication, and punctuality was important. I didn't like to keep people waiting. Doing all this as Gaeilge for the first time was a huge challenge. A child needs to eat and will listen very carefully to all those new instructions. You need to learn on the job. You have a greater incentive to learn when there is a relevance to what you do. Learning the language wasn't the objective – doing my job was the priority and the added value was learning to speak Gaeilge properly, for the first time. *Chuaigh* – went, past tense of *téigh* – to go. Most of us were introduced to '*chuaigh*' at an early age

Caibidil 10: *A fly is a small thing until it gets in one's eye*

and it was one of the verbs that we got a good handle on. Depending on whether you are from Malin or Mizen it is pronounced differently. Up above it sounds like *hooey* and down below it is very similar to *cúig*. Much like '*raibh*' – was – up north it sounds like *row* and down south it gets *rev*. The title of this book has different phonetics too: 'Beg tú alright' *síos an tír* – down the country – agus 'bay tú alright' *suas an tír* – up the country. Some say 'tomato', others say 'tomayto'. Put a Kerry man and a Donegal man in a room speaking English and we won't pretend that we have different versions of the same English language – even though we do in a dialectical sense. Dig deep and draw on all your basic rote learned vocabulary from back in the day. There's a lot in there, similar to a volcano waiting to erupt, an active volcano and not a dormant – *ina codladh* – type

A creative and fun learning construct demands your attention. In a nice way. Experiential learning, no matter how young you are, is a great motivating tool. I learned years earlier through my work with *daoine fásta* – adults – that their own life experiences provided an enlightening gateway to their learning. When I think back to my own school days, I associated the learning of Irish with thoughts of *brón* – melancholy – *eagla* – fear – and *dúr* – surly/grim. I didn't realise at the time that I was questioning its relevance and fun. Very few in my social circle spoke Gaeilge and the fact that it felt like a daily drudgery didn't endear the language to me. Five decades later, my three children ask the same questions of me that I was too afraid to ask back in the day. They also throw out challenges, such as, 'Not the Irish again Daddy!' Nonetheless, we are making progress. We had outdoor classes in the garden during lockdown. I also do simple directional phrases and when they are bored in the car we do '*Tím le mo leathshúilín focal ag tosú le ...*' – 'I spy with my little eye a word beginning with ...'. They also enjoyed this very much in school with their teacher.

When you are ready to move, you move on, and only then. If you treat this as a theoretical exercise, you are doomed from the start. You need to 'jump start' the language muscle in your brain and train it to speak to you when you least expect it. Your world is predominantly an English-speaking environment, and you are in a 24/7 *Béarla* immersion programme. You need to take control of that *timpeallacht* – environment. You're on your computer and you're asked for a password, why not pick one as Gaeilge? I recently started using Irish words that I haven't come across for setting a new password. Good on the security front but taxing on the memory front! You're setting up your Gmail account, why not as Gaeilge? You're writing your address, why not as Gaeilge? You're sending a text, why not as Gaeilge? You meet someone in the shop who says hello as Gaeilge, why not answer as Gaeilge? You're in a waiting room with your eyes glued to English-speaking apps doomscrolling, why not a Gaeilge app? Duolingo perhaps? There is no shortage of Gaeilge apps out there. If you want to stay up to speed with the GAA, Score Beo will keep you right. Raise your awareness in shops as some companies are using Gaeilge to display their produce. You are setting up a reminder on your phone why not *Gaeilge agus Béarla*. Rather than an *ordóg suas* – thumbs up – use a GRMA (*go raibh maith agat* – *thank you*)! Or if you're really grateful GRMMA (*go raibh míle maith agat* – a thousand thank yous). From a thinking point of view, think of all the places you go to in your own head when you are driving, in bed before you go to sleep, in the shower, walking, jogging, in the gym, in a boring lecture, etc. You are thinking in English. You are talking to yourself in English. You are giving yourself a hard time in English. That needs to change. Bring *téigh* – go – to the pub with you, because when it's time to go it's time to go now please. Bring *ith* – eat – to the restaurant with you. Bring *feic* – see – with you to the *radharceolaí* – optician – literal translation: view expert. Bring *déan* – do – with you to work. Bring *clois* – hear – with you when you are listening to the radio or a podcast. Bring *faigh* – get – with you when you get the groceries. Bring verbs into your life and make them part of it. *Leanfadh muid ar aghaidh* – we move ahead.

Caibidil 10: *A fly is a small thing until it gets in one's eye*

Dála an scéil – By the way

Malachy Ó Néill is Professor of Irish and Director of Regional Engagement at Ulster University. He was born in *Tír Eoghain* and works in *Doire*. He started learning Irish when he was eleven years of age. Malachy and a considerable cohort of language enthusiasts in the North were disadvantaged because Irish was not on the curriculum. They did not let this hold them back and today they continue to converse as Gaeilge and advocate for the Irish language. Malachy is a tremendous ambassador for the Irish language and is a good man to have a yarn with during the Ulster championship.

Focail na seachtaine – Words of the week

1. *Rí*[24] – king
2. *Ordóg suas* – thumbs up
3. *Dúr*[25] – surly/grim
4. *Timpeallacht* – environment
5. *Díreach ar aghaidh* – straight ahead
6. *Go deimhin* – indeed / *Cinnte* – certainly
7. *Cuileog* – fly

Do thuras féin – Your journey

1. _____
2. _____
3. _____
4. _____

---

[24] *An Ríocht Abú* – Up the Kingdom!
[25] This has given us the word 'dour' in English, coming via Scots Gaelic.

Beidh Tú Alright: *Is beag le rá an chuileog nó go dtéann sí sa tsúil*

5. _____

6. _____

7. _____

> Teanglann.ie phrase:
> *Chas tú mo chuid cainte* –
> You twisted my words.

Caibidil 11

Ní bhíonn saoi gan locht

Nobody's perfect

The witching debate in the witching hour. Siobhán from Oideas Gael shakes her head. She's heard this record repeatedly. 'There are classes here all winter.[26] You were all raised with Gaeilge … you have Gaeilge … you just don't use it ….' And the place goes quiet. Siobhán's cousin Kevin gets things going, and a conversation begins. 'My grandmother had this expression: ní bhíonn saoi gan locht – *nobody's perfect*. My grandfather had this expression when working in the fields maireann an craobh ar an bhfál ach ní mhaireann an lámh a chuir – *the branch lives on the hedge but the hand that planted it is dead.*' The conversation is enriched with so many observations and reflections. Then, slowly but surely, the odd Gaeilge line is introduced and then a conversation begins. Tiocfaidh sí ar ais – *she will come back.* Like the 65 Massey Ferguson tractor – it takes a while to get going but when it does there's no stopping it. To be

---

[26] Thankfully the local community have taken up the invitation from Siobhán and the team at Oideas Gael, and the winter classes are growing all the time.

part of that experience is a joy. The speed of the interaction can be a challenge. But that's the way it should be – natural, free-flowing and galánta *– beautiful – and before you know it, it's* a dó a chlog ar maidin *– two in the morning. Shhh …* Ná habair! Am dul a luí. Oíche mhaith.

● ● ● ● ● ● ● ●

Sir Roger Casement – Gaelic League member, Irish Volunteer and a former diplomat in the British Foreign Office – led a crusade in the Irish language revival. Like many Irish citizens today, he couldn't converse as Gaeilge, but he knew the value of our language being part of our quest for independence. He walked the walk. Seosamh Ó Ceallaigh, in his book *As Smaointe tig Gníomh, Coláiste Uladh, an Ghaeilge agus 1916*, quotes from a letter Casement wrote, 'My subscription of £80 towards the building fund of New Hall is a personal gift to the people of Cloughaneely' (p. 274). In a conversation with Seosamh he told me that Sir Roger Casement referred to Cloughaneely as the 'hills of my heart'. Casement was inspired by three Protestant women from the Glens of Antrim: Íde Nic Néill, Margaret Dobbs agus Róis Ní Ógáin.

Margaret Dobbs used these profound words:

> Ireland is a closed book to those who do not know her language. No one can know Ireland properly until one knows the language. Her treasures are as hidden as a book unopened. Open the book and learn to love your language.[27]

Liam Ó Duibhir wrote in *The Donegal Awakening*:

> Roger Casement, who was captured following the failed attempt to smuggle weapons into Tralee Bay on 21st April 1916, was a visitor to the county in 1912. His visit was not for political purposes,

---

[27] Ó Doibhlinn, D. *Womenfolk of the Glens and the Irish Language* (Muineachán, 1996), p. 103.

but for his love of the Irish language and his desire to learn it. He walked from Ballymoney in County Antrim [*Baile Monaidh, Contae Aontroma*] to Lishally, crossed on the ferry to Culmore, proceeded over the Scalp mountain [*Sliabh Scailp*] in Inishowen, along the old road to Buncrana [*Bun Cranncha*] and then through the Gap of Mamore to Ur[r]is. He spent six months living among the people of Donegal and visited many areas of the county, including Fanad [*Fánaid*], Portsalon [*Port an tSalainn*], Tory Island [*Toraigh*], Coughaneely [*Cloch Cheann Fhaola*] and Glenties [*Na Gleanntai*]. The following is an extract from a letter from Roger Casement to his niece Blanche Constance, sent from Tory Island on 16 October 1912 (a few months after the sinking of the *Titanic*):

> 'This is a photo of me too – taken on Tory Island away off the far N. West Coast of Ireland – right out in the Atlantic. All the people in it speak Irish! – Not English – except me. They can speak English too – but prefer Irish their own tongue. Lots of the islands speak no English at all. I haste now – as I've things to do. Always your affectionate but lazy uncle. Roger.'[28]

This is an intriguing and *suntasach* – significant – historical connection, between my own county and a person who played an active role in the 1916 Rising. *Sliabh Scailp* – Scalp Mountain – also gets a reference. Logainm.ie has an archival record referencing 'Scalp Mountain' as '*An Scailp*' and includes this archival note:

> Scalp – signifies the fissure or separation. This is the old name of the hill and takes its name from a fissure, gap or separation on its top or ridge. This is a large barren rocky and picturesque hill.

---

[28] Ó Duibhir, L. (2009) *The Donegal Awakening: Donegal and the War of Independence*, Mercier Press (Cork), p. 31.

There's plenty of other examples of Scailps/Scalps/Sceilps throughout the country with some extraordinary, anglicised spellings. Scoltnacrappagh doesn't do justice to the beautifully named Scailp na gCnapán in Gleann Cholm Cille. Skelpatassony is another quare one in the parish of Cill Charthaigh (Kilcar) which replaced Sceilp an tSasanaigh (Logainm.ie #1397121). Etymonline.com defines scalp as 'The crown or top of the head (including hair)' and if you combine *Sasanaigh* (English), this is worthy of further conversation in John Joe's Bar, Kilcar on a winter's evening! Scalpnadinga (Sceilp na Dinge) in Dún na nGall and Scalpaconnaun (Scailp an Chonáin) in Galway are two phonetically correct examples but when written down, they look a tad ridiculous to say the least.

If you really want to be blown away with majestic scenery, take a trip to *Oileán Gabhla* – Gola Island – and take in the breath-taking wonder of *Sceilp Ó Dugain*. It's just *dochreidte* – unbelievable. There is a stone plaque at this spot marking the memory of two young men who lost their lives in the World Trade Center on 11 September 2001. Their grandmother, Mary O'Sullivan, left Gola when she was 18 years of age and travelled to *Nua Eabhraic* (New York).[29] There is a poignant inscription as Gaeilge: '*I gCuimhne ar Peter Milano agus Patrick Sullivan a cailleadh sa W.T.C 9/11 – 01*' – 'In memory of Peter Milano and Patrick Sullivan who were lost in the W.T.C 9/11 – 01'.

Casement's desire to get to know the people and the geography was matched with his *turas teanga* – language journey. We now live in a digital age, and while we are connected around the clock, you'll not beat the Gaeltacht experience if you really want to nurture your own *turas teanga*.

I was fortunate to be in the Department of Gaeltacht and Culture for the 2016 Commemorative Programme. It gave me a true insight into the interdependence that exists between language and history.

---

[29] Evelyn Sweeney, whose family hail from Gola, was able to trace Mary O'Sullivan's journey on a recent trip to Ellis Island.

John Concannon, who is now ambassador to Canada and envoy to Antigua & Barbuda, Jamaica and the Bahamas, played a key leadership role in the commemorative programme. A language is not just a communication tool. Rather than trying just to immerse yourself in the language, immerse yourself in your local history and, believe me, so many things will start to make a lot more sense. Roger Casements was the name of an amalgamated GAA club between *Na Dúnaibh, Fánaid* agus *Baile na nGallóglach* (Milford). Growing up, it was just a name. To learn all these years later that my local club was named after a hero to the indigenous people in the Congo, Peru, Brazil and Ireland is enlightening to say the least. Logainm.ie shows instances of the place name Milford/Millford across seven counties *Áth an Mhuilinn* – the Ford of the Mill – is the preferred original name for most, bar one. Milford in Donegal is the exception; the original name is *Baile na nGallóglach* – Town of the Gallowglasses (Logainm.ie #1416620). The *Gallóglaigh* (anglicised as 'Gallowglass') were mercenary warriors from Gaelic-Norse clans in Scotland in the thirteenth to sixteenth centuries. A battle between the Irish (helped by *Gallóglaigh*) and the English took place in the townland. Breaking down *Gallóglaigh* you get *gall*[30] – foreign, óg – young – and *laoch* – warrior/hero – revealing a more descriptive label for Milford: the town of the young warriors.

THAR LEAR/THAR SÁILE – ABROAD

'When I walk with two others, there must be one whom I can learn from.' This Chinese idiom comes to mind when I think back to my visit to Brazil in March 2018. The then ambassador, Brian Glynn, researched the remarkable life and sad death of Sir Roger Casement, who served as British consul in Brazil in the early twentieth century. In a fitting tribute to Casement, the ambassador laid a wreath at the temporary consulate of Ireland in Rio de Janeiro on the 100th anniversary of his

---

[30] *Gall* is the Gaeilge for foreign and *Gael* is the Gaeilge for native.

execution. He could surely have never imagined that there would be a representative of Ireland commemorating him in Rio 100 years after his death.

People asked me at the time would I 'keep up' the Irish in my new ministerial roles. That question was answered very quickly during my first visit to Kampala, Uganda. Then Ambassador Donal Cronin, from the Kingdom of Kerry, greeted me as Gaeilge, and we conversed as Gaeilge. My Gaeilge journey continued, and I also made sure to keep my study visits to Gleann Cholm Cille on the agenda too because at the back of my head was the thought, 'if you don't use it, you'll lose it'. I continued with classes in Gleann Cholm Cille every summer up until Covid-19, and I also taught an Irish class a few years after my appointment. My newfound love for Gaeilge whetted my appetite for other languages too. It opened a new world to me, and very quickly I realised that dialectal difference is the norm and is not just unique to Ireland. Bantu, Central Sudanic, Nilotic, Swahili, Luganda and English are the main languages spoken in Uganda. While visiting a community in Kampala I was intrigued to hear the greeting that was used by the local people. Phonetically, it sounded like an Irish phrase '*a la chara ar ndóigh*'. These familiar-sounding words would probably translate to 'of course friend' or something to that effect. While I don't know the literal translation of the Ugandan phrase, I like to think it means something similar. Words, sounds and expressions became an obsession for me. The language I had struggled with and fought with was now a language I was fighting for.

An tAthair Pádraig Devine founded the Shalom organisation and works out of Northern Kenya. We flew from Nairobi to Turkana and met with locals to understand the community rehabilitation and reconciliation efforts. It was a pleasure listening to a 'Rossy' (Up the Rossies) communicate in the native tongue, listening to his humour *as*

Béarla and employing his favourite line *as Gaeilge: nuair a thagann an crú ar an tairne*[31] – when push comes to shove.

Gaeilge started out in this wee world along with the likes of Swahili, Mandarin, Cantonese, and Arabic. Those languages have crossed paths over the years, they have evolved, they have changed and, to cut a long story short, I wanted to find out more.

DÁLA AN SCÉIL – BY THE WAY

I have a fond memory engaging with former Brazilian President Collor when I visited Brazil in 2018 as Minister for Education. President Collor was communicating in Portuguese and Ambassador Glynn was on hand to do the interpretation. I spoke as Gaeilge, which gave an added challenge to the ambassador. He responded in style, jumping between Gaeilge, English and Portuguese. Two years previously, Mark Hanniffy got me to read a section of *Ulysses* as Gaeilge on a visit to Edinburgh. Both were really enjoyable experiences.

FOCAIL NA SEACHTAINE – WORDS OF THE WEEK

1. *Dochreidte* – unbelievable
2. *Suntasach* – significant
3. *Caogaidí* – fifties
4. *Uladh* – Ulster
5. *Ar ndóigh* – of course
6. *Turas teanga* – language journey
7. *Nuair a thagann an crú ar an tairne* – when push comes to shove

---

[31] *Nuair a thagann an crú ar an tairne* – when push comes to shove. The literal translation refers to when a nail on a horse's shoe hits the road and pushes against the horseshoe.

Beidh Tú Alright: *Ní bhíonn saoi gan locht*

DO THURAS FÉIN – YOUR JOURNEY

1. _____
2. _____
3. _____
4. _____
5. _____
6. _____
7. _____

> Teanglann phrase:
> *Ná bain casadh as mo chuid cainte* –
> Don't twist my words

Caibidil 12

Bíonn báisteach uafásach san fhásrach

Rain is terrible in the desert

Caill uair ar maidin, is beidh tú á tóraíocht ar feadh an lae – *lose an hour in the morning and you'll be chasing for the rest of the day*. I ain't giving up just yet, there is a lot more to be told, and I am confident that if that early hour is used properly in the morning we won't be chasing, we will be leading. Use the time wisely though. Figure out what you like about me. Is it my construction? Is it my song and verse? Is it my 'oidhreacht' which encapsulates my heritage and my legacy. If I am to be fully understood, there is plenty of scope in all of these rich areas to explore the magic and beauty of my past. The cornerstone of my existence is my past. However, my responsibility is to this generation and the next.

● ● ● ● ● ● ●

Beidh Tú Alright: *Bíonn báisteach uafásach san fhásrach*

AR AIS AR SCOIL – BACK TO SCHOOL!

Darragh had just graduated from Rainbows[32] and was transitioning to junior infants when I was appointed Minister for the Gaeltacht in the summer of 2014. Aedín agus Oisín were in pre-school. Without their permission, I joined them on their Irish language journey through primary school. They still haven't forgiven me. Introducing them to *fosta* – also – when they were learning *freisin* – also – and *brachán* – porridge – when they were eating *leite* – porridge – added a bit of honey and spice – *mil agus spíosra* – to proceedings. I feel bad in hindsight as their teachers were doing a very good job at promoting Gaeilge in the school. I can say without fear of contradiction, my children didn't share the same drive and passion for learning as their Daddy. I've often thought about this. Ultimately, my children didn't get access to full immersion in those early years, simply because I wasn't about all the time. Being honest, even if I had been about all the time, would that have changed things dramatically? Who knows? As time moves on, I am more convinced than ever that full immersion at pre-school and early years at primary is critical for the future sustainability of the language. In 2015, Harold Hislop, then chief inspector in the Department of Education, facilitated a very important workshop between Roinn na Gaeltachta and the Department of Education, which led to the introduction of the voluntary Gaeltacht Recognition Scheme policy, targeted at all Gaeltacht schools, primary and secondary. That was an important first step. Civil servants have a key role to play in the advancement and development of the Irish language. They must be responsive, attentive, and courageous. Politicians need to be ambitious. Harold answered my call in 2015, and for that I will always be grateful. The baton has been passed along to dedicated teams in the Department of Education and the Department with responsibility

---

[32] Rainbows is a pre-school in Carraig Airt which gave a great start in life to my children.

for the Gaeltacht and Irish language. The success of the Gaeltacht Recognition Scheme to date can act as a template for future policy development outside the Gaeltacht.

A few minutes on the phone in the evening with my family wasn't going to be sufficient. Those years were the ideal years for them to hear the language, absorb it, get used to it and normalise it. While lockdown opened a window and provided more time with my children, the defence systems had already hardened considerably. Outdoor classes in the garden were positive and enabled the learning of words while moving. A derelict outhouse with no roof, windows or doors provided us with an excellent educational tool. Differentiating between *amuigh agus amach* and *istigh agus isteach* are very important distinctions.

- *Tá muid ag teacht amach* – we are coming out
- *Tá muid amuigh an teach anois* – we are now outside the house
- *Tháinig muid isteach* – we came in
- *Bhí muid istigh ansin* – then we were inside
- *Díreach ar aghaidh* – straight ahead
- *Tiontaigh ar chlé* – turn left
- *Bog ar dheis* – move right
- *Ag bogadh isteach* – moving in
- *Ag dul amach* – going out
- *Tá muid istigh* – we are in (Or *tá muidinne*[33] *istigh* if you're saying it the Ulster way)
- *Táim taobh amuigh* – I am outside

The big prize was getting to spend one-to-one time outside with the 'wains'. I'm not sure they enjoyed it as much as me! Working on creative ways to make irregular verbs less irregular worked to an extent; however, these lessons were seen for what they were – just lessons.

---

[33] *Muidne/muidinne/muinne* is the emphatic form of *muid*.

Oisín, the youngest, got more into the spirit of things. Our mornings deciding what the weather was like were fun and not a chore, I think. I hope! The weather never let us down:

- *Lá scamallach* – cloudy day
- *Lá fliuch* – wet day
- *Lá báistí* – rainy day
- *Lá tirim* – dry day
- *Lá gaofar* – windy day (*lá slamhlaigh* in Falcarrach)
- *Lá garbh* – rough day (pronounced 'garru' in the hills)
- *Lá grianmhar* – sunny day
- *Lá measartha* – middling day

So, what was preventing us ploughing ahead with full immersion at home? Was there a possible association with the troubled waters and the pressure I was under at the time that the children were picking up on? Probably. Was I bringing in too much negativity, *strus agus brú* – stress and pressure – to the house? Possibly. In hindsight, my home was my escape from my full immersion journey and provided a much-needed break from the intensity of my steep learning curve. I needed that sanctuary. I can't decide which of the following episodes caused most trauma: my awful experiences at the Joint Oireachtas Committee for the Irish Language, or my terrifying few days prior to my participation at *An tOireachtas* in Killarney a few months into my new role? Or maybe it was more to do with saying goodbye to my family on a Monday morning and not seeing them again until the weekend. Whatever it was, the dynamic wasn't right for us all to jump aboard the Irish language train, just yet.

DÁLA AN SCÉIL – BY THE WAY

In the English language 'last week' can be expressed in different ways. It can be described as 'the week that has just gone' or 'the week that

Caibidil 12: *Rain is terrible in the desert*

has gone by'. No doubt the Irish expressions for 'last week' have influenced things. In the hills you'll hear '*an tseachtain seo a chuaigh thart*'; around the middle you'll hear '*an tseachtain seo caite*'; and, further down the road, you will hear '*an tseachtain [seo] imithe tharainn.*'

FOCAIL NA SEACHTAINE – WORDS OF THE WEEK

1. *Millteanach/uafásach* – terrible
2. *Strus agus brú* – stress and pressure
3. *Lá scamallach* – cloudy day
4. *Lá báistí* – wet day
5. *Dufair* – jungle
6. *Tá muid istigh* – we are in
7. *Brachán/leite* – porridge

DO THURAS FÉIN – YOUR JOURNEY

1. _____
2. _____
3. _____
4. _____
5. _____
6. _____
7. _____

> Teanglann phrase:
> *Chlis an chaint, an chuimhne, an obair air* –
> words, his memory, the work, failed him.

Caibidil 13

Fásann níos mó i ngarraí ná a chuirtear ann

More grows in a garden than is planted there

I see them getting on buses and jumping out of cars. Teenagers and younger ones alike. They don't all talk in glowing terms about me. I've become a bit of a crá croí – *nuisance/heartache* – to some. In spite of all of that, I ain't searbh – *bitter*. I am dearfach – *positive*; dóchasach – *optimistic* – agus réalaíoch – *realistic*. I want to become ábhartha – *relevant* – again. I want to be the connection in people's lives, and I must make sense. There is no shortage of emotional connection to my past: an nasc go dtí an stair – *the connection to the past*.

● ● ● ● ● ● ●

Petah Tiqua is Hebrew for Gateway of Hope. I never lost hope. The people around me never allowed me to lose hope either.

Caibidil 13: *More grows in a garden than is planted there*

My brief sojourn engaging with the primary school curriculum rolled along faster than my time in primary school. Same school though. Hard to beat consistency! Second time around was my last chance saloon to get my head around those irregular verbs, all eleven of them. There were many words I had forgotten and words that were completely new to me. We had a fridge back in the 1970s, and with subsistence living, it was more of an ornament. A friend of mine reminded me recently that the only thing in his cuisneoir – *fridge* – back then was the light. Anyhow, I couldn't remember *cuisneoir*, it was like learning a word for the first time. *Mil* – *honey* – was another and no matter how hard I tried *duilleoga* – *leaves* – weren't on my radar. Some have repeated their Leaving Certificate or repeated sixth class; however, I've never known anyone who repeated primary school. My time in primary school has finished, but I get to dip back in and out with Oisín. Now that I get to spend time with him after school, we use the opportunity to practise our Gaeilge. When there's a football involved the Irish flows more naturally! I've moved on to secondary school with Darragh and Aedín in Loreto Milford, my old alma mater. *Groundhog Day* or what!? Both Aedín agus Darragh's *múinteoirí* – teachers – got straight into the *urú* – eclipsis – agus *séimhiú* – lenition – from the get-go. I was quite stubborn about the grammar and the rules of Gaeilge. I totally believed I was going to get by and prove that we can all get there without worrying about sweating the small stuff, the stuff that gave us far too many sleepless nights. Their *múinteoirí* – teachers – blew all that out of the water. *Bhí an ceart acu* – they were right. We all must face our demons at some stage, so why not now? Was I ready for this though? The answer was yes. The grammar rules were coming a lot easier to me than was the case in the 1970s and 1980s. The *fuaimeanna* – sounds – made sense. My ear had become attuned to the *urú* in the right place and the *séimhiú* in the proper place too. Looking at the list of tasks on Aedín and Darragh's worksheets frightened me at the beginning. The pressure was on big time as they assumed I was an expert at grammar! If they only knew. Maybe they did! If I had that level of competence back in 2014, I would have avoided all the *'Aire gan teanga, Aire gan clue'* shenanigans. I took another look at the worksheet and things started to click, even though I was looking at a plethora of bizarre scenarios. Imagine explaining to someone in Coventry or Connecticut that the Gaeilge for 'her' is *'a'*; the Gaeilge for 'his' is *'a'* and the Gaeilge for 'their' is *'a'*. This is where the *draíocht* – magic – begins:

Let's explore the wonderful Gaelic world of the apple:[34]

- *Úll* – apple
- *An t-úll* – the apple
- *Na húlla* – the apples
- *A úll* – his apple
- *A húll* – her apple
- *A n-úll* – their apple
- *Síolta úill* – seeds of the apple
- *An t-úllord* – the orchard
- *Níor thit an t-úll i bhfad ón gcrann* – the apple didn't fall far from the tree

Ar ais go dtí an Ghaeilge – back to the Irish and back to the *obair bhaile*:

- *Ár nAthair atá ar neamh* – our Father who art in heaven
- *Ár n-arán laethúil* – our daily bread
- *Ár bhfiacha* – our trespasses

When I struggled with my grammar the first time and second time round, I didn't realise that a lot was already lodged in my head from a long time ago. All I had to do was tap back into the prayer that I knew

---

[34] Check out *'Cúig Úll Dhearga'*, which can be sung to the tune of 'Ten Green Bottles', in *Broga Nua 2* by Áine Ní Shúilleabháin (2008, p. 29).

off by heart to see the necessary *urú* changes. Once I understood how the changes occurred from the prayer, understanding other changes became a lot clearer. *Mar shampla* – for example:

- *Ár* – our
- *A* – their
- *Bhur* – your (plural)

… all follow the same rule:

- *Ár n-uisce* – our water
- *Ár bhfuinneog* – our window
- *A n-eilifint* – their elephant
- *Bhur n-uibheacha* – your eggs
- *A n-óraiste* – their orange

In a nutshell:

- **n** before a vowel
- **bh** before f
- **d** before t
- **b** before p
- **s** before t
- **g** before c
- **n** before g
- **m** before b

There's no other way around this, you must learn these off. One hour as a total percentage of a sixteen-year learning programme is a small ask and a small fraction of a life journey.

The full circle has come around indeed. This time I'm enjoying unlocking the mystery around our much-debated, multi-faceted Irish grammar.

Shaking off the shackles of a complicated history with grammar is no walk in the park. Embracing Irish grammar, for some, is akin to pulling briars with your bare hands. However, my second stint in secondary school with Darragh agus Aedín has changed things for me.

Have I had a change of heart on the grammar front? Not really. Just like the offside trap in football, it's a question of timing. The conversation and chat have to come first, and the earlier the better. Sing songs, reach out to a drama group, organise sport through Gaeilge and make the learning of Irish a fun trip rather than a drudgery. Be creative, spontaneous and innovative – *cruthaitheach, spontáineach agus nuálach*!

Bring Gaeilge back into its rightful place in the centre, not on the periphery.

Dála an scéil – By the way

Once you get the basics sorted there is no shortage of material out there to help you master the Irish language. I am grateful for all the books I was presented with during my language journey. I now have the time to study and explore them! Sitting in front of me is a book by Micheál Ó Cearúil: *An Séimhiú, ar an ainm briathra agus ar an ainmfhocal éiginnte sa ghinideach ar lorg ainmfhocail eile* (2016).

Focail na seachtaine – Words of the week

1. *Fás* – grow
2. *A cóta* – her coat
3. *A chóta* – his coat
4. *Nuálach* – innovative
5. *Duilleoga* – leaves
6. *Na huibheacha* – the eggs
7. *Cruthaitheach* – creative

Caibidil 13: *More grows in a garden than is planted there*

Do thuras féin – Your journey

1. _____
2. _____
3. _____
4. _____
5. _____
6. _____
7. _____

> Teanglann phrase:
> *Bhí siad cnapánach le chéile* –
> they exchanged hard words/blows.

Caibidil 14

Ná déan aon rud san oíche a mbeidh aiféala ort ar maidin faoi

Don't do anything at night that you will regret in the morning

Did Covid-19 create a new space for Irish society to reflect and create a new template for living? The commemorations in 2016 allowed our country to reflect on our short 100-year history of independence and I featured at various stages during this comóradh – commemoration. Embedded in the success of this very symbolic period was the role played by primary schools. The 2016 commemoration of the 1916 Rising was a true recognition of a significant time in our country's history and a true appreciation of how important our oidhreacht – heritage – and culture is to present-day society. Every effort was made to include my good self as much as possible. All in all, I was visible, front-and-centre, and certainly not ignored. The schools were the cuisle – pulse – of the commemorative

Caibidil 14: Don't do anything at night that you will regret in the morning

programme. My hope is that I will be central to the learning environment in all schools in the future. When I consider my place in the overall ecosystem, I sometimes feel scoite amach – *detached. I can understand why this is the case on several fronts. Take as an example the curriculum in many English-medium schools: while I do feature, it is in a very compartmentalised way. Now let me be clear. Very, very clear. I know that there are English-medium schools who ensure that I am the 'cuisle' of the school community throughout the day. I have an allocated agenda and an allocated time for discussion; however, I still don't have a meaningful role. It's like the tactics employed by Jack Charlton as to why he didn't choose David O'Leary as his first choice* lánchúlaí láir – *centre back – on the Irish football team. Everyone who knew anything about football back then questioned why a world-class defender was not on the team. I felt his pain and I suppose the same could be said for Liam Brady. However, Jack had a plan and – to call a spade a spade – his plan worked. So, to put a plan together, for a more creative and relevant approach to my development, hard calls will have to be made, just like those Jack made.*

Many people know that I should be playing a pivotal role in the education system. If I had a say in these matters, which I don't ar an drochuair – *unfortunately – I would love to have a similar role to that of Eric Cantona when he played with Manchester United – a free role, a roaming role with my collar up, dropping deep into* lár páirce – *midfield – creating the time and space and creating something from an impossible situation: King Eric! One day I will be king again. Gaeilge Ríoga: Rí Theanga, arís – Royal Irish: the king of languages, again.*[35]

● ● ● ● ● ● ● ●

The Irish way of saying things can so often get lost in translation when chatting to someone from London or San Diego. The humour can also get lost in translation. The play on words can get lost in translation.

---

[35] *Strictly, [the] royal/regal Irish [language]*

Beidh Tú Alright: *Ná déan aon rud san oíche a mbeidh aiféala ort ar maidin faoi*

And this is through the medium of *Béarla*. The Irish language is still embedded in the Irish psyche. The Irish way of seeing things. The Irish way of interpreting things. The Irish way of describing things. The Irish way of painting a picture. The Irish way of telling a story. The Irish way is alive and well, no matter what was thrown at it.

On 31 May 2018, *The Guardian*'s Michael Billington reviewed Brian Friel's *Translations*. He had this to say:

> What strikes one is Friel's ability to find complex meanings in a simple story and to capture Ireland, in 1833 at a moment of historical transition. A rural hedge-school, where classes are conducted in Irish, is to be replaced by a national education system in which English is the official language. At the same time, British soldiers are engaged in an ordnance survey involving the anglicisation of Irish place names.

The context and history of how our beautiful language has evolved over time has been the cornerstone of my learning journey. The anglicization of our language was an incredible disruptor. We are very fortunate to have groups like Conradh na Gaeilge, who continue to advocate strongly for our native tongue. Legislative and policy interventions will enable more language accessibility for the public. Both Irish and English as separate languages can live and survive together. Watching how Gaeilge has evolved has been my learning beacon over the last ten years. Yes, some things will get lost in translation. This happened to me in London in 1990 when I was hod carrying bricks off Oxford Street. My English, and my English employer's English, caused confusion from time to time. Sometimes, things just became 'a little bit stuck' and got lost in translation.

A lovely example in an article by Frank McNally in the *Irish Times* after Rachel Blackmore's historic victory in the English Grand National highlighted a bit of Hiberno-English shenanigans. McNally observes:

Caibidil 14: *Don't do anything at night that you will regret in the morning*

After winning the English Grand National on Saturday, Rachel Blackmore couldn't believe she was *after* winning it and, saying so in those terms, confused at least one British newspaper. Deciding there must be a word missing from her expression of disbelief, *The Observer* inserted one in square brackets. The result read: 'I just can't believe I'm [talking] after winning the Grand National'. In fairness to *The Observer*, there may indeed have been a word missing somewhere, but not from Blackmore's sentence, which was impeccable Hiberno-English.

The Irish language is still standing after all that was thrown at it over the centuries. On 18 May 2011, Queen Elizabeth II, in a warm address in Dublin Castle, used these words: '*A Uachtaráin, agus a chairde …*'. *Is fada an bóthar nach bhfuil aon chasadh ann* – It's a long road that has no turning.

One of my excuses over the years was, 'I just don't have the time to go back learning Irish'. This excuse of excuses was blown out of the water within days of my new appointment. Leaving the Department of the Gaeltacht and Islands aside for a minute, my other day, night, and weekend job was in the Department of Natural Resources on Bóthar Adelaide. Secretary General of the Department Mark Griffan understood the pressure I was under in another part of the city and I was grateful for his support. This place was my sanctuary in the crazy early days. Driving from *Roinn na Gaeltachta* – the Department of the Gaeltacht – on Sráid Chill Dara across the city was a release from the intensity of full immersion Gaeilge. What surprised me in this department was that there were plenty people with Irish who were prepared to converse with me as Gaeilge. Ciarán Ó hÓbáin has beautiful Irish and we interacted regularly as Gaeilge. I launched a new publication, *An Geolaíocht ó bhun go barr*, as an accessible study guide to the basic geological and geographical processes relevant to Ireland. This was launched in Coláiste Ailigh, Leitir Ceannain. With less pressure, I looked forward to these weekly visits. The big learning for me was that, with less pressure, the whole Gaeilge interaction becomes more enjoyable. There was less of a focus on the language per se and more of a focus on learning new terminology and vocabulary in areas which were virgin territory for me *as Béarla* never mind *as Gaeilge*. Little did I know at the time that this learning immersion methodology would be the bedrock of a policy initiative I launched in the *Roinn Oideachas* – Department of Education – in 2019: Content and Language Integrated Learning (CLIL).[36]

Like any minister in a new portfolio, I was learning on the job. New terminology was being thrown at me left, right and centre. Not to mention the jargon! As internet coverage wasn't as readily available in 2014/15 as it is now, I relied heavily on the pocket dictionary in the car. It's still there. The dictionary – not the car. Here's a sample of what was in store for me:

- *Sinc* – zinc
- *Ór* – gold, and how it changed to *deannach óir* – gold dust
- *Luaidhe* – lead (Remember the *peann luaidhe* – pencil – from our schooldays!)
- *Gipseam* – gypsum
- *Gual* – coal
- *Ola agus gás* – oil and gas

The introduction of a new technical language in this department was a whole new learning in itself. Nonetheless, studying something new, bilingually, helped to reinforce my learning. Here's another few samples on the mining front:

- *Mianadóireacht* – mining
- *Mianadóireacht dromchla* – *opencast mining*

---

[36] The acronym CLIL was coined in 1994 by David Marsh, a member of a team working in the area of multilingualism and bilingual education at the Finnish University of Jyväskylä (Marsh, 1994).

Caibidil 14: Don't do anything at night that you will regret in the morning

- *Mianadóireacht faoi thalamh* – underground mining
- *Mianadóireacht plásair* – placer mining

On the inland fisheries side, I met several angling delegations to discuss fishing rights and conservation. This was a challenging sector. With fish stocks under pressure, it was understandable that rivers had to replenish. I learned about the angler and learned about their passion for angling. I worked closely with Denis Maher in this division. Another example of a civil servant who works around the clock. A delegation from one of the Gaeltacht angling clubs made their presentation as Gaeilge. Salmon, trout and eels were the main topics of conversation. Here's a look back at some of my new vocabulary:

- *Ag slatiascaireacht bradán* – angling for salmon
- *Bradán fásta* – adult salmon
- *Bradán fiáin* – wild salmon
- *Eascann* – eel
- *Breac donn* – brown trout

A native English speaker has a great advantage over speakers of Portuguese, French agus Gaeilge. English is a language of a very basic grammar. In 1923 William Butler Yeats was awarded the Nobel Prize for Literature, which brought the English language to new heights. The rationale for the accolade was *'for all his inspired poetry which in a highly artistic form gives expression to the spirit of a whole nation'* (Nobel Prize website). Despite writing in the English language, Yeats was a leading light in the Gaelic literary revival. Friel, Heaney et al followed in his footsteps, writing in English but under the influence of the Irish language.

The transition to fully immerse as Gaeilge is a big decision. I know many families in strong Gaeltacht areas have a native Irish speaking parent and another parent with very limited Irish or none at all. This makes it very difficult to fully immerse straight away. Despite this, there are small steps that can be taken on that journey. *Mo chomhairle duit* – my advice to you is that 'quick win' introductions at bedtime and mealtime are a good start. *Arís, tús maith leath na hoibre* – again, a good start is half the work. To get *maidin mhaith* in the morning can be a big victory, as it may be the only exchange that takes place once those teenage years arrive! *Cloisim na tuismitheoiraí* – I hear the parents – with small toddlers using one word when they are out and about 'goitse'[37] (*Gabh anseo* – hurry up). As the toddler gets older you may have to move on to *tar anseo, ANOIS!* – come here, NOW, or *ná bí dalba* – don't be bold. To learn any language, you must hear it. Foclóir.ie and Teanglann.ie have no shortage of sound recordings if you're finding it difficult to meet people with Gaeilge. Furthermore, you will get the breakdown for the different dialects. Rather than getting too hung up on the differences, I try to use this as an opportunity to train my ear to the range of words and sounds that make up *ár dteanga shaibhir* – our rich language. Try out the different versions of *madra* – dog – and the ulster version of *sionnach* – fox in the guise of *madra rua* – red dog (pronounced *madu rua* in West Donegal)!

Dála an scéil – By the way

Acquiring a new skill (in this case working on a new skill) is beginning to see new scientific evidence about brain impact. Neuroplasticity research is pointing to the positive benefits of learning any new skill, irrespective of age, on the development of the brain structure. However, a lot more research will be required in this area. Li et al. (2014)[38] present interesting research on the study of neuroplasticity as a function of second language learning.

---

[37] A Conamara variant is '*goile*', from '*gabh i leith*'.
[38] Li, P., Legault, J. and Litcofsky, K.A. (2014) 'Neuroplasticity as a function of second language learning: Anatomical changes in the human brain', *Cortex*, 58, 301–324.

Caibidil 14: *Don't do anything at night that you will regret in the morning*

FOCAIL NA SEACHTAINE – WORDS OF THE WEEK

1. *Aiféala* – regret
2. *Saibhir* – rich
3. *Bradán fiáin* – wild salmon
4. *Madra rua/sionnach* – fox
5. *Deannach óir* – gold dust
6. *Mianadóireacht* – mining
7. *Dromchla* – surface

DO THURAS FÉIN – YOUR JOURNEY

1. _____
2. _____
3. _____
4. _____
5. _____
6. _____
7. _____

> Teanglann phrase:
> *Déan mórán agus can beagán* – do much and say little.

Caibidil 15

Ar scáth a chéile a mhaireann na daoine

We live in each other's shadows

Cha mbíonn mil ar fheochadáin, ná ór ar dhreasóga i dtíortha eile ach oiread is atá sa bhaile – *there's no honey on thistles, nor gold on briars, in any other countries any more than at home.*

Is lom é – *it is bare* – was used to describe the wretched bare apartments housing the Liverpool Irish. It is understood that this was the origin of the word 'slum'. You will still hear my voice in Liverpool to this day. Remember Cilla Black and Blind Date *when she was closing the show with 'ta ra'?* This came from tabhair aire – *take care*.[39] Too many Irish left our shore, and so many never to return. There were no translation apps for the trans-Atlantic voyage on the Derry boat. However, I was on

---

[39] Similarly, the word '*smashing*' comes from '*is maith sin*' – that's good. So next time someone says you look smashing you can explain. The derogatory word 'latchico' is also Gaeilge, *thiochóg – tíochóg*. The opposite of a helpful, useful person!

Caibidil 15: *We live in each other's shadows*

that boat too. It was a frightening prospect for native Irish speakers (many with no English at all) entering a new world, armed with the knowledge that what came natural in a free-flowing conversation was going to be of little use on the other side of the pond. It took courage to face that head on. Those were acts of bravery.

● ● ● ● ● ● ● ●

Language is important. Words can get you out of trouble. Words can get you into trouble. Words can get the better of you. At times, we are lost for words. The least said the better, some say. In Donegal Gaeltacht areas there is an old expression for 'I heard' – '*mhothaigh mé* – I felt. *Chuala mé* – I heard – is the Gaeilge we learned. Did you hear the news? Did you hear the terrible news? Yes, I 'felt' the news – *mhothaigh mé*. Father John Joe Duffy used this in one of his homilies in the aftermath of the Craoslach tragedy, where ten innocent people lost their lives. We all felt the news. We felt the impact of utter devastation on families and on a community. Of course, we heard but, in the main, we felt. We felt the pain. We felt the hurt. We felt the enormous loss. The Irish language has a way of dealing with tragedy. It won't change things. It doesn't alter. But sometimes it can help soothe. At a time of grief people use words to say they have no words. However, words are important – and not too many. I have come across beautifully designed cards with the message '*ag smaointiú ort*' – thinking of you.

There's also:

- *Mo comhbhrón a dhéanamh leat* – to join with you in your sadness
- *Ar dheis Dé go raibh a anam dílis/Ar dheis Dé go raibh a hanam dílis* – May his/her faithful soul rest on the right-hand side of God
- *Ar dheis Dé go raibh sí/sé* is another expression used in my home county which translates to 'he/she is on the right-hand side of God.'
- *Is trua liom/linn do chás* – I/We are sorry for your loss.

An early-morning phone call from the late Bernard McGuinness gave me the news of a devastating flood in Inis Eoghain. Some areas experienced more destruction than others. On the night of 22 August 2017 Inis Eoghain was hit with a *tuile mhór* – big flood. No lives were lost that night, which was nothing short of a miracle when I think back on the destruction and level of devastation caused by the flood. Roads and bridges were washed away. Na hUillí, Rinn Uí Choigligh, Carn Domhnach agus Cnoc an Choiligh were badly hit. Cluain Maine agus Iorras saw a lot of devastation too. The older people were saying that this wasn't a once off, it happened before. Charles McGlinchey, *an fear deireanach den tslionneadh* – the last of the name – sheds more light on things:

> My mother was Síle Harkin. She came from Urris and finished up her life in the Glen and lived till she was ninety. She was born about the year 1824 for I often heard her saying that she was old enough to remember something of the *tuilte móra* – the big floods – that came in the winter of 1827. She remembered being up and through the house that night. These floods swept away all the bridges about the parish. The Meendoran bridge was built after the *tuilte móra* and lasted to the flood of 1945.

This is a little bit of history which is of great relevance to our generation who lived through the *tuilte móra* of 2017. And a little bit of Gaeilge too with the *tuilte móra* – big floods. Edited by Brian Friel and Nollaig Mac Congáil, his book, *The Last of the Name*,[40] captures life in northwest Inis Eoghain through the eyes of Charles McGlinchey.

I remember the late Charlie Doherty from Clonmany mentioning Charles McGlinchey to me in early 2000 and students in Carndonagh

---

[40] Charles McGlinchey (2015) *The Last of the Name – An Fear Deireanach den tSloinneadh* as told to Patrick Kavanagh, edited by Brian Friel, Nollaig Mac Congáil and Desmond Kavanagh.

Community School presenting me with an early Christmas present of the book on 10 December 2018. It was a thoughtful gift and reflected the interest those students and their teacher had in their local history. Brian Friel's opening and closing paragraphs in the introduction, under the title 'Important Places 1999', goes as follows:

> *The Last of the Name* is a collection of stories and reminiscences of life in a very small parish in the northwest of County Donegal in the northwest of Ireland. The narrator is Charles McGlinchey (1861–1954), a weaver; and the stories he tells of life in his parish have to do with the period of his own life and of the previous generation. He told these tales to his friend, Patrick Kavanagh, the local school-teacher who visited McGlinchey a couple of nights every week during the winters of the late 1940s and early 1950s. McGlinchey was then over eighty years of age and as he reminisced and wondered about life, Kavanagh wrote his words down because he knew that this was an acute and closely-observed record of a kind of life that would never be seen again.
>
> Meetiagh Glen is an important place, not in itself but because an astute man observed it with love and his observations bestow an importance on it, elicited its importance from it. And that simultaneous bestowing and eliciting is the act of art. *The Last of the Name* is the work of an artist.

One of the traditionally weaker Gaeltacht areas in Donegal is Mín an Lábáin, Gleann Domhain. *Domhan* meaning 'world' is usually spelled without the 'i', except in the genitive, *domhain*, meaning 'deep'. Looks similar but is a different word. In this context, *Gleann Domhain* means Deep Glenn. There is an archival note in Logainm.ie (#1166995) Gleann Domhain, Deep Glen 'is 1770 feet above the sea and is a steep and rugged mountain.' The local national school had 11 students enrolled in 1999 – the school peaked at *ceithre scór* – eighty – about 10 years ago. Stramore/Srath Mór national school is situated in this beautiful part of the world. However, there are challenges with student numbers due to rural depopulation. The language development in the school is going *ó neart go neart* – from strength to strength. Significantly, one of the key cornerstones to the future sustainability of this language journey is the construction of an onsite *naíonra* – an Irish-medium playgroup for pre-school children, which follows the principle of total early immersion. This is key to the *leanúnachas* – continuity – which *iar-phríomhoide* – former principal – Therese McMonagle often referenced. Therese pointed out to me that if we had a *naíonra* in the area to feed into the primary school, the education journey would continue to Coláiste Ailigh, Leitir Ceanainn for secondary school and finally to either Atlantic Technological University (Leitir Ceanainn) or Ollscoile na Gallimhe (Acadamh in Gaoth Dobhair). A complete Gaeilge education starting and ending in Dún na nGall. *Nach maireann* – the late – Ellen McDermott contributed to the development of a language plan for the area. Ellen's passion and love for the language motivated a community and this infrastructure is here today because of that passion and love. Ellen's words were important. Her determination was realised. Her contribution to the language will be remembered.

Dála an scéil – By the way

The Online Etymology Dictionary has this meaning for 'slum': 1845, from back slum 'dirty back alley of a city, street of poor or low people' (1825), originally a slang or cant word meaning 'room,' especially 'back room' (1812), of unknown origin.

Unknown origin comes up quite frequently! *Is lom é* – it is bare, would be a good place to start.

Caibidil 15: *We live in each other's shadows*

FOCAIL NA SEACHTAINE – WORDS OF THE WEEK

1. *Mothúcháin* – feelings
2. *Tuilte móra* – big floods (*tuile* – flood)
3. *Ag smaointiú ort* – thinking of you
4. *Paidreacha* – prayers
5. *Ar shlí na fírinne*[41] – on the path of the truth
6. *Ceithre scór* – eighty, literally 'four score'
7. *Ó neart go neart* – from strength to strength

DO THURAS FÉIN – YOUR JOURNEY

1. _____
2. _____
3. _____
4. _____
5. _____
6. _____
7. _____

> Teanglann.ie phrase:
> *Drochtheanga a thabhairt do dhuine* –
> to use foul words to someone.

---

[41] *Ar shlí na fírinne* – On the path of the truth or on the way to the truth. So people don't die in the Irish language – they journey on into the light.

Caibidil 16

Bíonn dhá insint ar gach scéal

There are two sides to every story

Head for east Belfast and you'll witness a mini revival going on in my name, where Rangers' supporters are learning that the eye on the Rangers crest is the eye of the broc *– badger – which lends itself to their stadium's name – Ibrox. Linda Ervine has been championing this crusade and has organised many classes in the Skainos Centre on the Newtownards Road. Skainos is the Greek word for 'tabernacle' or 'to pitch a tent'. One thing is for sure, Linda has pitched a tent for the Irish language with a strong inclusive message – the language is for everyone. Divisions are not my scene. I'm as content in east Belfast as I am in the Gaeltacht Quarter of west Belfast and fair dues to all for flying the one* brat *– flag. A flag in my name and nothing else.*

● ● ● ● ● ● ●

Caibidil 16: *There are two sides to every story*

A HARD SLOG

At the end of the Maigh Eo Greenway, coming from Acaill, there is a signpost with Slogar/Slaugar. Pretty appropriate after the hard 'slog' *ar an bhicycle*. Téarma.ie informs us that 'slog' is 'swallow'.

The late Dr Fiachra Mac Gabhann suggested that the Maigh Eo place name is a form of *slogaire* – quagmire or swallow-hole. In Ireland, to 'slog' is used in an educational and work context – Irish paper 1 was a bit of a slog. *Ag dreapadóireacht* – climbing – depending on the elevation, can also be a hard 'slog'.

The anglicisation of most of our Irish place names was done phonetically. An unscientific and lazy approach, one could argue. However, the other side of the coin is this, while the spelling has changed, the sound hasn't changed in some cases. Looking at some of these places at face value, they will make no sense. In my home county, the late Dermot Walsh highlighted the anglicisation of a place near my home – namely Lough Salt. This lake is embedded between a mountain and ridge – as deep as the mountain is high.[42] The lake is the source of freshwater for over 20,000 people in Letterkenny. So 'salt' in the name raises a *brat dearg* – red flag – straight away. Following Dermot's intervention, I asked *An Coiste Logainmneacha* – The Place Names Committee – to look at it and, following their research, they concluded that the correct Gaelic name is Loch as Allt (Logainm.ie #111273). It is said locally that *allt* is the Irish word for the space between the knuckles of the hand. In place names it usually means height or cliff. And, thanks to a local *coiste* – committee – *ón* Tearmann and funding from Údarás na Gaeltachta there is a signage erected with the original Irish name on each side of the lough. Overlooking the lake you will find an ancient standing stone, approximately 4500 years old, erected by our first Gaeilgeoirs.

---

[42] 803 feet according to the late Tony Walshe as Mhaigh Eo, who worked with the Land Commission.

Bearna(s) is the Gaeilge for 'Gap'. *An Bearnas Mór* – Barnesmore Gap is in Donegal (Logainm.ie #130315). The direct translation of Barnesmore Gap is 'Big Gap Gap'. It's big alright but certainly not intended in this way. In fairness, locals refer to it as 'The Gap'.

The editors of *Donegal History and Society* (1995) state the following:

> Bearnas, Barnesmore, is the name of the important mountain gap on the main east-west route through the south-centre of the county which marks the southern-eastern limit of Tír Chonaill. Significantly, Saint Patrick's biographer, Tírechán, who wrote in the last quarter of the seventh century, refers to Barnesmore as Bernes filiorum Conill 'the gap of the sons of Conall'.[43]

I'm not sure where the Gap of Dunloe in Kerry originated but '*Bearna an Choimín*' (Logainm.ie #101202) – *coimín* meaning commonage or common land – seems to be the original name. This gap had common lands in the vicinity. There will be many places where the anglicised version has no correlation with the original Gaelic name. For example, Maamcross in Contae na Gaillimhe is known as '*An Teach Dóite*' – the burnt house (Logainm.ie #131046).

The census is a great resource for making connections. Identifying relations who ticked the Irish speaker box might be of interest to you. Where better to start than in your own townland. I grew up in Claggan (Logainm.ie #15949) (An anglicized version of *cloigeann* which means head) – and as the landscape is elevated, 'headland' makes sense. An Cloigeann is in the townland of An Dún Mór (Logainm.ie #15725). Dunmore is close to Carrigart. *An Dún Mór* is used both in Scottish and Irish Gaelic – the Great Fort. There is another Dún Mór (Logainm.ie #15744) I'm thinking of in An Cheathrú Chaol (Kerrykeel) – the narrow quarter (Logainm.ie #1414067). Dún Mór in Port Láirge

---

[43] William Nolan, Liam Ronayne and Mairead Dunlevy (eds), *Donegal History and Society* (1995), Geography Publications.

also lays claim to *Dún Mór* in Dunmore East (Logainm.ie #1166999). There is also an international presence. You will find Dunmore in the Bahamas, Pennsylvania, Virginia, and Australia. The phonetic integrity of the *Dún Mór* – the Great Fort – is protected.

Moving over the road to Carrigart, Logainm.ie has a *bailiúchán* – collection – of similar titles: Carrigard, Carraigard, Carrickart, Carrig Ard, Carrigan. *Carraig Airt* is the official name – Art's Rock (Logainm. ie #15724).[44]

Now, there is also a rock called *Carraig Airt* in *Corca Dhuibhne* in *Contae Chiarraí* – not to be confused with *An Charraig Ard* – high rock – in Sligo (Logainm.ie #44636).

I bumped into my former geography teacher shortly after I was appointed Chief Whip in 2017. I had just finished an interview on Raidió na Gaeltachta, whereby I referred to myself as *Príomh Aire* – literally, prime minister. Throwing in a bit of humour, Dolores congratulated me on becoming Taoiseach! She proceeded to inform me that my new title was in fact *Príomh Aoire* – literal translation: chief shepherd – a subtle difference in phonetics made the world of difference. *Aire*, pronounced 'ara', and *aoire*, pronounced 'era'. *Aoire* – to watch – is very close to *faire* meaning 'to wake' (in the funeral sense) which is also 'to watch'. A significant intervention in more ways than one as I began to ponder my newfound status as chief shepherd. As a farmer's son, I knew only too well the pitfalls when it came to herding sheep. The difference in this instance was herding without any barbed wire or sheep netting or sheep dog. Some people likened my new job to *Ag buachailleacht na luchóga ag na crosbhealaí* – herding the mice at the crossroads – as described by former Donegal TD Dinny McGinley. The joys and tribulations of any new job I suppose!

The word *aoire* jumped out at me on signage outside Gleann Cholm Cille, Mín an Aoire – Meenaneary. Logainm.ie defines *mín* as mountain pasture. O'Donovan's note in Logainm.ie archives attribute

---

[44] Some locals say the original name was *Ceathrú Fhiogart* (Figart Quarter).

the townlands meaning as 'misk[45] of the shepherd' and records the local tradition current in 1835 that 'Here the tree that sprung from Columb's dart vegetates yet' (Logainm.ie #14655); Hill of the grassy or grazing plain and plain of the rising ground. Local knowledge would say that it is the low-lying plains where the sheep would be herded by the shepherd. En route home to Carraig Airt, an hour and a half later, my curiosity landed me in Mín an Lábáin (Church Hill) (Logainm.ie #1412960) outside Letterkenny. The Logainm.ie glossary again, heading south to Baile an Lábáin, Labanstown, in Contae[46] Lú there is an archival entry on Logainm.ie which records the local meaning in 1836 as 'town of the mire and refers to a yellow mud clay' (Logainm.ie #33996). The second element is *lábán mud, mire*. Back to Mín an Lábáin, is it possible that Church Hill was named because of its topography and soil type? George William Russell (A.E.) wrote a book titled *Letters from Mín an Lábáin*.

The Online Etymology Dictionary has a definition for 'clabber'; 'mud' 1824, from Irish and Gaelic *clabar*. Many days we were up to our necks in *clabber*. Returning to my own parish of 'Míobhaigh' to a townland near where we used to cut the turf – Mín Formail (Meenformal) (#15845). The Place Names Branch has not yet carried out full research on this name, but their archival records on Logainm.ie show O'Donovan's suggestion from 1835 – Mín Formail 'field on the round Hill'. This implies O'Donovan thought the second element was formaoil, 'round hill', which occurs in some thirty place names around the country (e.g. Formaoil/Fermoyle in Laois Logainm.ie #27959). Finally, Logainm.ie shows two entries for Mín na Croise (Meenacross), one in Machaire (Maghery) (Logainm.ie #14951) and the other in Gleann Cholm Cille. The latter entry on Logainm.ie shows O'Donovan's note from 1835 – 'misk greenfield of the cross'. I will stop here

---

[45] Misk: a damp, boggy, low-lying stretch of grassland.
[46] We say '*condae*' in Ulster but it's written '*contae*' in the *caighdeán*.

with the Donegal examples. In Cork, there's a phonetically correct placename – Meenaraheeny *as Béarla* (Logainm.ie #10687).

Logainm.ie shows an archival entry from 1840 suggesting Mín na Ráithínídhe – plain or level land of the raheens or small forts. In this case, however, John O'Donovan and his colleague Eugene O'Curry were simply guessing based on the current English spelling; they did not visit County Cork. The official name is Moing na Ráithíní: the evidence shows that the first element is in fact *moing* meaning rank vegetation, swamp.

In East Galway you'll hear 'manín' and 'ladín' in the *Béarla* vernacular. With *-ín* – small – at the end of a word you really are in terms of endearment territory. At a very young age, the song 'Báidín Fheilimí' – Feilim's little boat – was my first encounter. *Bóin Dé* – ladybird, but literally God's little cow – is the sweetest and most endearing of all.

Connecting with our past is both enriching and empowering. The answers won't always be there and some of the conclusions you may reach will be without foundation and empirical data, but they provide interesting food for thought.

Gleann Beithe in Kerry was anglicised to Glenbeigh (Logainm.ie #22290). Logainm.ie doesn't confirm the exact translation of *beithe*, but the archival records show O'Donovan's 1835 suggestion, Glen of the Birch. In Donegal, Gleann Bheatha was anglicised to Glenveagh (Logainm.ie #111180). In *A Dictionary of Ulster Place-Names* (1999), Dr Pat McKay also suggests that Gleann Bheatha is a development from Gleann Bheathach. Foclóir.ie and Téarma.ie both define *beatha* as 'life'. On a parallel theme, *uisce beatha* – water of life/whiskey – just like Gleann Bheatha – will take your breath away! Learning through place names is a great learning pathway for young children, and where better to start, than at home. Remember, this is not a mathematical equation, it is more a personal journey of discovery that you will take on your own or with others, where you will meet many and experience so much joy.

While hauling *gliomach* – lobster – and *portán* – crab – with Jerry Early off Árainn Mhór (Logainm.ie #14527), he pointed to

Poll an Mhadaidh Uisce – pronounced 'Pollawaddyiska' (Logainm.ie #1396852). The Irish name means 'hole of the water dog – the otter'. There are many places which we name phonetically and may not know the meaning. With Logainm.ie on hand, what better way to discover our own surroundings. Arraheera is in the Northern part of Fanad. When I canvassed this area with the late Peter Friel, back in 1999, my curiosity for meaning just wasn't on the radar. Roll on a couple of decades plus some, things have changed somewhat. Earra Thíre na Binne – coastal border of the country of the peak (Logainm.ie #15775) – was originally Earra Thíre – coastal border of the country, and today is anglicised as the ordinary one worded, Araheera. Logainm.ie shows the official Ordnance Survey spelling – Arryheernabin. The first part of the name *earra* is a development from *oirear*, as in Oirear Dhumhaí/Errarooey (Logainm.ie #14416) – coastal border of the sand-dune. Go to this place, there's a long stone wall[47] (Jimmy Sweeney's wish) near the Fanad Lighthouse on your right, like something out of a Robert Frost poem. 'Hope is a good thing, maybe the best of things and no good thing ever dies.' – *Shawshank Redemption*

Leslie W. Lucas, author of *Mevagh Down the Years*, approached me shortly before his passing more than twenty years ago. His lifetime of research, gathering and preserving history in one parish was something that he felt strongly about and he highlighted the importance of it. I bumped into a relation of Leslie recently and she let me know that all his work has been handed over to the Donegal library. *Mevagh Down the Years* is a great reference point and is a great resource for students who want to get to know their own townlands. Gleann an Ghiolla Ghrán[n]a – Glen of the Ugly Fellow – might be a good starting point!

---

[47] The construction of this wall was on the '*méar fada*' for over 20 years. Peadar Tierney and Cait Fealty made it happen.

Caibidil 16: *There are two sides to every story*

Dála an scéil – By the way

Ó mo chara ó Chonamara

> *Thíos atá na tíortha teolaí,*
> *Thuas atá na soilse sí,*
> *thoir a bhíonn an ghrian ag éirí*
> *ach thiar atá mo chroí*
> (South [below] is where the sun is brightest, north [above] is where the fairy lights are highest, east is where the sun she rises but west is where my heart resides.)

Focail na seachtaine – Words of the week

1. *Ag tafann* – barking
2. *Caoróg mhara* – sea pink
3. *Ag dreapadóireacht* – climbing
4. *Aire* – care/minister
5. *Aoire* – shepherd
6. *Príomh-Aoire* – chief whip
7. *Bóin Dé* – God's little cow/ladybird

Do thuras féin – Your journey

1. _____
2. _____
3. _____
4. _____
5. _____

Beidh Tú Alright: *Bíonn dhá insint ar gach scéal*

6. _____

7. _____

> Teanglann.ie phrase:
> *Beidh ort an chaint sin a shlogadh* –
> you will have to eat those words.

Caibidil 17

Rotha Mór an tSaoil

The Big Wheel of Life

Níl ionam ach ball de chorp san mo shinsir – *I am but a part of the body of my ancestry* – said Sean Ó Ríordain (1916–1977), our great poet, who also went on a *turas teanga*. *Why not try it? Dip your toes? Something you always threatened to do? A load easily carried? Something to leave behind? Something good? Sure, why not?*

● ● ● ● ● ● ●

The wheel comes around at a ferocious pace, but it doesn't feel like that at the time. It comes round though, eventually. On 14 November 2022 in the beautiful city of Prague in *An tSeicia* – Czechia – *bhí beirt* – there were two – expert translators on hand to provide the full suite of interpretation at an EU COSAC (Conference of Parliamentary Committees for European Affairs) meeting. The status of Irish as an official Irish language was agreed at an EU level in 2007 and the derogation delaying its official use was lifted in 2021, just in time for the celebration of fifty years of Ireland's EU membership in 2023. I listened attentively to our Irish interpretation when delegations from Romania, Germany, Denmark et al contributed. I made my contribution as Gaeilge. Alex, from Denmark, came up to me afterwards and said it was incredible to listen to the Gaelic tongue. This reminded me of a translator from Liverpool who I met years ago at a meeting of the Assembly of European Regions. I remember his anger more than anything. He said, 'I speak 14 languages with Gaeilge being the most beautiful of all, so why do you not just speak it?' It was one of those moments when you look for a hole to jump into, and then you can't find one as you're sitting on a bus. It stuck with me though, as I toured country after country within Europe, where I was presented with the rich linguistic diversity in different countries and regions. Karelia in Finland is one of those interesting regions as it straddles the Finish and Russian border. In the early 'noughties' I was not as attentive to the dialect nuances as I crossed over the border to Russia. Another time maybe? While I communicated with politicians in the universal language of *Béarla*, the native tongue was king in the shops, streets, and restaurants. 20 years later, we have ensured equality of access for the Irish language at a European level and opened opportunities for our graduates across the seven EU institutions.

The wheel has certainly come around from the time of the sad farewells at the Bridge of Tears – Droichead na nDeor (see Mám na Mucaise/Muckish Gap, Logainm.ie #111302) – Falcarragh and Glenveagh, where our immigrants bade farewell to kith and kin. A plaque is located near the bridge with an Irish passage that translates as, 'Family and friends of the person leaving for foreign lands would come this far. Here was the separation. This is the bridge of tears.' The Irish language has now got a commercial value through employment opportunities in the EU. Surely this will be good for the language in the long run?

The 2022 *Corn an Domhain* – World Cup – in football, had plenty of controversy. The Iranian players refrained from singing their national anthem as part of one protest. It made me think though. When you hear each of the French players belting out 'La Marseillaise' before

Caibidil 17: *The Big Wheel of Life*

kick-off, is there not a great opportunity for all our national players to do likewise? And let me be clear, I am just talking about the men's team because I have seen and heard the Irish women's team singing the national anthem with gusto on numerous occasions. I ain't canvassing for a job as I know there's plenty of people out there who would be more than happy to teach the players a few lines for starters. It would also be a chance for a bit of team-building between internationals. Irish captain Nathan Collins and a few others sing our national anthem with passion. And not forgetting the many supporters in the stands.

An cheist – the question: *Cén fáth nach mbíonn ár n-imreoirí sacair* [male] *ag úsáid ár dteanga roimh an chluichí móra idirnáisiúnta?* – Why are all our football [*sacair*] players [male] not using our language before international games?

Sin an cheist! – That's the question! The answer is taking a leaf out of the senior Irish women's team.

There is always hope that one day every Irish player will be able to sing 'The Soldier's Song' as Gaeilge before an international match.

> **Amhrán na bhFiann**
> *Sinne Fianna Fáil, atá faoi gheall ag Éireann,*
> *Buíon dár slua thar toinn do ráinig chugainn,*
> *Faoi mhóid bheith saor,*
> *Seantír ár sinsear feasta,*
> *Ní fhágfar faoin tíorán ná faoin tráill.*
> *Anocht a théam sa bhearna bhaoil,*
> *Le gean ar Ghaeil, chun báis nó saoil,*
> *Le gunna-scréach faoi lámhach na bpiléar*[48]
> *Seo libh canaig' amhrán na bhFiann*

---

[48] '*Na bpiléar*' is a reference to bullets; however it is also a reference to the 'peelers' – the police, so nicknamed after Robert Peel, former Prime Minister of the United Kingdom.

Beidh Tú Alright: *Rotha Mór an tSaoil*

WE'LL CHANT A SOLDIER'S SONG

Peadar Ó Cearnaigh (1883–1942) wrote the lyrics to 'Amhrán na bhFiann' – 'The Soldier's Song'. I had the honour of leading a commemorative ceremony at his grave in 2016 in Glasnevin. Peadar was a close friend of Michael Collins, who is also buried at Glasnevin. The national anthem appears in the back of the souvenir programme commemorating the first Dáil, titled *1919–2019: 100 Bliain de Dháil Éireann*.[49] Our country's history is complex, and our independence is still in its infancy. At the heart of our leaders' aspirations back in 1919 was to have Gaeilge at the heart of our democracy, as evidenced by the following about the first Dáil, as stated in the souvenir programme:

BHÍ AN GHAEILGE I GCROÍLÁR NA TURASCÁLA OIFIGIÚLA LE HAGHAIDH AN 21 EANÁIR 1919.
THE IRISH LANGUAGE WAS AT THE CORE OF THE OFFICIAL REPORT FOR 21 JANUARY 1919.

- *Tagraíodh do chomhaltaí mar theachtaí agus ní mar MP nó members of parliament; tagraíodh don spéicéir mar an Ceann Comhairle.*
  Members were referred to as *teachtaí* and not as MPs, the speaker was referred to as the Ceann Comhairle.
- *Tugadh ainm gach comhalta i nGaeilge amháin.*
  The name of each member was given in Irish only.
- *Bhí na himeachtaí féin i nGaeilge ar fad beagnach, cé is moite d'úsaid na Fraincise agus an Bhéarla chun sleachta áirithe aistriúcháin a léamh.*
  The proceedings themselves were almost entirely in Irish, the exemption being the use of French and English for reading certain parts in translation.

---

[49] Tuairisc Oifigiúil Dháil Éireann, 1919–1922, Arna fhoilsiú Eanáir 2019 ag Tithe an Oireachtas.

- *Úsáideadh an chlóscríbhinn Ghaelach le haghaidh gach gné den tuairisc inar úsáideadh an Ghaeilge.*
 Gaelic typescript was used for all the Irish language elements of the report.

Tip of the day: Do not be put off by the complexity of the Irish above. Use it as an opportunity to learn this about spelling Irish words: 'e' and 'i' stick together (slender vowels) and 'a', 'o' and 'u' stick together (broad vowels). Basically, *caol le caol agus leathan le leathan* (slender follows slender and broad follows broad) – the golden spelling rule.[50] If there is a slender vowel to the left of the consonant, it has to be matched on the other side with another slender vowel. You can't have a broad vowel and a slender vowel on either side of a consonant. This rule makes it easy to spell words. Go on, give it a try with some of those words above. E.g. *aistriúcháin*.

Interestingly, on 21 January 1919 only 27 TDs met in the Mansion House and their names were read into the record in Irish. There were another 35 TDs read into the record as being *fé ghlas ag gallaibh* – imprisoned by foreigners – in English jails.

Inniu/Today

We have many opportunities for using Gaeilge, 'un[be]knownst to ourselves'. Children use the language naturally in pre-school where it is second nature. Likewise, on the sports field, where the dominant focus is the sport, the language sits comfortably beside it. Young people can pick up Irish while listening to the charts on mainstream radio. Many presenters use a mix of *Gaeilge agus Béarla*. Or if they want to go the whole hog they can tune into Raidió Rí Rá.[51] This is a win-win for the Irish language as young people end up listening to the DJ speaking as

---

[50] See *irishforparents.ie*.
[51] Conradh na Gaeilge campaigned to get Raidió Rí Rá on mainstream FM radio in 2014.

Gaeilge 'unknownst to themselves', and is a clever way of engaging with the younger audience.

Many adults rekindle their affection for the language when abroad, particularly if they want to talk about something without being understood by those around them! Their ability to reconnect with the language on the tube in London or in a pub in Yonkers happens naturally and immediately. *Bíonn muintir na hÉireann uilig iontach bródúil nuair a bhíonn siad ag úsáid na Teanga Gaeilge* – Irish people are very proud when they use the Irish language.

Whether it is at home on the airwaves, in the school yard or in the underground in London or New York, the Irish language can be heard. Our language was heard in our parliament 100 years ago and can be heard today, over 100 years later.

Donegal captain Patrick McBrearty was a joy to listen to when he broke into Gaeilge after lifting the Anglo Celt Cup in 2024. President of the GAA Jarlath Burns and former presidents have used their public appearances to promote the Irish language.

Scoil Phadráig in Westport has answered the call with their rendition of 'Ireland's Call' as Gaeilge. You know something works *nuair a mhothaíonn tú an ghruaig ina seasamh ar do dhroim* – when you feel the hair standing on your back. Check it out on YouTube. It's just *thar barr* – brilliant. Incidentally, they also had a song '*Sam ar shiúl rófhada?!*' – 'Sam been gone too long!' (Maybe Enda Kenny should have asked me for advice the day he appointed me as minister.)

I watched the 2016 All-Ireland final with my former private secretary Rose Gaughan in San Francisco. Even though Mayo drew the game with Dublin, she knew the opportunity was gone. She proved to be right as Dublin won the final by a point. She was *croí cráite/croíbhriste*. Heart-broken.

Dála an scéil – By the way

Irish language enthusiasts can be found all around the world. The translator from Liverpool with 14 languages is the one who sticks out in my

Caibidil 17: *The Big Wheel of Life*

memory. Gaeilge was his favourite. Two other language enthusiasts who stand out are Alex Hijmans and Victor Bayda. Alex was born in the *Isiltír* – Netherlands – and Victor was born in *Rúis* – Russia. Both are fluent Irish speakers, and they continue to inspire.

FOCAIL NA SEACHTAINE – WORDS OF THE WEEK

1. *Corn an Domhain* – the World Cup
2. *Amhrán na bhFiann* – The Soldiers' Song
3. *Iontach bródúill* – very proud
4. *Droim* – back
5. *Rótha mór an tsaoil* – the big wheel of life
6. *Mol an lá um thráthnóna*[52] – praise the day in the evening
7. *Aistriúchán* – translation

DO THURAS FÉIN – YOUR JOURNEY

1. _____
2. _____
3. _____
4. _____
5. _____
6. _____
7. _____

‖   Teanglann.ie phrase: *briathra milse* – honeyed words.   ‖

---

[52] Another way of using this lovely expression is 'Ná mol an lá go dtí an tráthnóna – don't praise the day until the evening' (things can go wrong in between!)

Caibidil 18

Aithníonn ciaróg ciaróg eile[53]

It takes one to know one

In the Gaeltacht areas of Donegal, the term 'bealach mór' survives. It is used in many contexts, from giving directions to explaining where people live, and it also happens to be the main road, direct translation – the big pass. According to Téarma.ie, 'Bealach' is defined as a narrow mountain pass. 'Bealach Mór' – the big narrow mountain pass! If I am to be understood I need to be explained. Doing something for the sake of doing it rarely inspires..

- Thosaigh mé – *I started*
- Chonaic mé – *I saw*
- Bhí mé – *I was*
- Rinne mé – *I did/made*

---

[53] Literally: a beetle recognises another beetle.

Caibidil 18: *It takes one to know one*

- D'ith mé – *I ate*
- D'ól mé – *I drank*
- Dúirt mé – *I said*

These are some of the verbs school children learn by rote. Important yes, but just like advice on the football field – don't bunch everyone into the middle as it will get too congested. There is still too much of a focus on my mechanics while at the same time I'm not being explained. It's like a blind date doomed from the start. No chemistry, a cleamhnas – *marriage – of convenience, or in many cases inconvenience where I'm not fully understood, leading to flirtation and affairs. My good pal* Fraincis *manages to catch the stray eye.* Toujours – *always –* í gcónaí. *Such brief affairs leave a long-lasting impact and memory.* À gauche/à droite *or* ar dheis/ar chlé? Lámha suas – *hands up – which are you more familiar with?* Fraincis nó Gaeilge *for left and right? I'm also conscious of a less than positive Irish expression – that fella doesn't know his left from his right. It's up there with he's a harmless enough kind of a fella! Still though, you'd take that before being called a 'gulldie' or a 'gulping'! You certainly don't want to be called a* briollamán – *fool.*[54]

It is better to have loved and lost than never to have loved at all. Show me any bit of love and attention and I will respond to music, song, poetry, drama, stories … All I need is relevance and fun, with a little mischief thrown in for good measure. My friend Béarla *added a new word to her vocabulary recently: 'hangry' – a mix of hunger and anger. And thanks to a new friend of mine, we came up with a lovely sounding new word –* 'focrasach', *from* fearg agus ocras – *anger and hunger.* Bíonn fear ocrach feargach – *The hungry man is usually cross.*

Language experimentation should not just be the preserve of dominant languages. Children love muttering 'focras', *it's up there with* 'feic' – *to see. I overheard a conversation in Rio De Janeiro a few years back explaining the importance of my friends coming together and meeting*

---

[54] *Grammar of Ros Goill Irish*, Leslie W. Lucas (1979), QUB.

Beidh Tú Alright: *Aithníonn ciaróg ciaróg eile*

up – tiocfaidh muid le chéile lenár dteangacha – *we will come together with our languages.*

● ● ● ● ● ● ●

ON LEAVING POLITICS – *GAN AON AIFÉALA* – NO REGRETS

It was once said to me that there are three stages in life. The first is when someone says to you, 'you've put on a few pounds'; second, when they say, 'you've lost a few pounds'; and the third stage is when someone says, 'you're looking well!'

The depth, perspective and wisdom emanating from Irish people through ordinary discourse can be rich and often entertaining. The creative spirit is alive and well in our use of language for sure, and that awareness and ability to paint a picture and develop a story into something can be so beautiful. We are a creative people and no doubt our innate ability to develop a story has enabled the continued rise of our creative industry. I remember being approached by a constituent who wanted me to officially open his Red Rose Café in Carraig Airt. I spent weeks wondering where this cafe would be located, how had I missed the planning notice, and why had the work not started? Sometime later I got a letter in the post. I opened it and out popped a hand-crafted miniature café. Written underneath was the inscription, 'Thank you Joe for opening up my Red Rose Cafe!' The effort and detail that would have gone into that process was a labour of love no doubt. It was up there as one of my most memorable official opening ceremonies!

The same constituent also introduced me to the following saying about politicians: 'When all's said and done, there's a lot more said than done.' Poking fun at politicians is a national pastime. This didn't start today or yesterday and won't change any time soon. Some of it can be cutting but a lot can be quite entertaining, like the comment made at a public meeting. Three politicians, including myself (no, this is not a joke), were at the top table making a promise or two to fix something or other when this fella at the back had this to say; 'When all you boys get elected you go 'bleend' and 'deef'. The banter at public meetings was helpful when things were getting heated. However, when there was a serious issue on the agenda, some of these meetings were a tough place to be. Things have got a lot more cutting and targeted on social media though. It's a lot easier to hide behind a thumb. A possible way around this would be for politicians to stay away from social media. This would be a pity as the Irish language is alive and well online. The level of interaction has increased immeasurably over the years. I found it a helpful space when working on sentence construction and spellings. Likewise with text messages. Texting people on the same trajectory can be fun, especially when you see some of the spellings. In my initial days as Gaeltacht Minister, I tried too hard for perfection with my messages. I also struggled with starting sentences. While knowing the Gaeilge for going to the shop and going to the toilet, it was the basic start to sentences that seemed to hamper me most. Can you figure out GRMA, TFR & OMD?[55]

Politics can sometimes be described as a *druga* – drug – but there is a *leigheas* – cure – pronounced 'lace' in Conamara and 'liss' in Ulster. Not unlike the gambler in Kenny Rogers' song, you need to know when to fold your cards. A friend explained to me that '*Aoine sin a leigheas*' is an old Irish expression for 'to cure the want of'. *Aoine* meaning 'Friday' but also meaning 'without'. Politics, like any other job, is a job. However, there is a constant deadly preoccupation with proving your worth. Like boxing champions in their late thirties, considering one more crack at the title. It's the I'll-run-one-more-time syndrome. Time is the thing though. Life is no dress rehearsal, and we only get one stab at it.

The value of time started making more sense to me when Covid-19 visited our shores. I got to spend proper time with my family. My

---

[55] *Go raibh maith agat* – thank you; *Tá fáilte romhat* – you're welcome; *O mo Dhia* – Oh my God!

friend and colleague Brendán Griffen from the Kingdom of Kerry went on a similar journey. He said, 'The reason for this is straightforward. I have two young sons and I want to be around them more for the remaining years of their childhood.'[56]

During lockdown Darragh and Aedín spent a full day observing the movement, dietary intake, and work routine of our ten hens. An 'eggciting' and worthwhile 'eggsperiment'! Apologies! Oisín, the youngest, thought differently, as he threw his eyes to heaven and decided to kick a ball instead. Time for such a study would never have been found in our pre-Covid world nor, sadly, our post-Covid world either. We walked on back roads (within our 5k) for the first time and on a stretch of road we skipped and danced to the wonderful beat of songs from *The Wizard of Oz*. Good times for us, but I'm conscious that this wasn't the same for many others. The 'rare is wonderful' approach could also be applied to my language journey. And while it is not so rare for me now, it certainly was then. To be handed the rare privilege to speak and have a full conversation as Gaeilge is something I will always value and cherish.

Doing new things forces us out of our comfort zones. You will meet new people and experience new things. You will also learn. The Irish language tells a story. The story has several titles: How to live; How to maximize life to the fullest and how to treat people and work with people; How to understand our ancestors; How to discover ourselves; How to appreciate and understand our psyche and the way we are. Ultimately, the key thing that I've learned from my language journey is to be grateful. I am grateful for my life, grateful to be living a good life and grateful for the opportunity to meet people, get to know them, develop friendships, and to spend time with family. I am so grateful I had the opportunity to go back to learning Gaeilge, as windows of opportunity and doors of discovery opened for me along the way. New horizons appeared. Having taken this journey, I now see life through

---

[56] *Irish Examiner*, 31 January 2023.

a different lens. The journey taught me about the enjoyment of curiosity and life-long learning and the wonder of seeing things differently.

The late Mrs Treasa Coyle was my first teacher. She introduced us to 'Báidín Fheilimí' in junior infants – or baby infants as it was then! On a recent trip to Gabhla Island *bhí mé ag smaoineamh uirthi* – I was thinking of her. What a wonderful way to learn a language, through song. This experience was without a shadow of a doubt the single biggest help to me on my language journey back in 1975 and again in 2014, 39 years later. My first song this time out was a song by Antoin Ó Dochartaigh. *Scríobh sé sna fichidí* – he wrote this song in the twenties 'Cad é Sin Don Té Sin' – 'Oh What Is It to That Person'. The lyrics were added by Ciarán Brennan from Clannad for their album *Banba*, released in 1994. Belated apologies to all who had to listen to me in Gleann Cholm Cille back in the day; to say I was *rud beag meirgeach* – a tad rusty – would be an understatement. The key lines for me in 'Cad é Sin Don Té Sin' was this *thíos* – below:

> *Má tá mise sásta i mo chónaí i gcró*
> – If I am happy living in a hovel –
> *Ó cad é sin don té sin nach mbaineann sin dó*
> – O what is it to that person it doesn't concern.

At night I was in that hovel, to such an extent I wanted to stay there until long after dawn. Nevertheless, I had to plough on. The shower was my singing sanctuary. *Ceann agus Guaillí* – Head and Shoulders – didn't judge! Word by word and line by line I kept on singing.

Ba é 'Amhrán na Scadán' mo dhara amhrán – the 'Herring Song' was my second song. I listened to Éamonn Ghráinne Mac Ruairí a few times on you tube and learned four verses (the final verse is on my bucket list). The thing I love about this Oileán Thoraí – Tory Island – song is the story about the life journey of a fisherman and his appreciation for how he lived his life at sea. Éamonn 'Dooley' Mac Ruairí composed this song over one hundred years ago. He is a great-grandfather of Colm Joe

Mac Ruairí who runs the social club on Oileán Thoraí. I'm sure Colm Joe and Daniel Cullen, originally from Tír Leathan/Carraig Airt, would be only too delighted to give it a blast if you ever get a chance to visit the island. The first verse jumps straight into the excitement and anticipation of the day at sea, in sharp contrast to the way I felt in my early days in the Gaeltacht portfolio. Check out this opening verse:

> *Nuair a théim a luí san oíche, bím ag smaointiú ar an iasc*
> – When I go to sleep at night I am thinking of the fish.
> *Nuair a éirím amach ar maidin, bheirim rúid go dtí an bhinn*
> – When I wake up in the morning, I rush for the cliffs

To see the verb '*teigh*' (*nuair a théim*) in this context enabled my sentence construction in my early conversations as I was on the move constantly.

Further down the song, the following line stood out:

> *'s gan idir mé is an tsíoraíocht ach an t-éadach tana tarr*
> – All that is between me and eternity is the thin shirt on my back (also referring to the 'tarred cloth' which you would get at the bottom of a currach)

The following lines complete the cycle of the fisherman in a most descriptive manner:

> *Ach anois atá mé aosta is mé ag éirí lag breoite tinn*
> – But now I am old and getting weak and sick
> *Níl mé ag dúil go brách le biseach a fháil go síntear mé sa chill*
> – I am not expecting to improve until I'm stretched out in the grave
> *Bheirim altú do Dhia na glóire mar chuir mé isteach m'am*
> – I give praise to the Glory of God for putting in my time
> *Ar chreig i lár na farraige i measc éanacha na mbeann*
> – On the stacks in the middle of the sea amongst the wild birds.

This song and verse put things into context. The wheel of life is a short spin and it's up to us to decide what we do with the time afforded to us. *Ar an chúigiú lá dhéag de mhí Iúil, i 2014 thug Enda Kenny deis domhsa agus ghlac mé é* – On the 15th of July 2014, Enda Kenny gave me an opportunity and I grabbed it – *agus níor amharc mé siar* – and I haven't looked back since.

The next song was 'My Donegal'. Inspired by the Irish Pensioners Choir in London (their motto is 'ceol agus soul'!), I said to myself, this is the one to learn. To give me a break from the *Gaeilge* I wanted to learn this song *as Béarla* first. Nathan Carter and Lisa Mc Hugh do a brilliant job – certainly up there with my good friend Mickey Doherty ó Rinn Uí Choigligh – Quigley's Point. If Mickey gets to his feet he will be sure to follow with a rendition of the JCB buí.

After learning the song, I promised the choir group at ATU, Leitir Ceanainn that I'd translate it to Gaeilge. I went about it in my own way and, no doubt, with a litany of mistakes. I came up with the words below for the last verse and the chorus. Let me assure you there were plenty of grammatical mistakes in the beginning (and maybe still!) Finally, it's not a word for word translation as that is not the way Gaeilge rolls. I had my fun and that's all that matters!

Agus ansin amárach, rachaidh mé síos
Go dtí Naomh Mhuire insan Tearmann
Guifidh mé mo phaidreacha do na daoine 'tá ar shiúl
Agus mé ag súil go bhfuil siad iontach bródúil

's é seo mo bhaile, an áit ar rugadh mé
Cibé ceantar ina dtéim
Tá sé i m'anam istigh
Rachaidh mo chosa go míle áit
Ach tiocfaidh mo chroí ar ais go mo Dhún na nGall.

And then tomorrow I'll take a walk
Towards Saint Mary's, to a sheltered spot,
I'll kneel and pray there for the ones that are gone
And hope they are proud of their wandering son

This is my homeland, the place I was born in,
And no matter where I go, it's in my soul,
My feet will wander a thousand places
But my heart will lead me back home to my Donegal

These three songs were relevant to me in three different ways: the position I found myself in, in the case of *'Cad é Sin Don Té Sin'*; the natural circle of life, in the case of *'Amhrán Na Scadán'* and where I'm from, in the case of 'My Donegal'. Learning Gaeilge through song has rehabilitated my relationship with music again. Alison Moyet and Annie Lennox are in competition with Leonard Cohen and Bob Dylan. 'Human' by The Killers has been added to my repertoire and I'm really looking forward to Mundy's next song as Gaeilge.

Relevance was key during my learning journey – and still is. While in the Department of Education I initiated a pilot in English medium schools – *Corpoideachas as Gaeilge* – PE through Irish. Conradh na Gaeilge had campaigned for this. I know this is only the tip of the iceberg; however, it's a start. Full immersion in junior and senior infants is well worth considering right across the country.

David Walliams is a well-known children's author. Many will be familiar with his book *Gangsta Granny*. *Tháinig mé trasna* Mamó An Gadaí Mór *le deanaí* – I came across *Mamó An Gadaí Mór* (the Irish translation of this book) recently. The publisher Futa Fata ó Spidéal have done incredible work in translating and rewriting this book and others by Walliams: *Mr Lofa* (*Mr Stink*) and *An Billiúnaí Beag* (*Billionaire Boy*). On pages 76 and 77 of *Mamó an Gadaí Mór* there are no less than twenty-five variations of some of our irregular verbs. Why do I say this? Well, here we have a talented storyteller and the main verbs

Caibidil 18: *It takes one to know one*

he uses are the irregular ones. Remember, there's only eleven of them. So it's worthwhile putting a bit of time into them.

Máirín Ní Mhárta translated David Walliams' *An Billiúnaí Beag – Billionaire Boy*. Claire Hennessy in the *Irish Times, mí an Mhárta –* March – 2017 sums it up, 'The humorous, conversational tone of the original shines through, with Tony Ross's illustrations on hand to assist any readers whose Irish may be a bit wobbly'.

At the beginning of my language journey, the following came in handy when I was explaining my position on the language scale: *Tá meirg ar mo chuid Gaeilge nó tá mé cineál meirgeach* – my Irish is rusty or I'm kind of rusty. Between the jigs and the reels (and a can of WD40 in hand) I set about changing that and I've been motoring along nicely ever since!

In an interview on RTÉ with Claire Byrne on *4ú Mí na Bealtaine, 2021* – 4th of May 2021 – she commented on my Donegal dialect. To be fair, many people struggle with the dialects. However, it's important to point out that apart from the pronunciation, words can be different too. For instance, *chífidh*[57] is used in Ulster instead of *'feicfidh'* – will see. Here's a few other variations with the *síos an tír* – down the country – version first and the *leagan Uladh* – Ulster version – on the right:

- *Feicim/Chím* – I see
- *Ní raibh/cha raibh* – was not (*Cha raibh* is like Scots Gaelic)
- *Nua/úr* – new (*úr* is used nationwide to mean fresh; check out Jack's van, selling *iasc úr* – fresh fish – next time you're in Carraig Airt, Dún Fionnachaidh *nó san* Fhál Carrach)
- *Álainn/galánta* – beautiful
- *Leite/brachán* – porridge
- *Gach/achan/gach uile* – every

---

[57] I've come across numerous spellings across Ulster for 'will see': *tífidh, chífidh, tcífidh agus tchífidh*. I am going to stick with *'chífidh'* as the spelling covers Munster Irish too. *Feicfidh* is used largely in Conamara.

Beidh Tú Alright: *Aithníonn ciaróg ciaróg eile*

My decision to leave politics was certainly influenced by my language journey. While acknowledging that health and family were central to my decision, I do believe that going back to learn Gaeilge showed me that there are always new possibilities and challenges out there which reminds me of the Latin line *carpe diem* – seize the day.

'No matter how lang we hey, it'll nay be lang ...' (no matter how long we live, it'll not be long) is a saying my mother shared with me after a Sunday night ballroom dancing (her not me!) in Logues of Cranford. She heard it from a Donegal man with a beautiful dialect that incorporates the fusion of Ulster and Scotland. As it happened, a relation from Glasgow was with us when we discussed this unique dialect, and she shared the following Glaswegian insight:

> *Here's tay us*
> *What's like us*
> *Damn few*
> *And they're all deed.*

My quest and yearning for Irish words were coupled with an interest in discerning words that were somewhere in the aul' triangle of *Gaeilge*, *Béarla* and *Gadhlig* (Scots Gaelic).[58] Words like 'palavar', 'skunnered', 'scallywag' and 'gallivanting'. Words I had heard in dispatches – mainly from my mother and my mother's mother – from a very young age. For years I took them for granted and didn't think twice. Now my curiosity knows no bounds. Where did they come from? What do they mean? Can we find out? How did they arrive in our present-day vernacular and how will they change and evolve in the future? Developing a curiosity for languages was a critical component and necessary fuel for my own learning.

---

[58] Of course, Scots and Gaidhlig are different languages, just as speakers of Ulster Scots argue that they speak a language which isn't just a dialect of English.

I was brought up with the offering of 'a boul of hot broth': *sú baile* – homemade soup. *Anraith* – soup (in the rest of the country) wasn't part of our kitchen vocabulary. There must have been plenty of confusion in the northern part of the country down the centuries as *sú* – soup – and *subh* – jam – were pronounced in the exact same manner. Further down the country the distinction is made as the 'bh' is always emphasised in the same way as *dubh* and *raibh* are pronounced 'duv' and 'rev'. They are pronounced 'doo' and 'rao' up the road. More confusion reigns with porridge. Textbook-based Gaeilge learning in the 1970s introduced us to *leite*, which was bizarre considering my neighbours a few miles down the road were eating *brachán*. There may have been some Portuguese influence in different parts of our island as the Portuguese for milk is also leite.

The 'whole shebang' and a 'whole hanlin' are integral parts of our vernacular in some parts of our country. Words and phrases are in a constant state of flux, bumping into each other, evolving, changing, adapting and growing. We get so many beautifully crafted sentences from our renowned Irish writers and the words and expressions literally dance off the pages. I was reading Billy Keane recently and his expressions reflecting everyday parlance were a joy to read. 'In spite of himself' and 'gallivanting' are two of my favourites.

Dála an scéil – By the way

I met many delegations during my time as Gaeltacht Minister and Minister for the Islands. *Gach uile* (every) – pronounced *'chuile'* – came up quite frequently when meeting with representatives off the Galway coast. Enda Conneely and Paddy Crowe from Inis Oírr had a unique dialect compared to the dialects from Inis Mór agus Inis Méain. No doubt, the islands' proximity to An Clár/Clare had a bearing on this. One thing is for sure though, irrespective of dialects, the island

Beidh Tú Alright: *Aithníonn ciaróg ciaróg eile*

communities work together with one voice when it comes to representing their island communities. And a fine job they do.

FOCAIL NA SEACHTAINE – WORDS OF THE WEEK

1. *Galar* – disease
2. *Sceadamán/Scornach* – throat
3. *Sceadamán nimhneach* – sore throat *(Uladh)*
4. *Scornach tinn* – sore throat *(Síos an tír)*
5. *Chífidh mé thú* – I will see you *(Uladh)*
6. *Feicfidh mé thú* – I will see you *(Síos an tír)*
7. *An rud is annamh is iontach* – What is rare is wonderful

N.B. Check out *Labhair an Teanga Ghaeilge* on the 'Ceol agus Soul' CD by Anne Morrissey.

DO THURAS FÉIN – YOUR JOURNEY

1. _____
2. _____
3. _____
4. _____
5. _____
6. _____
7. _____

Teanglann.ie phrase:
Focal a chur i mbéal duine – to put words in someone's mouth.

Caibidil 19

Is fearr lúbadh ná briseadh

It's better to bend than break

From the railroads to the highways, I am inextricably linked to the vocabulary in the United States. I was in full flow during the construction of the railroads and highways in the seventeenth and eighteenth centuries – in some places right up to the twentieth century. The roads were built by many Gaeltacht speakers who had their tea breaks as Gaeilge. The Irish for road is ród. *Rhode/Ród in Offaly comes to mind. You may be thinking, 'sure the Gaeilge for road is* bóthar?' *It is, and was drummed into you, you may add. But you also know that the Gaeilge for cow is* bó. *The* bóthar *was the narrow path where the cows walked between fields and the byre. Things change, words change, and I have certainly changed. I also embrace change. If the* ród *or* bealach mór *has evolved into the narrow path where the cows walked, then* tá mé sásta le sin *– I'm happy with that. It would be interesting to find out what word was used for road during construction in the States. I would guess it was the* bealach mór *for the Donegal boys. Now that I'm on your radar. Now that I've got your attention. Now that your curiosity might be getting the better of you,* éist liom – *listen to me. This was never meant to be a forced marriage. Peig springs to mind here!* Tá mé, tá tú, tá sé, ta sí, tá muid, tá sibh, tá siad. Íosa Críost, *will you ever forgive me? Fortunately, we have moved away from this process and moved to a more* comhrá – *conversation – based learning model. The trick is to empower all our teachers to use the built-in flexibility in the new curriculum, to be creative in the approach and bring the fun back into the learning experience. Many teachers do this well, but some struggle. It can be a question of confidence but also of legacy issues around how some teachers were introduced to me. But let's dig a little deeper. Let's go back a few steps. When do German children learn German? When do Chinese children learn Mandarin? When do Irish children learn English? Not where, not how and not why – just when? You are correct: when they are young.*

• • • • • • •

Marino Institute of Education and Mary Immaculate College have made great strides in building the language capacity for primary and secondary school teachers. While this has been successful, conversations have meandered into pre-school. The language part of the brain in the younger child enables them to soak up new words like a sponge. The capacity is not there to do it now, and the teams at Marino and Mary Immaculate would be well worth talking to. No doubt, this is happening already in some pre-schools outside the Gaeltacht. However, here is an opportunity worth pursuing at a wider level. Gene Mehigan in Marino has thought about it and believes this could work. Organisations like Muintearas and Comhar Naíonraí na Gaeltachta have a wealth of experience to contribute to this important conversation. Fiontar agus Scoil na Gaeilge at DCU have a proven track record in delivering innovative teaching and research on digital projects. An Taoiseach Simon Harris has initiated discussions on publicly funded childcare facilities for early years. Could this be the opening for a bit of long-term planning and start building the teaching capacity for early years full immersion as Gaeilge?

QUICK WINS ...

Operation 'Fanacht' – To Hell or to FANACHT. One of the 'red tops' ran with the above headline during one of the many Covid-19 *dianghlasáil* – lockdowns. Very *cliste* – clever – and a nice win for the language. Do we do this enough? Not really. Campaigns by Conradh na Gaeilge, and vigilance by the Irish Language Commissioner has ensured that the language is all around us. You don't have to travel one mile in any part of Ireland to see our language on the road signs. And rightly so – *albeit in italics.* Grassroots organisations like Céim Aniar and An Chrannóg in Dún na nGall have a solid track record in the promotion of our language through drama and music respectively. The summer colleges continue to raise the bar in the Gaeltacht area of Gaoth Dobhair, Na Dúnaibh, Rann na Feirste, Gleann Fhinne, Cill Charthaigh, Árainn Mhór, Loch an Iúir, Conamara agus Chiarraí. Traditions in Port Láirge, Maigh Eo, An Mhí agus Corcaigh are alive and well *fosta* – also. And there's others of course.

Back to the quick wins. In 2016 the *mojito* was the most popular cocktail in Britain and France. Ireland has always led the charge in whiskey and Gin distilling and brewing of craft beer. What about inventing our own range of cocktails as Gaeilge? Maybe a *solúbtha*, which means flexible, pronounced 'soluppa'. I will leave that with all you cocktail experts. Having worked as a barman in Ostán Carraig Airt and Filideilfia I am by no means a cocktail expert; however just like the language you make it work for you in a creative way. Resilience is used frequently when discussing courage and perseverance. In searching for an equivalent focal as Gaeilge we hit the wall.[59] The expression (not an equivalent word) for resilience is *teacht aniar* – coming from the

---

[59] See note under *dála an scéil*.

Beidh Tú Alright: *Is fearr lúbadh ná briseadh*

West. With no disrespect to our east coast readers, if you're able to survive on the west coast of this wee island – *ar na Carraigeacha agus ar an bhfraoch* – on the rocks and heather – that's resilience. To keep everyone on board here, if you live on an island off the west coast of mainland Britain in the middle of the Atlantic Ocean, that's resilience! Cocktail *uimhir a dó* – number two – 'the *Teacht Aniar*'. We were flat out learning the past tense, conditional tense, present tense, and future tense – even though the present was bleak in those Irish classes, never mind the future. One of the lesser-known tenses is the *modh foshuiteach* – but it features in some very well-known expressions: *go raibh maith agat/go ndéana a mhaith duit*[60] – thank you, but literally 'that good may come on to you'.

Similarly, *go dtaga do ríocht* – thy kingdom will come. We have mentioned what we gave to the English language but this one (kingdom) we gave to the German language: 'Reichstag' comes from our own Irish and you can add at least four or five hundred other words given by the Irish monks who reintroduced learning to Europe after the Dark Ages. Cocktail number three – the *Modh Foshuiteach* – pronounced 'Mow fuh hee cha'.

A quick win for the Irish language is when the state intervenes when naming a new public *togra* – project. When building a new tram service for Dublin City the naming of this new project was a master stroke: *Luas* – speed. Paradoxically, the quick-witted Dubs refer to it as the 'snail on the rail'. Also, they couldn't call the designated tram lanes on the road '*lána luas*' because it means 'fast lane'! This word is embedded in our psyche and, to be honest, I didn't realise it was an Irish word until a few years ago. Travelling on *Bus Átha Cliath* – Dublin Bus – is a great opportunity to brush up on the Gaeilge, with a mini lesson at every stop. Hats off to all the state and semi-state agencies that have Gaeilge front and centre under the Official Language Act, and

---

[60] In the Gaeltacht regions of Dún na nGall you will hear '*Go ndéana a mhaith duit*' – very similar to '*go raibh maith agat*', emphasising 'that good is made for you'.

hopefully there will be more to come outside the state requirements.[61] *Teagasc* – teaching – the state agency providing research and education in agriculture and *Coillte* – woodlands. *An Bord Bia* – the food board – is another, and *An Bord Pleanála* – the planning appeals board – is one that is etched in the psyche. We need to move into this space more ambitiously. SOLAS: *An tSeirbhis Oideachais Leanúnaigh agus Scileanna* – Further Education and Skills Service – is one of the new recruits. A more recent recruit is 'Cuan Síochána – Vulnerable Citizens Suite', which was officially opened by Minister Helen McEntee this year. *Mar eolas, An Garda Síochána,* which has been abbreviated to 'The Guards', was a very considered title when named by Michael Collins and the Irish government in 1923. It translates as 'guardians of peace'. No doubt we all strive for some *síocháin* from time to time. It's time to make peace with our great language and seize the quick wins through meaningful interventions that make sense and are relevant.

DÁLA AN SCÉIL – BY THE WAY

'Hitting the wall' is a lovely expression but try this as Gaeilge: the manager's back is to the wall at present – *tá lámh an bhainisteora i mbéal an mhadra faoi láthair* – literally, the manager's hand is in the mouth of the dog now!

FOCAIL NA SEACHTAINE – WORDS OF THE WEEK

1. *Dianghlasáil* – lockdown
2. *Iontach cliste* – very clever
3. *Fanacht* – waiting
4. *Teacht Aniar* – coming from the west (Resilience)

---

[61] Julian de Spáinn, *Ard Rúnaí* at Conradh na Gaeilge, and his team were instrumental in ensuring the Irish language can be seen and heard, morning, noon and night.

Beidh Tú Alright: *Is fearr lúbadh ná briseadh*

5. *Togra* – project
6. *Solúbtha* – flexible
7. *Luas* – speed

DO THURAS FÉIN – YOUR JOURNEY

1. _____
2. _____
3. _____
4. _____
5. _____
6. _____
7. _____

> Teanglann.ie phrase:
> *Níl dochar san fhocal nach gcantar* –
> Unspoken words cannot hurt.

Caibidil 20

Níl bua gan dua

No pain, no gain

I'm thinking of the Irish mammy and daddy who stood at Droichead na nDeor — *the Bridge of Tears — and waved goodbye to their son or daughter, in the full knowledge that seeing them again was not a given. While they probably said their goodbyes as Gaeilge, there was an acceptance that I would be of little assistance on the streets of New York, in the tunnels near Cricklewood or in the cattle ranches of New South Wales. In fairness, when people's backs were to the wall, the far-away fields didn't have much need for me. In fact, I was a bit of a hindrance. Working on the building sites of London, being sent for 'sky hooks', 'glass nails' and 'glass hammers' was through the medium of* mo chara — *my friend* — Béarla. *Mind you, when the Irish speakers wanted to have their own private discourse, they always reverted to their native tongue, and rightly so.*

● ● ● ● ● ● ●

Beidh Tú Alright: *Níl bua gan dua*

If we park the *mothúcháin* – emotion – and the *fíordhroch-thaithí* – raw negative experience – we can make a start. Let's enjoy what we're doing, let's experiment, and let's be inquisitive as to why a place in the United States of America is called Baltimore – *Bailte Móra* – a collection of big towns? Where did the expression associated with the east coast of the United States 'Do you dig it?' come from? *An dtuigeann tú* – do you understand? A language does not stay under lock and key – it travels, it evolves, it infiltrates … and while the *Béarla* dominates now, it lacks curiosity and intrigue. The beautiful, almost Spanish-sounding word *solúbtha*, meaning flexible, traversed into *Béarla*/Ulster Scots to give the word *supple* to describe the agility of a person.

Whether or not we have full documented proof of how a language transitions or words originated we shouldn't get stressed out in that space. Remember, one man came up with 1,700 new words in one lifetime. Shakespeare did this by combining words, changing nouns into verbs, adding prefixes or suffixes, and so on. Some words stayed the same and some didn't.

The Course of Irish History, first published in 1967,[62] highlights the excuse used by Henry II, King of England to enter Ireland in the twelfth century:

> For Henry had sought from Pope Adrian IV permission 'to enter the Island of Ireland in order to subject its people to law and to root out from them the weeds of vice', 'to enlarge the boundaries of the Church', and to 'proclaim the truths of the Christian religion to a rude and ignorant people'. The poets, with their long tradition of native learning, knew how unfounded was the description 'rude and ignorant people'. They knew that in the very century in which Henry came to Ireland the leaders of their own profession had reorganised their craft and had laid the basis for a prescriptive

---

[62] T.W. Moody & F.X. Martin (eds), *The Course of Irish History*, Radio Teilifís Éireann in association with Mercier Press (1967), (1984), p. 108.

Caibidil 20: *No pain, no gain*

grammar of Irish, the first such grammar of a western European language. They knew of a revival of learning which had taken place in the eleventh and twelfth centuries in the great monastic schools and of which they had seen material evidence in the form of manuscripts and in the decorative metalwork of the period.

We live on an island surrounded by water. We have a history of people taking an interest in our country for the right and the wrong reasons. With all the challenges over time, the Irish language has always been at the heart of who we are as a nation. Our Irish language is in our DNA. It has survived turmoil, invasions, and conflict. It will survive in the time ahead.

Consider some of the vocabulary that traversed Ulster over hundreds of years:

- *A thaisce*
- *Lig do sgíth*
- The house fernenced me
- A full-scale hanlin
- A halihan
- Scallywag
- A quare haems of a job
- The boul in the scullery
- Steebie
- A hash of a man
- Screenging for money, or food
- I was foundered with the cold
- The bothy

My father and his brothers love using the title 'Tamheedledee' as a term of endearment (I hope). Less endearing terms like 'guldie', 'greeshin', 'clouster' and 'gulping' were labels to be avoided![63]

Words and language are in a constant state of flux, and nothing is permanent. As Heraclitus quipped one time about flux, 'You can't put your foot in the same river twice'. Zeno went further with, 'You can't put your foot in the same river once'. Maybe those two boys had too much time on their hands! Both perspectives highlight the complexity of flux and how some things are not just *dubh agus bán* – black and white. Words meet, they grow together and sometimes they disappear. The 'whole shebang' has unknown origin and is still alive and well in modern day vernacular. In parts of Inis Eoghain, in my own county, 'corpse house' is used instead of wake house. Or as Gaeilge, Teach na Faire. While 'corpse' is of Latin origin it has been used in Gaeilge conversations down the centuries right through to *Béarla* exchanges *inniu* – today. Now we have *Corpoideachas* – Physical Education (PE), literally education of the body, on the Leaving Certificate curriculum.

Growing up in Dún na nGall, a '*futterer*' was a far from glowing description of someone doing a piece of work. Little did I know then that the Gaeilge word *fútráil* predated 'futtering' or being a 'futer'.

Old words still exist today and stay strong. The spelling of banshee has been anglicised, but the same phonetics takes us back to the basics: *bean sí* – fairy woman.

Dictionary.com maintains the origin of 'Bothy' from 1560–70 is probably from Scots Gaidhlig: *bothán*, hut. I've been told that the Balmoral show has its origins in the Irish language: *both mór* – big hut! The Oxford Learner's Dictionary maintains 'bothy' is a small building

---

[63] James Fenton, *The Hamely Tongue* (2006), pp. 59, 63, 45, 96, 140, does a great job in highlighting Ulster Scots in County Antrim with the following: As thran as a donkey; Like a drooned rat; Cooterments; hard tae bate; Niver's a lang time.

in Scotland for farm workers to live in or for people to shelter in. It also states that the word origin is from the late eighteenth century obscurely related to Irish and Scottish Gaelic. There is nothing obscure about the origin of bothy. Surely it is *bóithigh* – cow house. Most of these cow houses adjoined the main household. There were many times the household itself got the title 'bothy' as the cows sometimes stayed in the main household to keep families warm at night. There was an annual transit of seasonal workers throughout the nineteenth and twentieth centuries for the purpose of *'tattie hoking'* (potato gathering) in Scotland. Accommodation for workers was less than desirable even at the best of times. The 'bothy' or the *'bóithigh'* may have been introduced to Scottish vocabulary during these times by the hard-working *'tattie hokers'* from Donegal, Mayo and elsewhere. The Kirkintilloch tragedy of 1937 highlighted the substandard accommodation made available to the *'tattie hokers'* from Achill Island. At Kirkintilloch just outside Glasgow, in the early hours of 16 September 1937, tragedy struck: a fire claimed the lives of ten young men and boys between the ages of 13 and 23. According to the *Irish Times* (Friday 17 September 1937): 'The place where the youths died was a death trap; just a low shack, walls of brick, roof of tar – tar that added its fuel to the deadly conflagration. Arriving from Edinburgh last night to begin work, twenty-six Tawtie-hokers were given shelter by their employer, Mr Graham in this bothy'. The *Atlas of Donegal*, edited by Jim McLaughlin and Seán Beattie,[64] describes the Árainn Mhór disaster of 9 November 1935. Nineteen people lost their lives returning from potato harvesting in Scotland.

The transit of Irish men and women from Donegal and Mayo to Scotland for work wasn't a one-way street. Listening to people in my own parish, many Scottish people came to Downings to work on the boats during the herring season.

---

[64] J. MacLaughlin and S. Beattie (2013) *An Historical, Environmental and Cultural Atlas of Donegal*, Cork University Press.

Beidh Tú Alright: *Níl bua gan dua*

Dála an scéil – By the way

Without going into too much detail, let us look at the word '*corpoideachas*' (PE) and how it changes. When a word precedes it, e.g. 'PE kit', it changes to '*éide chorpoideachais*'. My admiration and respect for translators and interpreters is growing all the time. The Gaeilge construct is complex for sure so take it one step at a time.

Focail na seachtaine – Words of the week

1. *Corpoideachas* – physical education
2. *Sióg* – fairy
3. *Bothán*[65] – Bothy/bothie, house/hut
4. *Loch Garman* – Wexford
5. *Fíor* – true/real
6. *Droch* – bad/poor/negative
7. *Taithí* – experience

Do thuras féin – Your journey

1. _____
2. _____
3. _____
4. _____
5. _____

---

[65] Raphoe – Ráth Bhoth (Logainm.ie #810) – *Both*: hut, cell; and *ráth*: ring-fort. Logainm has a note from O'Donovan; 'many ancient Irish churches were erected within the rings of pagan raths and cashels'. Also, 'the circular enclosure was a consistent feature of early monastic sites' – Norman 7 St. Joseph, p. 90.

Caibidil 20: *No pain, no gain*

6. _____

7. _____

> Teanglann.ie phrase:
> *An focal maith, géar, feirge, magaidh –*
> good, sharp, angry, mocking words.

Caibidil 21

Tír gan teanga, tír gan anam

A country without a language is a country without a soul

Many parents struggled during lockdown when it came to teaching Gaeilge. Irish learning is far from a walk in the park when English is staring and blaring[66] at us around every corner. Nonetheless, I sense a new attitude whereby the appetite is there to start again. It will be different though. Through technology, innovation, visual arts and drama, new platforms are helping enormously in my development. You can re-capture my very essence, which lies dormant in your consciousness. Ar scáth a chéile a mhaireann na daoine – *we return to that ancient saying which goes back to people's early preoccupation with shadows.*

● ● ● ● ● ● ●

---

[66] Did this word come from Gaeilge too? *Bladhair* – shout/bellow.

Bob Geldof in an interview with Tommy Tiernan[67] had the following to say:

> So I was with Bruce Springsteen last week, and I don't know if you read his book, *Born to Run*, but it's spectacularly good ... The guy's a writer, and he's got the Irish thing The Rats have ... That's the Irish thing. I mean, it really is. We have the words, and I've often said in the UK – 'I'm Irish, you know, we have the words.' It is a thing we do. It's absolutely part of the game here.

Tommy himself is some man for one man to pull words and phrases down from the clouds. When the words start bursting out of him there's no stopping him as he takes you places that you thought never existed.

Micheál Óg Mac Aoidh along with Tom Sailí Ó Flaithearta agus Beartla M. Ó Flatharta (Rua) make a great effort in moving Gaeilge into the twenty-first century with their play *Aislingí Grádha Oídhche Lúghnasadh – A Mid Summer Night's Dream*.

Here's a sample:

Tommy
Unprovoked, mo thóin! Bhí an slíomadóir sin ag shift-áil Méadhbh taobh thiar do mo dhroim. Agus, íocfaidh sé go daor as – Unprovoked, my arse! The sneaky, slimey snake there was shifting Meadhbh behind my back. He will pay dear for this.

Diarmuid
Ní raibh mé ag déanamh dada taobh thiar de do dhroim agus maith atá a fhios agat é – I was doing nothing behind your back and well you know it.

---

[67] Reproduced in the book *Winging It* (Penguin Ireland, 2020).

Tommy
Bhí tú! Ghoid tú Meadhbh uaim – You were! You stole Meadhbh from me.

Diarmuid
Ah, in ainm Dé! Get real – Ah, in God's name! Get real.

Tommy
Tabharfaidh mise 'get real' duit, a mhaicín, idir do dhá shúil – I will give you 'get real', son, between your two eyes.

There is no limit to what people can do with a language. *Níl aon teorainn leis* – the sky is the limit. *Triail* – experiment – *agus cruthaigh* – and create. Park up the *eagla* – fear – (pronounced 'ugla' up north). If you were in any way afraid all those years ago, that *eagla* was in you, it was on you, in your fingertips, in your toenails and it was part of your life. The description as Gaeilge is very apt. *Bhí an eagla* ORM – the fear was on me, in me, right through me and part of me.

To be described as 'a harmless enough sort of crator' is not really a compliment. It means you can be safely ignored. In comparative terms, the English language is harmless enough compared with the richness and complexity of Gaeilge. The English language came up with the very harmless 'just in case'. In comparison the Gaeilge equivalent is *'ar eagla na heagla'* which directly translates as 'for fear of the fear'. You get the picture. To further confuse things, let's look at a few variations of 'man' – as if there were only a few variations.

- *Tá an FEAR ag caint* – the man is talking
- *Tá na FIR ag caint* – the men are talking
- *Éist le caint an FHIR* – listen to the man talking
- *Labhair leis an bhFEAR* – speak to the man
- *Labhair leis na FIR* – speak to the men
- *Fireannach* – male
- *Dia duit, a FHIR mhaith* – hello, good man
- *Dia daoibh, a FHEARA* – hello men

Caibidil 21: *A country without a language is a country without a soul*

There you have it, five variations of man/men. Men were a lot more complex back then! And that's before we even get to Fear Dia (Ferdia) from the Cú Chulainn story.

The late Tommy Friel from Fánaid recalled that in days gone by *'mar a deir an fearaide'* was used widely by the native Irish speakers in his community which translates to, *'as the man says'*. Man-a-man was used by a man from *Carn na nGabhar*/Carnagore. Leslie Lucas recorded *a fheara breá* – boys-a-boys – in his work.[68] If you happen to be travelling through Ferbane in County Offaly, pull the car *isteach ar chlé* – into the left – and have a wee gawk at the road sign. It will read *Féar Bán*/Ferbane – white grass (Logainm.ie #1416831). There happens to be a local song called the 'Green Grass of Ferbane'. The good people of Ferbane will know the score in the naming of the village, and why it's not Ferglas. Logainm.ie has a note on the great county of *Fear Manach* (Logainm.ie #100014). Note that there is no fada on *'fear'* (pronounced 'far') which would indicate that the original name was *'Fear Manach'* or *'Fir Manach'*. The man or men of *Manach*. The meaning of *Manach* is 'Monk'.

It is important to navigate carefully between the words 'white' and 'woman' – *bán agus bean*, pronounced 'bawn' agus 'bann' respectively. Even though in Ulster we pronounce both words 'bann'. When you consider the varieties of English dialect from Cornwall to North Carolina and from the East End of London to the west coast of Ciarraí, there is quite the range. This is against a backdrop of advanced communication systems and a bombardment of English and American media dominance. When describing a lack of gullibility there is a great expression used by people who lived on the banks of the Mulroy, *cha dtáinig mé aníos an Mhaoil Ruaidh i mbairille* – I didn't come up the Mulroy in a barrel. This is quoted by Leslie Lucas in his *Cnuasach Focal as Ros Goill*.[69]

---

[68] Leslie W. Lucas, *Grammar of Ros Goill Irish* (QUB, 1979), 248, 708.

[69] Leaslaoi Ú. Lúcás, *Cnuasach Focal as Ros Goill* (1986), Acadamh Ríoga Na hÉireann [Royal Irish Academy], p. 30.

Beidh Tú Alright: *Tír gan teanga, tír gan anam*

Dála an scéil – By the way

If you really want to experience the fear in Fear Manach give the FEARmanagh Adventure Race a go and you'll learn all you need to know about FEAR! Derrygonnelly/ Doire Ó gConaíle is a majestic location and it will test you in many ways, as I recently found out!

Focail na seachtaine – Words of the week

1. *Ár nAthair* – our Father
2. *Ár gcairde* – our friends
3. *Ar eagla na heagla* – just in case, literally for fear of the fear
4. *Triail* – experiment
5. *An tráthnóna sin fadó* – an evening long ago
6. *An Mhaoil Ruaidh* – The Mulroy
7. *Tír gan teanga, Tír gan anam* – a country without a language is a country without soul

Do thuras féin – Your journey

1. _____
2. _____
3. _____
4. _____
5. _____
6. _____
7. _____

|| Teanglann.ie phrase: *Fonn gan focail* – song without words. ||

Caibidil 22

Téann focail le gaoth

Words are like the wind

Look at these two lovely fadas near each other on the number scale: séú – sixth – agus tríú – third. Two other beauties with the fadas side by side include 'God's little cow': bóin dé – ladybird – agus báúil – sympathetic. In relation to the fadas, get up on your tip toes and stretch those vowels. With two fadas side by side, just stay on your toes that little while longer. If you wish, you can mimic the mac tíre – wolf (literally 'son of the land') – when you are pronouncing báúil – Baaaaaauuuuuuuuil! Maybe not in company.

● ● ● ● ● ● ●

I encourage you to open your eyes and heart to endless possibilities. Bí ag lorg – be explorative – bí fiosrach – be inquisitive – bí i do dhuine féin – be yourself. Try and remember words and expressions used by parents and grandparents and neighbours. Some told us a good 'smack' would do us no harm. Others beg to differ. In fact, if we look at the Gaeilge for control – smacht – and introduce faoi smacht

– under control – there may be some connection between 'smack' and '*smacht*' – a journey of discovery. Speaking of wains (wee ones) and dubious parenting skills, 'scolding' comes to mind. The Online Etymology Dictionary points to Old Norse skald 'poet'. *Scamhailéireacht* – scolding – is found in Foclóir.ie. In many parts of Donegal, you will hear the word 'scawling' in the same sentence as 'the wains'. At the tip of Inis Eoghain you will hear the following in relation to someone getting a good telling off – 'He got a right skalding'. Our word for the day is '*scamhailéireacht*' – what a great word.

Spend twice as much time speaking as writing. Keep it real. Former US Charges d'Affaires Stuart Dwyer once said, 'if I break my leg, I won't be saying *bhris mé mo chos* – I broke my leg – I'll be saying, "Call me a god d*** ambulance!"' This was after he spent a few classes trying to learn a *cúpla focal*. Stuart was making the point that rote learning sentences would not benefit him in an emergency. Classes are important, grammar is equally important, but everyday discourse must be on the menu too. Like many aspects of life, it's the little things that count. The work environment is a great place to start. The ushers in Leinster House were very much part of my learning journey. There were different standards, but the enthusiasm and willingness were the same. It may have just been a twenty second exchange, but it was enough to keep the practise going. A simple *Dia is Muire duit* reply to *Dia duit* – hello. A simple *maidin mhaith* – good morning – at the start of the day and a departing *oíche mhaith* – good night – goes a long way. *Táim tuirseach* – I'm tired – was conveyed on many occasions during late night/early morning legislative sessions.

As always, have Foclóir.ie, Téarma.ie, Teanglann.ie, Abair.ie and Logainm.ie on hand to experiment with new words and new sentences. *Mar shampla, lá amháin bhí mé ag ól cupán tae* – for example, one day I was drinking a cup of tea – *agus ní raibh an focal agam fá choinne 'saucer'* – and I didn't have the word for saucer. Low and behold, I was presented with '*fochupán*'. Some people use *sásar*, however the interesting thing here is '*fo*', which is the Gaeilge for 'sub'. Branching out

Caibidil 22: *Words are like the wind*

from the knowledge that a saucer is a 'sub-cup' we can move on to so many other terms such as the examples below:

- *Aonad Fo-uisce an Gharda Síochána* – Garda Sub-Aqua Unit
- *Fobhaile* – suburb
- *Fochoiste* – subcommittee
- *Fochonraitheoir* – subcontractor
- *Fo-chomhfhiosach* – subconscious
- *Fochultúr* – subculture
- *Foroinn* – subdivision
- *Foghrúpa* – subgroup
- *Fo-cheannteideal* – subheading
- *Fo-urlár* – subfloor
- *Fodhaonna* – subhuman
- *Fo-eagarthóir* – subeditor
- *Fotheideal* – subtitle
- *Fomhuiréan* – submarine

One of my biggest challenges was panicking at the beginning or middle of a sentence and then searching in desperation for the translation of English words. This is a bad place to be. Firstly, we have two separate language constructs and secondly when you are searching for the *Béarla* word you are thinking *as Béarla*, and you need to get out of that trap like a herd of turtles, well, maybe a bit faster than that. I needed vocabulary that would fill the gaps and buy me time.

Here are a few standalone phrases with no complications which will add to your vocabulary.

- *Mar sin féin* – nevertheless
- *Ba chóir dúinn* – we should
- *Sílim go dtuigim* – I think I understand
- *Má theastaíonn uait* – if you want to

- *Áfach* – however[70]
- *Go deimhin* – indeed
- *Lig dom* – let me
- *Ní ligfidh mé* – I will not let
- *Más mian leat* – if you wish
- *De réir* – according to
- *Sin ráite* – that being said
- *Mise ba chiontaí* – I was to blame
- *Ná bac le sin* – don't bother with that
- *Ná bí dalba* – don't be bold

And if you want to start a row with someone I would suggest the following:

- *Bíodh ciall agat* – have some sense!

Having the confidence to throw a shape at a conversation is important. The ultimate judge as to who decides what goes into that conversation is you. You have the power over your words *as Béarla*, the same applies to *Gaeilge*. *Tá an chumhacht* – the power is – *istigh i do lámha* – in your hands. Like so many life challenges, there is a voice holding you back. *Ná bac le sin* – don't bother with that. *Ar aghaidh leat* – onwards!

One of the advantages many of us have in our word arsenal is rote learning from our childhood. Much of this was through song and learning poems by heart. Despite a lot of this data being buried as time moves on, if we dig deep enough some of the prayers, for instance, are still with us. Whether you are still practising, taking time out, never practised or on a permanent sabbatical from religion, I would strongly suggest going back over some of these prayers. I found out very quickly that while I could reel off the Gaeilge versions of the 'Our Father', the

---

[70] *Áfach* (however) is never used at the start of a sentence, *áfach*!

'Hail Mary' and the 'Glory Be to the Father', I had never taken the time out to analyse and compare them with the English versions. *Tabhair* – to give – has a big part to play in the 'Our Father':

Ár n-arán laethúil tabhair dúinn inniu – Give us this day our daily bread. This one sentence is a great example of how Irish words do not mirror the same version in English. If you translate directly from Irish to English in the same order of words, the sentence would go like this: 'Our bread daily give us today'.

Below are another few examples of how to use our verb *'tabhair'*. Can you spot the *modh coinníollach* – conditional mood?[71]

- *Tabhair dom é* – give it to me
- *Tugann siad airgead* – they give money
- *Thug mé faoi deara* – I noticed
- *Níor thug mé faoi deara* – I didn't notice
- *Thabharfadh sé an léine dá dhroim duit* – he would give you the shirt off his back
- *Cothrom na Féinne a thabhairt* – to give an even break
- *Tabharfaimid seans dóibh* – we will give them a chance

DÁLA AN SCÉIL – BY THE WAY

Ár n-arán – **Our** bread: this is the second time we see *Ár*. We are introduced to *Ár* at the beginning of the prayer with *Ár n-Athair atá ar neamh* – Our Father who art in heaven. *Arán* – bread – and *Athair* – father – both begin with a vowel so both take an 'n' once we introduce *Ár*.

I practised a lot to get my tongue up to the roof of my mouth with the Irish *urú* 'n', something the native Irish speaker has been practising since birth.

---

[71] *Tabharfadh sé …* – he would give …

Beidh Tú Alright: *Téann focail le gaoth*

- *Ár ndoirse* – our doors
- *Ár n-Athair* – our Father
- *Ár ndeora* – our tears

FOCAIL NA SEACHTAINE – WORDS OF THE WEEK

1. *Ciaróg* – beetle
2. *Siongán* – ant
3. *Ár n-áran* – our bread
4. *Tabhair* – give
5. *Níor thug mé faoi deara* – I didn't notice
6. *Tabhair dom é* – give it to me
7. *Ná bac le sin* – don't bother with that

DO THURAS FÉIN – YOUR JOURNEY

1. _____
2. _____
3. _____
4. _____
5. _____
6. _____
7. _____

‖ Teanglann.ie phrase: *Fuighle fáis* – empty words ‖

Caibidil 23

Níl eagla ar an mac tíre roimh an ngadhar a bhíonn ag tafann

The wolf does not fear the barking dog

I am grateful that so many people still believe in me. I have a purpose. I have a reason for getting out of bed in the morning. Make every séimhiú and urú count. If it takes you a while to learn the where, what, when, how and why of my construction, then that's ok. While perfection might be the goal, the enjoyment is making plenty of mistakes along the way. That's where the real learning happens.

● ● ● ● ● ● ●

Beidh Tú Alright: *Níl eagla ar an mac tíre roimh an ngadhar a bhíonn ag tafann*

TÁ CRÓGACHT AN MHIC TÍRE SA SLUA AGUS 'SÉ AN SLUA CRÓGACHT AN MHIC TÍRE – THE STRENGTH OF THE PACK IS THE WOLF, AND THE STRENGTH OF THE WOLF IS THE PACK.

And they're back! Wild Ireland in Inis Eoghain, Donegal have facilitated the return of wolves to Ireland after over 200 years. Killian & Katie and their team have brought history alive in south Inis Eoghain with the re-introduction of the *mac tíre* and the *béar*. For all you Mahoneys and Mahons, you come from the Irish word for bear – *mathúin* – and that's the bare truth of it! (*Oso*, the Spanish word for bear, might interest all you Oisíns out there). Killian uses the Irish language to describe his timeline and, in the process, brings authenticity, understanding and relevance to an amazing tourism project. By tracing the paw steps of our native animals, this *tearmann* – sanctuary – is already becoming a must for local schools and beyond. The memory of the wolf lives on in Irish place names, e.g. Knockaunvicteera in County Clare – little hill of the wolf. There are several words in the Irish language to describe the wolf. *Fael, faolchú, madra allta* and *faelcu* were also used. My introduction to another variation was Falcão in 1982. He starred in midfield along with his Brazilian teammates Zico, Eder and Socrates. Maybe there was a connection with Portugal and Ireland back in the day! On an even more obscure connection, it was said to me that the late, great Pele's name came from '*ag imirt peile*!' – as I said, obscure indeed!

When building a house, the *bunchloch* – foundation – needs to be right. In addition, there is a sequence to be followed rigidly. The foundation, damp course, the square, the RSJ and then the *díon* – roof. *Ag tús mo thurais* – at the start of my journey – I didn't have a proper structure or sequence to my learning. It was as close to full immersion as one could get. I will always be grateful to Joe agus John, not alone *ag obair mar thiománaithe* – working as drivers – but also *ag obair mar múinteoirí* – working as teachers. I was surrounded by people who were speaking to me as Gaeilge. Living so close to the Gaeltacht was

Caibidil 23: *The wolf does not fear the barking dog*

a plus but realising so many people outside the Gaeltacht were *líofa* – fluent in our native tongue was a real eye-opener.

Bhí an t-ádh rua ormsa – I had red luck – that Noeleen Fagan came into my life as *mo rúnaí príobháideach* – my private secretary. A fluent Irish speaker, with a healthy abundance of common sense and humour, Noeleen created a safe space for me to manage my learning in conjunction with my day job. Barra, Maura and Micheál were on hand to deal with this very unusual situation. My late granny's philosophy that everything happened for a reason was my default position!

The civil service code kicked in, the officials had a job to do, the new minister had arrived. In fairness, the support from the officials for a newly appointed minister was exceptional under very difficult circumstances. Not only did they deal with my day-to-day business they also had to deal with the daily criticism and media requests. Furthermore, I was very fortunate to have Minister Heather Humphries alongside me as my senior minister. Her cool-headedness and common-sense approach to everything in the Department was a big help – and Heather practised what she preached by heading up the road to the Donegal Gaeltacht in Gleann Fhinne.

Overall, it was mainly *dearfach* – positive. The little things kept biting me though, for example, addressing an audience of *dhá chéad duine* – two hundred people – I started off by saying 'Cad é mar atá tú', which was effectively addressing one person. I should have used '*sibh*' – you plural – not '*tú*'! Noeleen was on hand to warn me not to make that mistake again. I learned *ag treabhadh ar aghaidh* – ploughing ahead – *ar mo chéad lá* – on my first day. While my appointment as Minister for the Gaeltacht garnered a considerable degree of publicity agus *agóid* – protest – a good lively *díospóireacht* – debate – ensued. It is important to get the word out that you are *ag foghlaim nó ag ath-fhoghlaim* – learning or relearning. You will be met with enthusiasm and support from people you've never met before. Unlike me, you won't have to deal with media pressure, and you won't have to stand in front of your peers reciting prose and poetry. I met many people who were there to help, the personification of the noble art of helping someone when stuck in a *shuch* – a slow-moving stream/quagmire. Keep out of the '*shuch*' though, stay between the ditches and stick to the *croíbhóthar* – heart of the road. Some of the satire was clever; however some of the criticism was persistent.

Bíonn blas ar an mbeagán – Small portions are tasty

Thinking back about the bizarre circumstances that were presented to me, I didn't know amidst the chaos that something structurally unusual was taking shape. Because of the public nature of my journey, my support structure came to me rather than me having to seek it. The support is there for you too, the difference being you will have to ask for it, which is no bad thing. I would dearly love to present my chaotic learnings to you in a more systematic way. However, *ní mar sin a bhíonn* – that's not how it is. I recommend getting less hung up on grammatical mistakes and look at this journey as a lifelong project with a beginning, a series of unknowns, surprises, bumps on the road and discovery. You may say I'm over-egging it, but I can truly say that the last decade was transformative from a *féinmhuinín* – self-confidence – point of view.

In 2009 a study was carried out in the University College of London, and this question was asked: how long does it take to establish a new habit?[72] The results revealed that it takes on average 66 days to acquire a new habit. A few months into my language learning journey I had formed a habit. Good and bad habits are hard to break. This is a habit of the good! Yes, go to your class for a week or a few weeks; however, build into your learning a daily routine that brings you to that habit-forming milestone. It will be worth it. I promise.

---

[72] Lally, P., Van Jaarsveld, C.H.M., Potts, H.W.W. & Wardle, J. (2009) 'How are habits formed: Modelling habit formation in the real world', *European Journal of Social Psychology*, 40(6), 998–1009. DOI: 10.1002/ejsp.674.

Caibidil 23: *The wolf does not fear the barking dog*

D́ALA AN SCÉIL – BY THE WAY

Caithfidh gach duine a t-iomaire atá rompu ar threabhadh – everyone has to plough their own furrow ahead. However, another wise Irish saying kicks in too: *ní neart go cur le chéile* – there's no strength without unity.

FOCAIL NA SEACHTAINE – WORDS OF THE WEEK

1. *Croíbhothar* – heart of the road
2. *Dearfach* – positive
3. *Díon* – roof
4. *Díospóireacht* – debate
5. *Agóid* – protest
6. *Ag treabhadh ar aghaidh* – ploughing ahead
7. *Féinmhuinín* – self-confidence

DO THURAS FÉIN – YOUR JOURNEY

1. _____
2. _____
3. _____
4. _____
5. _____
6. _____
7. _____

> Teanglann.ie phrase:
> *Tá gaol idir an dá fhocal* –
> the two words are connected

Caibidil 24

Nach tapa a imíonn an t-am nuair a bhíonn tú ag spraoi

Time flies when you're having fun

Time did not fly for some. Time almost stopped. I know that some of you had a very negative experience in the classroom. Battle lines were drawn, lines were crossed, bad things were done, and there I was, caught in the middle. Caught in the middle, with big people on one side and much smaller, more vulnerable people on the other. Children. This was so wrong. I am sorry. I am sorry you had to go through this. Irish homework badly done, aimsir chaite *in the future,* séimhiú *missing, poems not learnt off by heart, etc. had terrible consequences for you. Again, I am sorry. These bad memories are associated with me.* Arís, tá brón orm.

● ● ● ● ● ● ●

Caibidil 24: *Time flies when you're having fun*

Where's a good place to start? The beginning maybe? Baby infants perhaps? In an ideal world, maybe. Nonetheless, if you want to start early, it most definitely needs to be pre-school. By junior infants, you've missed a beat already! What about the rest of us then? There's no script or manual here. My perpendicular learning curve took on a life of its own. My learning was relevant to what I was doing and, as time wore on, had a fun element. On reflection, it had an added perspective. I had ownership of my learning. It was haphazard. It was all over the shop. It was chaotic. It was illogical. And while it was all these things, I owned and created my learning systems. It was an individually crafted learning programme based on a multitude of parts. I had tutors and teachers in all shapes and forms dipping in and dipping out along the way: the little nuggets; the dialect nuances; the language intrigues; the overlap between *Béarla agus Gaeilge* and the insight. Finding out for the first time that when you break *Céadaoin* – Wednesday – into its component parts you get '*céad*' and '*aoin[e]*' – first Friday – was a revelation. Wednesday was the first fast day and Friday was the second fast day. With two days a week fasting, forty days of Lent and an odd trip to Lough Derg, maybe there's something in this fasting that we should be paying more attention to. Irish monks did more fasting than their continental counterparts!

In essence, the cornerstone to my learning was my desire to find out more. I was curious. I hit – and still do – many cul de sacs. Cul de sac has French origin, however, 'cul' has triggered my curiosity as *cúl* is the Gaeilge for back, behind or goal. *Cúl báire* is a goalkeeper.

The Online Etymology Dictionary has the following for cul de sac:

> 1738, as an anatomical term, 'a diverticulum ending blindly,' from French *cul-de-sac*, literally 'bottom of a sack,' from Latin *culus* 'bottom, backside'. Application to a street or alley which has no outlet at one end is by 1819.

Beidh Tú Alright: *Nach tapa a imíonn an t-am nuair a bhíonn tú ag spraoi*

One word led to another. One expression became a gateway to another 'aha' moment. My appetite for learning merely accelerated. During all of this I was learning in an environment that was fun, creative, and explorative. Most importantly, it was my learning design. A learning manuscript designed to my specifics and my rules. I had autonomy; I was my own boss.

BUILD YOUR OWN FOOTBALL TEAM

Here is one such learning design that I worked on with my children and my nephew Tom. We were all struggling with the irregular verbs. How do you bring those irregulars to life and create a self-designed learning construct? This was the conundrum. The native Irish speaker didn't have this challenge as all this stuff was presented to them between the ages of two and three, if not earlier, when they soaked it all up. The first thing I needed to find was an area of interest and common ground. Sport was the common denominator. As there were eleven irregular verbs,[73] football (the eleven-a-side one) was the landing zone. With this, I got them to build their very own football team. Starting with the goalkeeper, each of them came up with the same verb for the goalie between the sticks: *BEIR* – to catch. All good so far. In nominating *BEIR* for goals I was able to explain more about the term 'irregular' and why it was ascribed to these chosen verbs. I explained that it was the words' ability to be *ildánach* – versatile – when moving from the past to present to future and the verbs' agility and ability to change, e.g. from *beireann/bheir sí* to *rug sí* – she catches/she caught. I also pointed out that '*beir*' is the verb 'to be born' which changes to '*rugadh mé*'. All motoring along nicely so far. One down, ten to go. To maintain the self-construct, self-participation and ownership of their team, each of them had a choice of formation. In the main, it was either 4-4-2 or 4-3-3. The fun part began when they got to pick

---

[73] Beir, faigh, clois, feic, ith, tabhair, tar, téigh, bí, déan, abair.

Caibidil 24: *Time flies when you're having fun*

their real-life players. It was all about relevance. Young people invest much of their time learning the names of football players passively because it's their thing. It's interesting. The 2022 World Cup, allegedly the best World Cup ever, shortened a pretty difficult winter for some of us. Young people picked up new names that will be forever etched in their memories in the same way Ardiles, Cruyff, Rossi, O'Neill, Armstrong, Whiteside, Hamilton, Platini, Zico, Socrates, Karl Heinz Rummenigge and Falcao remained with us slightly older crew. Their first job was to choose a goalkeeper. There was no point me pushing for Shay Given, Packie Bonner or Conor Martin when Alisson Becker and David de Gea were on their minds. I asked them who and where they would position *FAIGH* – to get – and *TABHAIR* – to give. I got the following proposition: 'two centre midfielders, one who is a grafter and wins almost all the tackles and "gets" the ball and the other who is a great passer and "gives" the ball.' Two modern-day players were assigned to the positions, namely Modrić and De Bruyne. Each player is associated with the appropriate verb. Now we have the basis of a team. A goalie and two centre midfielders. *CLOIS* – to hear – became a right full-back as he 'listened' attentively to the call for the offside trap. The left full-back was carrying a few extra pounds. He was *ITH* – to eat! *ABAIR* – to say – was never stuck for things to say and shouted instructions to her teammates. *FEIC* – to see – kept an eye on any quick breaks as *scuabadóir* – sweeper. *TAR* – to come – covered a lot of ground and came back to help the defence a lot as a right midfielder and the left midfielder *DÉAN* – to do – was a hard worker covering every blade of grass and did a lot of work over ninety minutes.

In the team I built, I had Jean Tigana playing centre mid as the verb *DÉAN*. *TÉIGH* – to go – was one of the two strikers up front along with *BÍ* – to be. *BÍ* had the same freedom as Eric Cantona and could just be herself. Amber Barrett got the nod here to play up front. Refreshingly, she will always 'be' herself. *Téigh* – to go – was assigned to Blackburn Rovers player Tyler Toland as she would 'go' all over the pitch.

The fun and relevant part for young football supporters' is creating a story involving their chosen footballers. A good place to start is in the past before moving into the future and conditional tense. C*honaic* Ronaldo, *d'ith* Messi, *rug* Kelleher, *thug* Salah, *tháinig* Rashford, *fuair* Pele, *chuaigh* Toland, *rinne* Zidane, *bhí* Barrett, *dúirt* Houghton *agus chuala* McGrath.

As I lay on my bed that first week in Gleann Cholm Cille I was studying my irregular verbs. They were coming back to me easy enough; however, the retention bit was the difficulty. Like gathering potatoes, the words all looked the same, just different sizes with the odd *lofa* – rotten – potato thrown in for good measure. On reflection there was too much coming at me at once. I was fire-juggling.

The words and phrases on the conveyor belt needed to be singled out and graded, not unlike the potato sorting machine. This happened naturally. Context provided for this. People, place, and memory were my three triggers for this to happen. Unlike a bucket of spuds and not knowing which drill the spuds came from, my words and sentences were backed up with a memory hard drive through association. The picture of the *bóin dé* – ladybird – will be with me forever as it climbed the bathroom wall in Milwaukee. The councillor who whispered in my ear to use the phrase *sár jab* – great job – in advance of a speech I was delivering at a Gaeltacht event. Politicians are experts at praising even before you do something! Climbing Muckish Mountain up through the Miners path helped reinforce a beautiful word I couldn't remember from before – *Ag dreapadóireacht* – climbing. This word became my gateway word for so many others. When building my eleven-a-side football team, I had a particular fondness for my sweeper who was *ag scuabadóireacht* – sweeping!

There is a beautiful set of Gaeilge words ending in '-*dóir*'. My youngest said that he loves *an focal* '*scuabadóir*'. Perhaps there could be a connection with 'matador'! Other job titles which may be of interest to you are as follows:

Caibidil 24: *Time flies when you're having fun*

Scuabadóir – sweeper – We all remember *scuab* – don't we?
Tumadóir – diver
Peileadóir – footballer
Grianghrafadóir – photographer
Garraíodóir – gardener
Díonadóir – roofer
Dreapadóir – climber
Seanadóir – senator
Siopadóir – shopkeeper
And finally, *slíomadóir* – a sneaky/slimey sort of a person!

I will never forget my eleven-a-side team of irregulars. They are etched in my memory forever more. *Mar a bhí ar dtús, mar atá anois agus mar a bheas go brách, le saol na saol, Áiméan* – as it was in the beginning, is now and ever shall be, world without end, Amen.

DÁLA AN SCÉIL – BY THE WAY

Days of the week were Christianised by monks: *Dé* – God – in front of them all, e.g. *Dé Luain* – Monday. *Dé hAoine* – God's fast (Friday); *Dé + céad + aoin* = God's first fast (Wednesday); *Dé + idir + dhá + Aoine = Déardaoin* – God between two Fridays (Thursday).

FOCAIL NA SEACHTAINE – WORDS OF THE WEEK

1. *Céad* – first
2. *Aoine* – Friday
3. *Céadaoin* – Wednesday
4. *Bolb* – caterpillar
5. *Lofa* – rotten
6. *Sár jab* – great job
7. *Ag scuabadóireacht* – sweeping

Beidh Tú Alright: *Nach tapa a imíonn an t-am nuair a bhíonn tú ag spraoi*

DO THURAS FÉIN – YOUR JOURNEY

1. _____
2. _____
3. _____
4. _____
5. _____
6. _____
7. _____

‖ Teanglann.ie phrase:
Níor creideadh mo ráite – my words were not believed ‖

Caibidil 25

As an obair a fhaightear an fhoghlaim

Learning is gotten through work — don't make your work a drudgery though!

One last take on the fadas for now, in recognition of Des Bishop's travails in In the Name of the Fada. *Take the Gaeilge word* 'fear'. *For all you men out there, don't be 'afeared' that there's a connection between the Gaeilge word* 'fear' *and the* Béarla *word* 'fear'. *Fear as Gaeilge (pronounced far) is man, féar (pronounced fair) is grass and 'is fearr' is best. The fada is a key part of the Irish language and there's no mystery around it. Your fada raises your vowel.* Ár — *our* — *and* ar — *on or at* — *pronounced* 'are' *and* 'air' *respectively. Good relationships need good communication. Transmission breaking down in so many ways over the centuries didn't help. Experiments were aplenty. A Gaeltacht in County Meath?*[74] *There was a communication problem straight away. Different languages? Níl. Different dialects? Tá. I am one and the same. People in different parishes have different ways of saying things, never mind counties. The Fál Carrach ones say* carr *(kar) for car and the Gaoth Dobhair ones say* carr *(kerr) – or is it the other way around? They say* lá garbh *for a rough day in Na Dúnaibh but I've also heard* lá giobach. *In Conamara* giobach *describes how people look after a night on the beer. A sore throat in West Cork is* scornach tinn, *whereas in Donegal it's* sceadamán nimhneach *– poisoned throat – and just outside Ard an Rátha on the road to Gleann Gheis (Glengesh) there's a townland called Sceadamán as the mountains in the background are in the shape of a throat. In a nutshell, people see me differently and have different opinions of me. I don't waste time worrying about what people think of me. That would be energy badly spent.*

●●●●●●●

Lean ar aghaidh

As Aedín got into the car after primary school one day she had a beautifully designed placard with the words '*lean ar aghaidh*' written in different colours. She likes art. She is creative. This was a clever way of bringing Gaeilge into the creative space. Job done. *Lean ar aghaidh* – move on! We also worked on our 11-storey building story using our 11 irregular verbs during Covid-19. Each storey was assigned a verb and a story was built around this pictorially and with words. *An chéad urlár, an dara hurlár, an tríú hurlár*, etc.

Enda Kenny, the then Taoiseach, sent me a message the day after my appointment to the Department of the Gaeltacht. Two words:

---

[74] According to *Comhairle Chontae na Mí*, the Meath Gaeltacht consists of the two adjacent villages of Ráth Chairn and Baile Ghib. In the 1930s, the Irish Land Commission undertook a remarkable social engineering project involving Cork, Kerry, Mayo and Donegal.

lean ort – on with you/plough on/follow on or words to that effect. Words of wisdom from a friend of mine about procrastination wasn't going to cut the mustard for me. 'Put off to tomorrow what you can do today as you might have nothing to do tomorrow!' Former Taoiseach Leo Varadkar followed in Enda's footsteps and appointed me to the Gaeltacht for a second time. There was less controversy second time round. Like Enda, he has a passion for the Irish language and used the opportunity in the Dáil on many occasions. Katherine Licken, former Secretary General of *An Roinn Turasóireachta, Cultúir, Ealaíon, Gaeltachta, Spóirt agus Meán,* was on a similar Irish language learning journey and used every opportunity to converse as Gaeilge.

Looking towards the future is probably the best space to be in when embarking on any new venture, particularly when it is difficult to begin with. Goal-setting is the objective. We probably have enough baggage between us all to fill an airport carousel or two. I don't buy the philosophy or mindset that 'past performance is a good indicator of future performance', I'm more of a Beckett fan:

'Ever tried. Ever failed. No matter. Try again. Fail again. Fail better.'

I can relate to Aristotle too: 'here is only one way to avoid criticism: do nothing, say nothing and be nothing.'

Little did I know when feeding the pigs all those years ago, the panoramic mountain view of 'Muckish' from the farmyard had such an obvious direct connection. The mountain is in the shape of a pig's back. Logainm.ie has two entries for the Mountain – '*An Mhucais*' as Gaeilge agus 'Muckish Mountain' *as Béarla* (Logainm.ie #111301). One of the archival records from 1835 includes the following local explanation: '*Mucais* – pig-like – It looks like the back of a pig.' This ancient name is in fact a compound of *muc* – pig + *ais* – back (of a human, an animal, a hill, etc.) The second word is still in use in phrases like *ar ais, le hais. Chuaigh mé ar ais ar scoil* – I went back to school.

Chuaigh mé suas an sliabh den chéad uair sa bhliain naoi déag ochtó a naoi – I went up the mountain for the first time in 1989 – *le mo chairde* – with my friends – Cormac, William agus Robin. *Chuamar sa gheimhreadh agus bhí an sliabh clúdaithe le sneachta* – we went in the winter and the mountain was covered in snow. *Ba é ár spreagadh cuairt a thabhairt ar an teach tabhairne ina dhiaidh sin* – Our incentive was our visit to the pub afterwards. *Cúpla seachtain ina dhiaidh, chuamar ag dreapadóireacht na hEaragaile den chéad uair* – a couple of weeks after we went climbing Errigal for the first time.

Benbulbin in Sligo is a mountain I haven't climbed; nonetheless the mountain's name and majesty drew my curiosity. *Binn Ghulbain* – jaw-shaped peak/cliff or the peak of Gulban (Logainm.ie #112008). *Gulba*, genitive *gulban*, is an old word for jaw; but in the Fiannaíocht tales Gulban was also explained as the name of a mythological pig who inhabited the mountain. The archival record in Logainm.ie is '*Gonais Gulban gheirfhiacal muc neimhe do bhí a nGullbain ... on muic sin do hainmnigheadh Benn Ghulban.*' I struggled with this translation. I'll leave you to do a bit more digging here. I got as far as a *'sharp tooth of heavenly pig'*! Interestingly, the mountain has the same shape as Muckish, hence the pig reference. As an aside, *gob* is Gaeilge for beak, a word commonly used in English conversations that can, on occasion, be rudely aimed in one's direction under the instruction to 'shut your gob!' Additionally, there was Conall Gulban, a son of Niall of the Nine Hostages, who had an association with the mountain. I will get my good friend Frank Feighan, who would be more familiar with Sligo to organise a climb one of the days with historian Michael Gibbons. Frank managed to organise a double-decker bus from Boyle to Stuttgart in 1988 so he will have no problem making this happen.

- *Droim Seanbhó, i gContae Liatroma* is the beautiful Irish place name that has been anglicised to Drumshambo – the ridge of the old cow in County Leitrim.
- *Cloiseann muid níos mo fuaimeanna ar na sléibhte* – we hear more sounds on the mountains.
- *Chualamar coiscéimeanna troma sa sneachta* – we heard clumping footsteps in the snow.

Caibidil 25: *Learning is gotten through work – don't make your work a drudgery though!*

- *Chualamar na héin ag ceol* – we heard the birds singing.
- *Chualamar an ghaoth ag éirí níos láidre* – we heard the wind getting stronger.
- *Chualamar an gáire* – we heard the laughter.

In your world, you will be surrounded by unique sounds. *Éist leo chun iad a chloisteáil* – listen to them to hear them. *Éist liom* – listen to me. One of the challenges I had was how to differentiate between the different forms of the prepositions '*leo*' – with them – '*linn*' – with us – and '*libh*' – with you all; '*sibh*' – you all – and '*sinn*' – we/us. Going back at them a second time, I made the fundamental mistake of putting them all into the washing machine *le chéile* – together – again! *Botún mór* – big mistake. Different colours in a hot wash is not good. *Mo chomhairle duit* – my advice to you – choose a context for each, give them all breathing space and stay clear of the temptation to rote learn. Still confused? If so, look at what I've given to you just now. I have given you two separate examples: *Éist liom* – listen to me – *agus mo chomhairle duit* – my advice to you. You can use these two examples as a starting point and grow out from there. There are many examples which I have stored away over the years. Here are a few:

President Barack Obama visited Ireland in 2011 and got a rousing Irish reception on College Green accompanied with '*Is féidir linn*' signage. This was a translation from his 2008 presidential election slogan 'Yes we can'.

A former colleague of mine always talked about people who had no interest in protecting the environment. He would say, '*Is cuma leo*' – They don't care.

This *seanfhocal* – proverb – which was given to me by Francie Cullen struck a chord with me. *An duine a thagann chugat le scéal amháin imeoidh sé uait le dhá scéal* – the person who carries a story to you will depart from you with two stories.

A night-time routine with my children has also afforded a family opportunity to practise some Gaeilge. It started off with a one-liner, *oíche mhaith* – good night – and we kept adding every few weeks. The nightly exchange is as follows, depending on how *tuirseach* we all are:

> Joe: *Tífidh/Chífidh (Feicfidh) mé ar maidin* sibh – I will see you (all) in the morning.
> Na páistí: *Tífidh/Chífidh muid ar maidin* thú – we will see you in the morning.
>
> Joe: *Beannacht Dé oraibh uilig i gcónaí* – God's blessing on you all, always.
> Na páistí: *Beannacht Dé ort i gcónaí* – God's blessing on you, always.
>
> Joe: *Mo ghrá libh go léir* – all my love for you all.
> Na páistí: *Ár ngrá leat go léir* – all our love for you.
>
> Joe: *Ar aghaidh libh* – onwards with you all!
> Na páistí: *Ar aghaidh leat* – onwards with you!

Coinnigh do chluasa oscailte – Keep your ears opened.

Nó, da mbeifeá i do chónaí i nGaoth Dobhair – foscailte! – or if you live in Gaoth Dobhair, *oscailte* acquires an initial 'f'. I remember getting into trouble on Raidió na Gaeltachta one time for using the word *'foscailte'*. The complaint was from a person in Rann na Feirste and I was told that *'foscailte'* is only used by Gaoth Dobhair people! I heard since that it's also used in Cloch Cheann Fhaola!

Hats off to all the born-again Gaeilgeoirí who took the plunge later in life. You know who you are so tell your nearest and dearest you're after getting a mention in this book! So how do we turn a negative into a positive? I know many of you have had a pretty grim experience not just with learning Irish but also with the general methodology of learning when the stick was the preferred choice over the carrot. *An bhfuil cead agam ...?* – Do I have permission ...? I don't think

Caibidil 25: *Learning is gotten through work – don't make your work a drudgery though!*

it's possible to park up the bad experiences, however, I do think it's possible to separate the language from the baggage. To be clear, not everyone had a bad experience.

Start anew. Start afresh. *Leanaigí oraibh* – on with you!

Dála an scéil – By the way

Dr Brian Lacey, Michael Gibbons and Seán Ó Coistealbha are covering a lot of ground exploring our physical landscape. If you're interested in finding out more about connections to your past, this eclectic group will shed a shining light. I learned a lot from these men on the banks of *An Mhaoil Rua*, the foothills of *Na Beanna Beola* in Conamara and in Mevagh graveyard. *Go raibh maith agaibh uilig.*

Focail na seachtaine – Words of the week

1. *Lean ar aghaidh* – onwards
2. *Botún mór* – big mistake
3. *Mo chomhairle duit* – my advice to you
4. *Le chéile arís* – together again
5. *Is féidir linn* – (yes) we can
6. *Is cuma leo* – they don't care
7. *Mo ghrá libh go léir* – all my love for you

Do thuras féin – Your journey

1. _____
2. _____
3. _____
4. _____

5. _____

6. _____

7. _____

> Teanglann.ie phrase:
> *Is beannaithe rá do bhéil* – blessed are the words you speak.

Caibidil 26

Briseann an dúchas trí shúile an chait

Nature breaks through the eyes of the cat

Remind me again – how and where do I exist? In a classroom? In a textbook? In a poem? In a prayer? In a song? In the Gaeltacht? In a ciorcal comhrá *– conversation circle? If you're not thinking of me, I'm out of sight and I'm out of mind. If I'm not on your radar you're not going to get to know me. I'm one of the good guys, I'm great company – and please don't feel I'm being desperate. I just get lonely when I'm on my own. Don't be shy about touching base from to time. To be honest, I don't mind the people giving out about me. It's when I'm being ignored is the hard part.*

● ● ● ● ● ● ●

Beidh Tú Alright: *Briseann an dúchas trí shúile an chait*

Curiosity is dangerous territory for the cat. To all you cat lovers out there, I have nothing against cats. My children adore *ár* Spotty. One of the most profound Gaeilge idioms involves the cat – *briseann an dúchas trí shúile an chait* – nature breaks through the eyes of the cat. Next time you look at your cat, bear this in mind. When your cat's away you can think on the *seanfhocal thíos* – below – which is part and parcel of today's English vernacular – *nuair a bhíonn an cat amuigh, bíonn na luchóga/luchain ag rince* – When the cat's away, the mice will play/dance. 'Like father like son' is a frequently used expression in the English language. It's certainly not as descriptive as the Gaeilge, *cad é a dhéanfadh mac an chait ach luch a mharú* – what will the son of the cat do but kill a mouse? The stories Irish people tell through the medium of English captures the way Irish was spoken. This skill to paint a picture and tell the story has been passed on, albeit in English. This is still a positive though. It's part of who we are, *ár ndúchas* – our nature/our innate quality/our native place/heredity. There is no English word that can encapsulate the deep meaning of *dúchas*.

In Brendan Kennelly's introduction to *The Penguin Book of Irish Verse* (1970, 1981), he writes:

> Today it is clear that though history nearly always sundered Irish from Anglo-Irish, the imagination has nearly always brought them closer together so that now, in retrospect, the cultures they both produced may be seen as a compact imaginative unity ... Frank O'Connor has made available in English some of the finest poems in early, middle and later Gaelic ... On the whole I have elected to allow early Ireland to speak through O'Connor's mouth. And what a singing, eloquent mouth it is!

Whether it is prose, short stories or poetry, with our Irish poets and writers a richness and beauty emanates from their writing. While the English medium has been the conduit in recent centuries, it is

Caibidil 26: *Nature breaks through the eyes of the cat*

clear that the legacy of the Irish language in previous centuries still echoes. The creative writing ability of Seamus Heaney, James Joyce, Samuel Beckett, William Butler Yeats, John Boyne, Sally Rooney, Edna O'Brien, Anne Enright *agus* Brendan Behan is nurtured by the historical capacity of the Irish language to tell a story in pictures and in a very descriptive way. It is important to capture the contribution of all our great writers. A wander to Price's Lane in Dublin makes a good attempt at setting the record straight. Historical accounts on the wall there read:

> We Irish love to bathe in the reflected glory of our great writers, but do we really? We love Joyce, Yeats, Behan and Co. but never seem to notice that we unconsciously always think men. Is Irish literature our intellectual bathing place, our 40 foot? Did Ireland produce great female writers? Yes, it did and many. Why is this little known? ... Kate and Edna O'Brien, Elizabeth Bowen, Iris Murdoch were the equal of the men and we should celebrate them.

The Kerrywritermuseum.com website whets the appetite of hungry readers:

> Ignite your imagination and discover a dreamworld, a whole world of magic told by the Seanchaí – the bearer of Irish folklore. Embark on a journey set against the canvas of some of the greatest wordsmiths the country has ever seen. There will be mystery, there will be murder, there will be love, there will be comedy and then there will be more magic ...

John Banville's book *Snow* uses the words 'jalopy' and 'shenanigans', words we were brought up with but are not sure where they originated, or did we even question? Checking in with the *Oxford Learners Dictionary* it states 'shenanigans' is mid-nineteenth century, of unknown origin. Similarly, for 'jalopy' the *Oxford Dictionary* states, '1920s (Originally US): of unknown origin'. Words which were part of our everyday conversation with a potential *nasc* – link – to our *teanga dhúchais* – native tongue. One of the anonymous poems translated by Frank O'Connor in *Irish Verse* is titled 'The Sweetness of Nature'. This is one of the songs of the mad king Suibhne Gealt, from a twelfth-century romance, the material of which dates to the eighth century. In this poem Suibhne is flying from the battlefield, driven mad by the sight of the broken bodies. Was he heading for *Caisleán na dTuath* – Doe Castle – in north Donegal? The River Bann and 'Derry' and 'Moyra' are referenced. Here is a flavour:

> Endlessly over the water
> Birds of the **Bann** are singing;
> Sweeter to me their voices
> Than any churchbell's ringing.
> -
> Over the plain of **Moyra**
> Under the heels of foemen;
> I saw the people broken
> As flax is scutched by women
> -
> But the cries I hear by **Derry**
> Are not of men triumphant;
> I hear their calls in the evening,
> Swans calm and exultant

O'Connor references flax being 'scutched by women'. Flax was an integral part of industry and commerce in Ulster in the centuries that followed the twelfth century. *Scutching* is a word which was used by local farmers in my parish through everyday conversation. It would be interesting to know which word O'Connor came across when translating, or maybe this was the original word used as Gaeilge for

Caibidil 26: *Nature breaks through the eyes of the cat*

this particular part of the flaxing process? I remember a set of 'flails'[75] hanging up in my father's barn when I was growing up. I never saw them in use, but they would have been used for scutching corn and, as my father pointed out, removing the seed from the corn stalks. This would have been a similar procedure for removing 'lint' seed, and once removed the stalks were used for thatching. Incidentally, people who couldn't afford lint (flax) stalks used *mearphriontaí* – rushes, but literally, fingerprints. However, the Gaeilge word for fingerprints is *méarloirg*. My father suggested I speak to the older people to get more information and then he suddenly realised he's at the northern end of *ceithre scór bliain d'aois* – eighty! Time pulls no punches and that is why it is incumbent on all of us to capture, record and store our history for the generations to come. Let no person deter you from your language journey which is a gateway to your ancestry and history – *ó ghlúin go glúin* – from one generation to the next. Literally, from knee to knee, which is a more descriptive Irish version of passing something on from one generation to the next. The visual here is that of a baby sitting on their parent's knee and to imagine the baby growing up and potentially having a baby on their knee sometime in the future.

One of the things I learned from my own journey is that there must be a relevance to one's learning. I know I keep saying this. I'm doing it for emphasis so my apologies. My own case was exceptional, in that if I didn't learn quickly, I would not have lasted too long in the job – forced relevance you may say! The kibosh was never far away from ending my early ministerial apprenticeship. A fellow Gaeilgeoir from Ard Mhaca was the first to draw the word 'kibosh' to my attention. Etymology Online has an extended note on 'kibosh' which may be of interest to you. While it states that it is of unknown origin – 'despite intense speculation', it also references an Irish connection – one candidate is

---

[75] *Súiste* is the old Irish word for flail. It was made of wood and leather to separate the seed. Then the flax was left in pools of water to rot. Dictionary.com: 'to separate the fibres from the woody part of (flax) by pounding.'

Beidh Tú Alright: *Briseann an dúchas trí shúile an chait*

Irish *caidhp bháis, caipín báis* – cap of death – sometimes said to be the black cap a judge would don when pronouncing a death sentence. However, some scholars have discredited this source of the word as there is a Hebrew connection meaning 'to conquer'. I must say that it is good to see the Online Etymology Dictionary making a sterling effort to be proactive on the Irish links and not just leaving 'unknown origin' hanging out there in the ether. Foclóir.ie has the following spelling for death cap – *caidhp bháis*. Incidentally, on a recent walk along the banks of An Mhaoil Rua[76] – Mulroy Bay – I was introduced to a local word, *bairéad* – cap. It's a beautiful sounding word that you can practise and compare the pronunciation with 'Mairéad'. This brings me nicely along to the man and woman of the moment, Colm Bairéad agus Cleona Ní Chrualaoi – the two amazing people behind the film *An Cailín Ciúin*. Cleona's mother is from the Na Dúnaibh Gaeltacht, and it was great listening to her being interviewed on Raidió na Gaeltachta after the film received its Oscar *ainmniúchán* – nomination. The first ever Gaeilge film to be nominated for the Oscars – and with a Na Dúnaibh connection too. *Comhghairdeas libh arís* – congratulations to them again. Interestingly, *The Quiet Man* was the first feature film to have Irish in it. Maureen O'Hara confesses that she had John Wayne sleep in a '*mata codlaidh*' – a sleeping bag! Paul Mescal being interviewed at an award ceremony as Gaeilge *ar an bhrat urláir dearg* – on the red carpet – was a significant step for the language.

Another thing that added relevance to my learning was my insatiable desire to find out more about where I was born, more about the people who came before me and certainly more about my own country and its interaction with the world. Gaeilge was my vehicle for brushing up on my *stair* – history. Historically, my relationship with *stair* was up there – or down there, more accurately – with my frail relationship with Gaeilge. The mathematics of two negatives making a

---

[76] A walk organised by Róise Nic Laifeartaigh which included Dr Brian Lacey, Michael Gibbons and Seán Ó Coistealbha.

Caibidil 26: Nature breaks through the eyes of the cat

positive comes to mind. The hat (not the *caidhp bháis*) that fitted me is not necessarily a perfect match for everyone. *Tuigim* – I understand.

DÁLA AN SCÉIL – BY THE WAY

The nature of politics these days can be divisive. Maybe this was always the way but now it is more visible. In regard to my learning journey, I had a lot of support across the political divide. Councillor Micheál Choilm Mac Giolla Easbuig was fast out of the traps to question my appointment. As time wore on he became very supportive of my learning crusade at both a private and public level. Never got his vote though! However, I'm happy to be corrected on this assumption.

FOCAIL NA SEACHTAINE – WORDS OF THE WEEK

1. *Ár ndeora* – our tears
2. *Luchóga* – mice
3. *Méar/méar fhada* – finger/long finger
4. *Mearphriontaí* – rushes (*méarloirg* – fingerprints)
5. *Ár ndúchas* – our nature
6. *Bairéad* – cap
7. *Caidhp bháis* – death cap

DO THURAS FÉIN – YOUR JOURNEY

1. _____
2. _____
3. _____
4. _____
5. _____

6. _____

7. _____

> Teanglann.ie phrase:
> *Thug sí scrabha den teanga dó* –
> She had a few sharp words to say to him.

Caibidil 27

Ní neart go cur le chéile

There is no strength without unity

Umojo ni nguvu – *Unity is strength*
 I have enough friends to go around. They're not all dead – I bump into Swahili from time to time. The more we get to know each other, we find we have so much more in common. Umojo ni nguvu – unity is strength – is a Swahili expression. Ní neart go cur le chéile – *there's no strength without unity*. Then there's my good friend Mandarin, who has a similar expression for strength and unity – tuan jie jinshi liliang. Bhíodh Arabic agus mé féin – *Arabic and I have been* – around the block a while now. Think *Last of the Summer Wine*. That's us!

● ● ● ● ● ● ●

As time wore on, my *stór focal* – vocabulary – started to grow. Confusion reigned when new words appeared on ministerial scripts and policy papers. I battled through and came up with my own way of dealing with the intensity of full immersion. In one instance I narrowed my learning down to words beginning with the letter 'R'. I did this on the basis that very little changed with words beginning with 'R' and I was getting *traochta tuirseach* – as tired as you'll get – with so many changes to the words beginning with a vowel. Remember *ubh?* it changed more times than my career! It was a nice break knowing that there would be no *urú* nor *séimhiú*, causing me bother for a while. Of course, there would be changes at the end of the word for example *rang* – class – became *ranganna* – classes. I could deal with this as I was only focusing on the end of the word. Basically, I wasn't burning the candle at both ends or biting off more than I could chew. Throw computers into the mix: it's *ríomhaire*, so computer classes become *ranganna ríomhaireachta* and the computers became *na ríomhairí*. In my political world rules and regulation were omnipresent. Plenty of government-related words began with 'r', including Government itself. The following two words can be tricky to differentiate but when you put the two together it helps: *rialachán* – regulation – and *riarachán* – administration. As there is only one letter of difference, I came up with the following: the 'L' in *rialachán* is for legislation and the 'R' in *riarachán* is for red tape, something that Governments excel in, of course! *Rialtas* – Government – and *rialacha* – rules – were my two danger words as there would be somebody somewhere getting upset. Compartmentalising my learning aided and abetted my desire for an expanding *stór focal*. *Ríomh phost* – email – was a big part of my world during my time as minister. Initially I thought this a very clever construct – the mail before the mail – but later I realised that '*roimh*' is the Gaeilge for 'before' and *ríomh* is coming from computer (*ríomhaire*). In essence, it's just a computer mail, which is fair enough. I had email correspondence aplenty back in 2014, before the other social media platforms started to dominate. *Raibh* – pronounced 'row' or 'rev' (depending on where you live) – was already in the bag from a long time ago. We all know *go raibh maith agat*. What I didn't know at the time was this tidy little combination was part of the wonderful world of the *modh foshuiteach* – the 'possibility form' of the verb. I do remember hearing about it back in the day but what

Caibidil 27: *There is no strength without unity*

it meant was another day's work. *Ríocht* – kingdom – is a powerful title for one's county. *Rí* is 'king' and *Ríthábhachtach* is 'all important'! If you're passing through Athenry one of the days take a good look at the signage – Baile Átha an Rí – townland at the fjord of the king (Logainm.ie #19599).

'*Go dtaga do ríocht*' – thy kingdom come – is a lovely example of *an modh foshuiteach*.

Other examples include:

- *Nár laga Dia do lámh* – that God may not weaken your hand
- *Go n-éirí leat* – that you may succeed (good luck)
- *Go mbeirimid beo ar an am seo arís* – that we will be alive at this time when we meet again

That last one is a beautiful expression and can be used as a toast and a parting statement when leaving good company. A friend of mine told me his mum always says this as they take turns mixing the ingredients for the Christmas cake. *Galánta*!

Ag rith – running – became *Bhí mé ag rith* – I was running. No change to the word – happy days. My 'R's' kept on giving. Running was an appropriate description for what I was trying to do during those crazy days. Running to stand still. The treadmill of politics is the essence of flux. Many years before I had dabbled with philosophy at *Ollscoil Mhá Nuad* – University of Maynooth – where I came across the two lads Heraclitus and Zeno. The two spent a bit of time thinking about the flux concept and elements of change. Flux summed up my time in Maynooth with an eclectic band of brothers who worked hard on happiness and laughter – and graduated with honours. Our lead maestro Ciarán Keon isn't with us any more *ach tá muidinne ag smaointiú air i gcónaí*. Things change in the world of politics from hour to hour. In more recent years, minute to minute. Things would be going grand and then you'd hit a speed bump. Something was always being stoked up behind the scenes by somebody somewhere throwing a spanner – and sometimes a whole toolbox or garage – into the works. The Irish word *roimh* – before – took on a whole new significance. The preparatory work was critical. Preparing the ground was paramount. Being blind-sided by decisions which went against the wishes of communities wasn't a good place to be and I hope lessons were learned.

Bringing my 'R's' to a conclusion. *Réimse* – realm; *réise* – span; *ráig* – outbreak; *ráite* – expressed; *ráithe* – quarter; *reatha* – current; *réidh* – ready.

These were some of the words that kept popping their heads up in everyday discourse with Department officials. Through focusing on the 'R's for a few weeks it helped me remember them. Being relevant to my work was key and when they kept reappearing on scripts and policy papers, there was plenty of opportunity for reinforcement. If I had a good memory, I would probably be a doctor or dentist today. Or a *Know Your Sport* champion, which was won by my friend Seamus Wilhare in 1995. I had to work hard at memorising. Political satire welcome here! I try to encourage underage teams to use their weaker foot to 'kick start' a part of the brain that would otherwise lay dormant. Learning Irish is no different.

During my first stint in Gleann Cholm Cille, I bumped into a language enthusiast from Ard Mhaca – Armagh – and he informed me that *an chéad lón* – the first meal – is the Gaeilge for breakfast and *an dara lón* – the second meal – is the term for dinner, and not *dinnéar*. I suppose the overlap from our Norman history would account for the overlap with the French 'dîner'. It is my understanding that the first meal and second meal concept is the custom in *An tSín* – China – also.

Uladh

I was witness to positive momentum in language development throughout the province of Ulster. This was a great motivator during my language journey, especially considering the constraints faced by many in their quest for language rights and recognition. I also learned about the distinction for courage. In *Uladh* – Ulster – you will hear *uchtach*, and *síos an tír* you will hear *misneach*. Whether in west Belfast or east Belfast, County Derry or Londonderry, the Irish language was here long before us all. Wouldn't it be great if it is stronger here, long after we're gone?

A shoutout to all the leaders involved in the 'Líonraí Gaeilge'[77] Irish Language Networks and the 'Bailte Seirbhíse Gaeltachta'[78] – Gaeltacht Service Towns. The Gaeltacht Act 2012 created a legislative basis for the language planning process. Foras na Gaeilge and Údarás na Gaeltachta are the lead organisations in this language planning process. I was witness to the heavy lifting at the beginning of this process and like a lot of work that civil and public servants do, it goes unnoticed. A lot of the preparatory work was initiated in the Forbacha offices in Gallimhe. The officials in that section work hard and were a pleasure to work with during my time as minister.

The team of officials in the Forbacha were instrumental in progressing the many important capital projects in the Gaeltacht. These included Teach an Phiarsaigh in Ros Muc, Teach Solais Fhánada, Amharclann Ghaoth Dobhair, Ionad Cuimhneacháin na nImirceach, Carna agus Ionad Naomh Fionnán, An Fál Carrach. The re-development of Coláiste Ros Goill is progressing, and a lot of preparatory work has gone into it by Céim Aniar. Dealing with the people who were advocating for these *tograí* – projects – was a pleasure, notwithstanding the odd battle or two at an official level along the way, which is par for the course! Having said that, engineering inspector Eamon McGill was the official on the ground who helped make these projects happen.

---

[77] Irish planning officer Dónall Ó Cnáimhsí explained to me recently that the language development planning in Gaoth Dobhair is in a good place because of the constructive engagement between the schools and the community.

[78] Collaborative work by Letterkenny Chamber of Commerce and Líonra Leitir Ceanainn with Dr Finbarr Bradley held a forum recently on 'Identity & Authenticity in Business – Making the Irish Language Work for You'.

New capital projects only happen with the support of communities. Leaders come to the fore. I have witnessed exceptional leadership and it was my pleasure to deal with you all.

DÁLA AN SCÉIL – BY THE WAY

Chatting with my former colleagues Joe agus John, both native Irish speakers, I asked why *lá fada* – long day – doesn't take a *séimhiú* (h) and *oíche fhada* – long night – takes a *séimhiú*.[79] Neither of them knew why but both knew the correct way to pronounce both. Two fluent speakers. A lesson for us all for sure. Séamus Mac Giolla Chomhgaill who worked in Roinn na Gaeltachta introduced me to the *rialacha* – rules – around the *séimhiú* and the relationship with the *guta* – vowel – and *consan* – consonant. He also introduced me to the changes when dealing with the 'teens'. If a word ends in a consonant there is no *séimhiú* in the *'déag'*, *mar shampla: dhá aspal déag* – twelve apostles. When a word ends in a vowel there is a *séimhiú*, *mar shampla: dá mhí dhéag* – twelve months. GRMA a Shéamuis. [I'm worried here now that there's an exception to this rule and I've just got Séamus into bother!] *An locht ormsa* – my fault!

FOCAIL NA SEACHTAINE – WORDS OF THE WEEK

1. *Ríomhaire* – computer
2. *Roimh* – before
3. *Reatha* – current
4. *Réimse* – realm
5. *Rialacha* – rules
6. *Rialachán* – regulation
7. *Riarachán* – administration

---

[79] The *séimhiú* changes the sound of the word and its spelling. It literally means 'a softening' and involves adding the letter 'h' after the first consonant.

Caibidil 27: *There is no strength without unity*

DO THURAS FÉIN – YOUR JOURNEY

1. _____
2. _____
3. _____
4. _____
5. _____
6. _____
7. _____

‖ Teanglann.ie phrase:
Focal údair i mbéal amadáin –
words of wisdom on the lips of a fool. ‖

Caibidil 28

An t-eolas a mhúineadh do dhuine

To show someone the way

In Boston I overheard a conversation about the origin of 'schlep', a word which is used extensively in the United States and Ireland when 'pulling' and 'dragging' is involved. I am reliably informed by my good friend Yiddish, that the origin is from the verb 'shlepn' – 'to pull, drag'. Yiddish words appear here and there in the composition of Béarla. 'Spiel' can be used to describe a lengthy speech and is often greeted with skepticism. Politicians heed! Again, Yiddish spelling is 'shpiel' – *a sales pitch or speech intended to persuade* – and there's also a German influence with 'spielen', meaning 'to play'. In Béarla *the following Yiddish words are now part and parcel of daily interaction:* 'shemozzle', 'glitch', 'chutzpah', 'bagel', 'schmuck'. The one I find interesting is the Yiddish word 'shamus' – 'detective' – or more than likely an Irish lad, Séamus, who went on tour and never came home!

● ● ● ● ● ● ●

Caibidil 28: *To show someone the way*

De réir mar a thuigim – as far as I understand – there is hope in the idea of 'teaching the old dog new tricks.' It is more challenging, but certainly possible. Going back to learn a language in my forties did present a challenge. I got a text with the word *'galar'* in it a few years back. For the life of me I couldn't figure it out. A quick visit to Téarma.ie and up pops 'disease'. The context of the message was in relation to Covid-19 and the sad passing of a young person from the disease. I will always associate that text/word with the difficult days many people had to endure in 2020–2022. *'Galar'* will always stay with me. In reaching out to people with Gaeilge you can stockpile a lot of new vocabulary by associating the new word with the person who passed it on. I have built up my vocabulary by using this technique. I was presented with *'suntasach'* – significant – and *'slat tomhais'* – yardstick – from two Na Dúnaibh locals; one from the far side, and the other from 'the other side'. *'Sceadamán nimhneach'* – sore throat – was given to me by a Donegal woman at a conference in Galway. I have many of these examples and I am indebted to everyone who has passed the baton along the way. Don't shy away from correction either. I got a 'scouling' in Fánaid for mixing up my *'samhradh'* and *tSamhaidh'* at an event in the middle of winter! At an event in the Múscraí Gaeltacht of Cork, I used the focal *'scoir'* – concluding – at the end of my speech and pronounced it 'score'. At the end of the event a man came up to me and advised that *'scoir'* should be pronounced 'skir'. I was grateful for the intervention, and I've used *'m'fhocal scoir'* – my final word – at the end of many speeches in Munster and Conamara. I had to dig deeper rather than just accept it was a difference in dialect. The word 'score' in English – as in 'what's the score?' – also means twenty. The Online Etymology Dictionary accounts for its origin with the following:

> Late old English scoru 'set of twenty', from old norse skor 'notch, tally, twenty; of Germanic origin, related to shear, the verb (late middle English) is from old Norse skora 'make an incision'.

Once again, no reference to the Gaelic language where for thousands of years our ancestors would have used *ceithre scór bliain d'aois* to celebrate reaching the eighty years of age milestone.

Cnuasach Focal Ros Goill[80] references its uses down the centuries:

- *Goidé an scór?* – what's the score?
- *Goidé an scór a ndéanfá thusa sin?* – why would you do that?
- *Goidé an scór nach dtáinig tusa inné?* – why did you not come yesterday?

I digress! The lovely Gaelic expression for 'digress' is *'téigh ar strae' nó 'téigh ar seachrán'*.

There is a lovely song, *'Tráthnóna Beag Aréir'*, in which Seán Ban Mac Grianna describes how he was set/led astray by a beautiful woman. Clannad do a great version of it and it's well worth a listen. *'Is í sheol mo stuaim chun seachráin tráthnóna beag aréir'*. The good thing about reaching out for a song from Clannad is that you will never be disappointed with many more. *'Teidhir Abhaile Riú'* agus *'Dúlamán'* should get you started!

DÁLA AN SCÉIL – BY THE WAY

Tír Eoghain man Cathal Ó Manacháin set me right: 'In the genitive (*focal scoir*), Ulster dialect wouldn't differ much from the other dialects. It would sound like "skirr", whereas "scor" on its own without the genitive would sound like "skorr"'. The beauty and richness of life is diversity and we have it in abundance through the Irish language.

---

[80] Leaslaoi U. Lúcás (1986), *Cnuasach Focal as Ros Goill*, pp 38.

Caibidil 28: *To show someone the way*

FOCAIL NA SEACHTAINE – WORDS OF THE WEEK

1. *De réir mar a thuigim* – as far as I understand
2. *M'fhocal scoir* – my final word
3. *Téigh ar strae* – digress
4. *Goidé an scór?* – what's the score/story?
5. *Cnuasach* – collection
6. *Cnuasach focal* – word collection
7. *Eolas*[81] – information

DO THURAS FÉIN – YOUR JOURNEY

1. _____
2. _____
3. _____
4. _____
5. _____
6. _____
7. _____

|| Teanglann.ie phrase:
roiseadh cainte – rush/spate of words ||

---

[81] *Tíreolas* – geography (information about the country).

Caibidil 29

Is fearr go mall ná go díreach ag an am ceart

You're better late than dead on time (Better late than never)

I love Arabic: as-salamu alaykum – *peace be upon you;* shukran agus habibi – *thank you and my beloved friend. I just love the sounds. I love the flow. We have both been around a very long time. Our ancestors spoke the same words back then. It feels great having a connection to our respective pasts. Words have been passed down through generations. The baton of wisdom has been passed along. We are the better for that.*

● ● ● ● ● ● ●

I enjoyed breaking up words into different component parts. Take *grianghrafadóireacht* as an example. By learning this word, I learned four words for the price of one; *grian* – sun; *grianghraf* – photograph; *grianghrafadóir* – photographer; *grianghrafadóireacht* – photography.

Caibidil 29: *You're better late than dead on time (Better late than never)*

Another method I had was bringing similar sounding words together with different meanings. The hat trick of C's. Take the focal *ceathair* – four – and see how close it is to *cathair* – city – agus *cathaoir* – chair. To add to the challenge here, there's no fadas to help differentiate. Let's get our *teanga* – tongue – working here. *Ceathar* is pronounced 'keher', *cathair* is pronounced 'kahir' agus *cathaoir* is pronounced 'kiher'. You may want to go to Foclóir.ie to hear for yourself the very subtle difference between 'four' and 'chair'. One of the positions I managed to avoid at Donegal County Council and made up for it in the Dáil is the position of *cathaoirleach* – chairperson. There is no gender differentiation regarding this role in the Irish language. Chairman arrived through the English language and in more recent times has been made redundant. The committee chairs in the Houses of the Oireachtas have changed from the English title to *Cathaoirleach*. In 2011, I was Chairman of the Good Friday Agreement Committee and Co-Chairman of the British Irish Parliamentary Assembly. Roll on to 2020 and I was elected *Cathaoirleach* of the European Affairs Committee and *Cathaoirleach na gCathaoirleach* – Chair of Chairs. Like all things in life, this came to an end as did my time in politics. Additionally, 'cathedral' comes from the Latin word '*cathedra*' which is the seat/church of the bishop and, no doubt, *cathair* (chair) came from this.

Interestingly, the number four describes the nature and origin of the word for cousins. The Gaeilge word for cousins is *col ceathracha*. This is because four parents are participants in the cousin relationship. *Col* means relation and *Col ceathracha* are four-way relations. *Col seisir* is a six-way relationship, so a second cousin.

I remember attending an Údarás na Gaeltachta event a few years back and listening to Cathaoirleach Anna Ní Ghallachair, who eloquently explained the momentum of an Údarás project which had just been launched and was gaining momentum. She explained in a descriptive fashion that the project was *ag gluaiseacht* – taking off – like an *eala* – swan. I'm thinking that maybe '*gluaisteán*' isn't the right word for car. Many in west Dún na nGall will agree, as the Irish word '*carr*' is the preferred choice!

Former secondary school teacher Micheál Mac an tSaoir, *ina chónaí i mBiorra* – living in Birr – was an early-day gamechanger for me. Originally from Dún na nGall, the Fánaid Gaeilge dialect was clear and similar to its unique clarity *as Béarla*. Identifying Gaeilge speakers from your home community is a big asset as you build your resource base for your language journey. *GRMA a Mhicheáil.* In Birr, the late Tony Hogan gave me a taster session in the Gallimhe Gaeilge dialect before I headed off west to Conamara. This was helpful because the officials in the department in the Forbacha were mainly from Galway and I wanted to be able to say hello to them at least. GRMA Tony.

An early-day phone call (as Gaeilge) with Paddy McKinney, from *Baile an Droichid* – Ballindrait – outside *Leifear* – Lifford – to wish him a *'Lá breithe sona duit'* – was another confidence-building step in my long journey ahead. After one week, I realised I was not on my own. There is a core group of Irish people who offer their help in the spirit of the *meitheal* – a choice word for a coming together of neighbours to bring in the harvest. My own memory of this cooperative spirit was from many moons ago when we were 'thrashing' the corn. Neighbours came together to help and at times all that could be heard was the belt of the thrashing mill on the PTO, the crackling of straw and silent tongues. Only to be interrupted by laughter when a *luchóg* – mouse – appeared and tears and screams if a *luchóg mhór* – rat – appeared.

People were willing to help me along. Many wanted me to get there. That's when 'fear' took a permanent back seat. I wasn't doing this in isolation anymore. I had a full team in place ready to do battle. Joe and John, my right-hand pilots, were on hand to keep the car between the ditches but also to go native on the conversation front – *Gaeilge amháin* – a *Béarla*-free zone. Early morning chats were of a very basic form. The weather dominated. *Lá gaofar inniu* – a windy day today. The condition of the road featured too: *tá an bealach an-sleamhain inniu* – The road is very slippery today. As the day wore on, we talked about who was *marbh* – dead – where we'd be putting our heads down for the night and what was on the *clár* for *amárach* – agenda for tomorrow. What do you talk about most when you're driving from *Corcaigh* – the marshy place – to *Cluain Dolcáin* – the pasture of Dolcán – or *Maigh Eo* – the plain of the yew tree? Which way now?! There appears to be two words in Irish for 'yew': *'eo'* agus *'iúr'*. This would make for a very interesting conversation in a pub in Loch an Iúir after a Donegal/Mayo game.

When the head hits the pillow at night, the little planner for the next day goes to work. I was flat out talking to myself. I got advice to train myself into talking as Gaeilge, and while talking to yourself you can make all the mistakes you want – with no judge or jury. When you're searching for a word or two, have a dictionary on the bedside table. I had one in the *leithreas*, one in the car, one in the office and so on. However, as we're all online, Foclóir.ie, Teanglann.ie (including an electronic version of Ó Dónaill's Irish–English dictionary) and Téarma. ie will never see you stuck. And, if you meet someone during the day with a Gaelic surname, check out Ainm.ie.

DÁLA AN SCÉIL – BY THE WAY

Bunching words together worked for me. This may not work for everyone. Experimentation and exploration are key drivers in my Irish language journey, which is effectively a mechanism for my life-long learning journey.

- *Toradh* – result
- *Torthaí* – fruit
- *Tórramh* – funeral (in Dún na nGall; the word is *'sochraid'* síos an tír)

Beidh Tú Alright: *Is fearr go mall ná go díreach ag an am ceart*

FOCAIL NA SEACHTAINE – WORDS OF THE WEEK

1. *Eo/iúr* – yew
2. *Ag gluaiseacht* – taking off
3. *Cathaoirleach na gCathaoirleach* – chair of chairs
4. *Grian* – sun
5. *Grianghraf* – photograph
6. *Grianghrafadóir* – photographer
7. *Grianghrafadóireacht* – photography

DO THURAS FÉIN – YOUR JOURNEY

1. _____
2. _____
3. _____
4. _____
5. _____
6. _____
7. _____

> Teanglann.ie phrase:
> *Sin le rá* – that is to say; in other words

Caibidil 30

Ní mar a shíltear a bhítear

All is not what it seems

Think of me. Use me. Get to know me. When you think of me, I will think of you every minute of every day. When your head hits the pillow and you're thinking of the travails of the day just gone or in trepidation of the day to come, think of me. Think of Gaeilge. Talk the words through in your head … I'll be with you; I'll stay with you. You will never be alone. Coinneoidh muid le chéile – we will stay together – and if you go for that shower or jog in the morning … or any other time you're on your own, think of me, talk to me, sing with me, text with me, email with me, write notes with me even down to an líosta siopadóireacta *– the shopping list.*

● ● ● ● ● ● ●

The title of this chapter is a profound expression which sums up where our beautiful language is at. *Ní mar a shíltear a bhítear* – all is not what it seems. *CLG Charn Domhnaigh* – Carndonagh GAA club – in north Inis Eoghain started a *cúpla focal don lá* – couple of words for the day – a few years back. A great idea. *An dul chun cinn* – momentum – in Carn. The abbreviated 'Carn' covers both the original Gaeilge name and the anglicised version. During a recent trip to Carn GAA HQ in Carrickafoden it was great to see Gaeilge visible on the building. The revival of hurling and Gaeilge in this community reminds us of the *díocas/paisean* – passion – *agus aisling* – dream – that Roger Casement had for all things cultural in his quest for independence.

In 1996 I returned to Ireland after spending a year in the Middle East. Before my departure, I asked one of my teammates on the Dubai Creek football team to keep an eye out for any job opportunities after I would leave for home. The travel bug wasn't completely out of my system. He put it to me very bluntly: 'Out of sight out of mind Joe, and when you're gone, you're gone.' Alas, I never returned to the Middle East (apart from a brief ministerial visit in 2019 – I hardly recognised the place) and the rest is history. I've really thought about his words since my journey started with Gaeilge again. To be honest, the language wasn't out of sight pre-2014. It was on all the road signs and on the world wide web. Most public documents were available as Gaeilge. TG4 agus Raidió na Gaeltachta were there to be watched or listened to and the language could be heard on any trip to the Gaeltacht. *Tháinig mé trasna ar an Ghaeilge i gcónaí* – I would always come across an Ghaeilge. So why was it off my radar for a quarter of a century (1989–2014)? Maybe this might help to explain it: *Seachnaíonn súil ní nach bhfeiceann* – the eye avoids what it doesn't see.

This *seanfhocal* – proverb – spoke to me in so many ways. The eye avoids what it doesn't see. 'Seeing is believing', as is so often said. For those twenty-five years, I saw the language, I still believed in the language but my curiosity to explore just wasn't there. Plus, I really didn't believe I could master our beautifully spoken word. In fact, I had convinced myself that I was useless with all languages. Fast forward a couple of decades, plus some, it is a case of my eye looking around the *coirnéal* – corner – to find out more. *Mo chomhairle duit* – my advice to you – *ar aghaidh leat* – go for it! Before you know it, you will be *ag gluaiseacht*.

Driving through Monaghan you will see a sign for *Droim Dhamh Íochtarach*, which whetted my curiosity. This was anglicised to Drumganus Lower which is reflected on the road signage. The Irish name *Droim Dhamh*, which means ridge of the oxen, was rendered 'Dromgawe' (1630) in English and then subdivided into two 'Dromgaues' (1637). Drumganus is the modern anglicised form of that corruption. Logainm.ie shows that this corruption had influenced the Irish name and local Irish speakers in 1835 did not understand '*druim ganas*', trying to explain it as 'Ridge of the Hatred'. The man who will be able to shed more light on this is Brendan Ó Dufaigh, the inspirational *Gaeilgeoir ó Chontae Mhuineacháin* – from County Monaghan. Brendan has left a rich language and cultural legacy in County Monaghan. He inspired and encouraged me on my journey and for that I will always be grateful. My thoughts are always with the Ó Dufaigh family who lost a wonderful young son and brother, and continue to show so much courage in keeping his memory alive.

'A laser-engraved picture of Ógie, as he was known, playing in Enniskillen on the night of his death, has been etched into the highly polished black granite surface [of his headstone]. The inscription written in Irish reads:

> *Nuair a shéidfear an fhideog domhsa ag deireadh mor é,*
> *Agus a sheasfaidh mé os comhair Chathaoir Bhreithiúnas Dé,*
> *Go ndeire an Réiteoir Mór liom, Rí na bhFeart,*
> *Rinne tú cion fir, a mhic Ógie – d'imir tú mar is ceart.*

This translates as:

> When the final whistle for me has blown,
> And I stand at last before God's judgment throne,
> May the great referee when he calls my name …
> Say, you played like a man, Ógie; you played the game.'[82]

Ag smaointiú oraibh uilig – thinking of you all.

Dála an scéil – By the way

Na Clocha Liatha – Greystones – (Logainm.ie #128825) is the Irish name of a Wicklow town and is a direct translation. However, *An Clochán Liath* – the grey stepping-stones – in the Donegal Gaeltacht is not a direct translation. You can find out how and why it came to be called Dungloe in English in the note on Logainm.ie (Logainm.ie #1414074).

Focail na Seachtaine – Words of the week

1. *Díocas* – eagerness
2. *Díomas* – pride, arrogance, contempt
3. *Ní mar a shíltear a bhítear* – all is not what it seems
4. *Seachnaíonn súil ní nach bhfeiceann* – the eye avoids what it doesn't see
5. *Aisling* – dream
6. *Dul chun cinn* – momentum
7. *Díocas/díograis/paisean* – passion

---

[82] *Irish Independent*, 27 November 2022

Caibidil 30: *All is not what it seems*

DO THURAS FÉIN – YOUR JOURNEY

1.
2.
3.
4.
5.
6.
7.

> Teanglann.ie phrase:
> *briathra trua* – piteous words

Caibidil 31

Níl aon tinteán mar do thinteán féin

There's no place like home (Or there's no hearth/fire like your own hearth/fire)

My survival held firm in the ceantracha scoite amach/iargúlta/forimeall – *peripheral areas*. Places where there were more stones in the fields than potatoes. Places where survival wasn't a given. Places where large families were sub-divided and dispersed to the far corners of the globe. Places where I still call home. Through caint laethúil – *daily discourse*; amhráin – *song*; seanfhocail – *proverbs*; ceol – *music*; searmanais eaglasta – *religious ceremonies*; agus tráchtáil/gnó – *and trade/commerce*, people kept breathing life into me. Together, we persevered and to this day I will always acknowledge the native Irish speaker of the Gaeltacht for securing my destiny. You carried me. You still do.

● ● ● ● ● ● ●

Caibidil 31: There's no place like home (Or there's no hearth/fire like your own hearth/fire)

It is important to keep the head busy. When my father turned 81, I asked him 'are you still able to handle the *sábh slabhrach* – chainsaw?'

He said, 'I'm not ready for the *coirnéal* – corner – just yet.' He plays bridge and solo and his feet have no desire to leave the *urlár damhsa* – dance floor – any time soon either. My mother is in the same boat, and when they're not in the boat together, they're swimming in the sea. 'Get busy living or get busy dying' as both Andy Dufresne and Ellis Red Redding famously said in *Shawshank Redemption*. In the movie *City Slickers* (1991), Curly said, 'Just one thing. You stick to that, and the rest don't mean shit.' Mitch asks: 'But what is the one thing?', to which Curly replies: 'That's what *you* have to find out.' Finding out more about who you are, about where you're from and what your ancestors got up to through a language that is part of your DNA might just be the something different you've been looking for. If learning Irish doesn't rock your boat, there's an opportunity to learn about the Irish as a gateway to your past.

Ná déan nós agus ná bris nós[83] – don't start a habit and don't break a habit. I'm not sure how appropriate this advice is. My interpretation is don't start a bad habit and don't break a good habit. Something new can be anything. For me, something new was not just learning to speak Irish. It was about going back into education. I had been in the educational wilderness during my time as a politician. I would advise the new crop of politicians not to fall into this trap. My Irish language journey has increased my appetite for reading again. Furthermore, I am on the final stretch of a MSc in Positive Health Coaching at RCSI.[84] I am fortunate to have a great group of classmates who are on their own individual journeys and passionate lecturers who are breaking new ground in positive psychology coaching. The most important step in making a decision is making the decision. Much like the Chinese

---

[83] I got this line from former TD Éamon Ó Cuív. He's the man to talk to about its meaning.
[84] RCSI University of Medicine and Health Sciences.

idiom, the most important step on a 10,000-mile journey is the first step. Grab that decision by the scruff of the neck: 'I'm going to do this!' *Is féidir leat imeacht gan aon aiféala ort* – you can walk away with no regrets.

DÁLA AN SCÉIL – BY THE WAY

Francie Cullen insisted that I still had to learn stuff. You know the stuff. The not too exciting stuff. I resisted as best I could as I was happy with my new 'free spirit' approach to learning. He managed to grind me down in the end. He made me learn the prepositions. *An t-iomlán dearg acu* – the whole blessed lot of them!

FOCAIL NA SEACHTAINE – WORDS OF THE WEEK

1. *Gan aon aiféala* – with no regrets
2. *Is féidir leat imeacht* – you can leave
3. *Ná déan nós* – don't start a habit
4. *Ná brís nós* – don't break a habit
5. *Sábh slabhrach* – chainsaw
6. *Coirnéal* – corner
7. *Urlár damhsa* – dance floor

DO THURAS FÉIN – YOUR JOURNEY

1. _____
2. _____
3. _____
4. _____
5. _____

Caibidil 31: *There's no place like home (Or there's no hearth/fire like your own hearth/fire)*

6. _____

7. _____

> Teanglann.ie phrase:
> *Chuaigh mé tríd/fríd an amhrán* –
> I forgot the words of the song

Caibidil 32

Leanfaidh muid ar aghaidh le chéile

We will follow each other forward together

The flame is still burning signaling a strong ambition for even brighter days ahead. T.P. Ó Connchubair, ó Bhaile na nGall, was asked one time to predict my future. He replied with the following – mol an lá um thráthnóna – *praise the day in the evening time. I tend to agree with T.P. when I think about my own* todhchaí – *future. We will wait and see how this story unfolds.* Mar sin ráite – *that being said* – táim iontach dearfach – *I am very positive.*

● ● ● ● ● ● ●

Gaelscoileanna agus Gaelcholáistí sprouted up outside the Gaeltacht with the help of many Irish speakers from Gaeltacht communities. *Bun an Phobail* (Moville) have the *dul chun cinn* – momentum – in driving culture and language forward in Gaelscoil Cois Feabhail. On your left, en route to Greencastle, stands a modern school and just outside grows a *crann darach* – oak tree. The strength of the oak representing the strength of the school's ambition to keep the language strong. Communities know the value of the Gaelscoileanna and Gaelcholáistí movement. Gaoth Dobhair siblings Róisín Ní Chumhaill agus Colmán Mac Cumhaill were at the helm, along with the Donegal town community to build a state-of-the-art school, Gaelscoil na gCeithre Máistrí. It may feel that the wheel is turning slowly from the outside looking in. The reality is different. Good things are happening and the Irish language capacity building continues apace.

Legend has it that Roy Keane was given three great pieces of advice in the early days of his football career. While Roy was playing with Nottingham Forest, Brian Clough told him to concentrate on three things, namely: pushing forward into the box, tackling, and passing. My advice, for what it's worth, also comes in three: *cleachtadh, cleachtadh agus cleachtadh* – practise, practise, practise. This will help you engineer the confidence to show off some of your newfound vocabulary.

THIG LEAT DUINE A BHAINT AS AN PHORTACH ACH NÍ THIG LEAT AN PORTACH A BHAINT AS AN DUINE
YOU CAN TAKE THE PERSON FROM THE BOG BUT YOU CANNOT TAKE THE BOG FROM THE PERSON[85]

You've heard the word 'bog' before, no doubt. Sometimes, it is used instead of *leithreas* – toilet. *Tóg go bog é* – take it easy. What about the 'bogey man'? Many times, I was threatened with this infamous character when I was younger. Bogey is an evil and mischievous character. Dictionaries also define bogey as a piece of nasal mucus. 'Down under',

---

[85] *Caint Cois Tineadh/Fireside Talk*, Donnchadh C. Ó Laighin & Anna Marie Ní Ghallchobhair (2014).

bogey is an act of swimming or bathing. Additionally, it's a term golfers try to avoid, and certainly not a double bogey! *Is maith leis an gcapall seo talamh bog* – this horse likes it when the going is soft. *D'éirigh an t-im bog* – the butter went soft. And what about *Baile Uí Bhogáin* – Ballyboggan (Logainm.ie #1831)? One of the archival records on Logainm.ie, from 1836, refers to O'Bogan's town. That makes sense and might contradict any suggestion that there would be any drainage issues. How many times have we been 'bogged down' with work? Some of us have happy/unhappy memories of the bog. Not dissimilar to some of our experiences in Irish class. It was an ordeal to go there, and when we got there, we were counting down the seconds to go home. At least there was a clock at the top of the class. Sure, didn't both experiences toughen us up? The bog still held on to some Gaeilge – the *sleán* is used for cutting turf. Some of the other unique expressions may have come from Gaeilge: paring the turf, holing the turf or rickling the turf (piling it up in ricks) on the peat banks (peat binks where I come from). Leslie Lucas, in *Cnuasach Focal Ros Goill*, references rickling' with the following: *Bhí sé ag rickliú na móna* – he was rickling the turf. This is just another example of a word I used and assumed was *Béarla* but came from Gaeilge. The place where we threw the turf out is known as the 'brew' or the 'bank'. I'm wondering if it comes from the word *brú* – pressure? I came across '*bruach an locha*' recently, possibly describing the pressure from the lake but more than likely the bank of the lake. Again, possibly! Lastly, 'on the brew' was slang for someone claiming unemployment assistance. I'm not sure where that reference came from. Could it be pressure again, from not being able to get a job? Or on the *bruach* – edge, margin, bank. Thinking back, the days on the hill were a hard 'slog' but good days. *An teachtaireacht thuas* – the message above – is to encourage you to explore words and language, in all their nuances, all its forms and interpretations. Seek out their origin, their meanings and trace your own footsteps in the *gaineamh* – sand. Your own life experience will help reawaken and rekindle words and expressions that you've heard before. Acclimatise your ear to become more attentive to words and expressions that people use in everyday discourse.

Just the other day my mother used an expression she probably used when we were younger, '... as happy as Ned in the *coille*'. She heard it from her own mother and passed it on. Interestingly, my mother learned for the first time that the expression meant 'as happy as Ned in the wood'. My mother was born *ar imeall na Gaeltachta* – on the border of the Gaeltacht – in *Leathardán* – Lathardan (Logainm.ie #15927), beside the *Gleann Bhairr* – Glenvar – Gaeltacht (Logainm.ie #130379) literally, top of the glen. She didn't speak Gaeilge, nor did her parents. *Leathardán* is a place name that also features in Waterford, Clare and Sligo. Logainm.ie doesn't confirm the exact meaning of *Leathardán*. Observing the topography of my mother's birthplace one can assume that *leath* – half – and *ardán* – elevation/platform – explains a townland halfway up the side of the hill. Next time you are in 'The Parish' (outside Buncrana) you will see this hill across *Loch Súilí* – Lough Swilly. This is a special place where the townland starts halfway up the hill and ends at the breakwater that moors punts, currachs and half-deckers. The sun will be shining, even on a rainy day. My own curiosity will take me to Leathardán in the other counties one day, *le cuidiú Dé* – with the help of God. Up the road from where my mother was born is *Ráth Maoláin* – Rathmullan[86] – (Logainm.ie #16046), explained by O'Donovan in 1835 as 'Mullan's Rath'. Rathmullan History Society brought the rich history of this place to the fore in the past few decades. In 2007 a unique and significant four-hundredth anniversary commemoration of the 'Flight of the Earls' took place here.

---

[86] Preservation works have been carried out on the Old Abbey in conjunction with Donegal County Council and the Department of Housing, Local Government and Heritage. Extensive preparatory work is under way to develop the 'Battery' by the 'Way Forward' group. Rathmullan Abbey was built in 1508. The Battery was built in 1812 along with six other batteries or Martello towers on the banks of Lough Swilly. The English built them in fear of a Napolean invasion.

Charlie Dillon, in conjunction with the Royal Irish Academy (RIA) and with support from Roinn na Gaeltachta, has embarked on an ambitious project, *Foclóir Stairiúil na Gaeilge*, comparable only with the *Oxford English Dictionary*. This extensive work incorporates the period of the Flight of the Earls, in 1607, and tries to trace words that were used during that period, examining their origin, their meaning and how they have evolved into present day vernacular.

The rich tapestry of resources available through *Foclóir Stairiúil na Gaeilge*, Dúchas.ie, Bealoideas.ie, Foclóir.ie, Téarma.ie, Abair.ie, Logainm.ie and Teanglann.ie opens new windows for our primary and secondary school students, and many more. The work is a testament to many people past and present who dedicated their lives to the language in the full knowledge that what they were doing was and is integral to the legacy of our language. The language is not just a means of communication but a relevant useful tool in further understanding our social and cultural environment.

My father was born *ar imeall na Gaeltachta freisin*, bordering Droim Mhic an Leadra[87] – known locally as Droim (Logainm.ie #15758). My father didn't speak Gaeilge, nor did his parents. According to Logainm.ie it is a combination of *droim* meaning ridge and Mac an Leadra, suggested by O'Donovan in 1835 to be a family name. He was born in a place called Coole (Logainm.ie #15754). Logainm.ie doesn't confirm the Gaelic name for Coole, however O'Donovan's notes in the archival records for Coole Upper and Coole Lower would suggest that 'Coole' is an anglicised version of *cúl* – back. Anglicised Cool[e] more often represents Irish *cúil* – corner or nook.

I'm sure that living close to two Gaeltacht districts would have impacted on the English dialects over the years. I was born *ar imeall Na nDúnaibh agus Charraig Airt Gaeltacht* and didn't speak Gaeilge in

---

[87] Thousands of placenames were anglicised to Drum, Drom, Drin, etc. Check out placenames close to you, e.g. *Droim C(h)aim* – ridge of (the) pile of rocks. There is a Drumcarn in three counties of Ulster, according to Logainm.ie.

Caibidil 32: We will follow each other forward together

the house growing up. History does repeat itself, but it doesn't necessarily mean we are defined by it. *Anois* – now – three generations later, *tá Gaeilge agam* – I have Irish – and I am as happy as Ned in the *coille*! *Nó, chomh sásta le madra a mbeadh dhá eireball air* – or, as happy as a dog with two tails. *Nó chomh sásta le muc bheag sa gcac* – I'll leave that for you to figure out yourself!

DÁLA AN SCÉIL – BY THE WAY

In my ten years I haven't learned any 'curse' words as Gaeilge. I'm told they exist, but I never went looking for them either. If there are any Gaeilge curse words I'm going to take a guess and say they're not as coarse as the curse words *as Béarla*. I've started a habit of eliminating those horrible *Béarla* curse words from my vocabulary. Starting today!

FOCAIL NA SEACHTAINE – WORDS OF THE WEEK

1. *Ar aghaidh le chéile* – forward together
2. *Tóg go bog é* – take it easy
3. *Ag ricliú na móna* – rickling the turf
4. *Teachtaireacht* – message
5. *Gaineamh* – sand
6. *Eireball* – tail
7. *Talamh bog* – soft ground

DO THURAS FÉIN – YOUR JOURNEY

1. _____
2. _____
3. _____
4. _____

5. _____

6. _____

7. _____

‖ Teanglann.ie phrase: *Fear tostach* – a man of few words ‖

Caibidil 33

Fhad is a bheas an mhéar ag sileadh bíonn an teanga ag moladh

While the hand is giving the tongue is praising

Many parents struggle speaking Gaeilge; many sports teams communicate through the medium of English; playground conversations and play itself is through the medium of English in the main; and invariably, most grandparents converse through the medium of Béarla. This is the stark reality for so many families. If young people don't want to eat their glasraí – vegetables – that becomes a daily battleground. Similarly, if the young person struggles with the relevance of learning Gaeilge, the battlelines harden. The word 'an ghráin' – hate – is thrown into the heart of these deliberations, which is a shame for all concerned. How do we avoid this? It's not easy. However, it is possible to try something different. There must be a labour of love. There must be desire. There absolutely needs to be passion. The individual can be empowered in this space. The learner must be put at the heart of their own educational journey.

● ● ● ● ● ● ●

I found it *iontach deacair* – very difficult – to read books as Gaeilge at the early stage of my language journey – I still do! However, it was a great way to push myself to learn new words. Some sentences reveal how colourful English expressions we use today came from beautifully constructed Irish phrases. Seán A. Mac Mathúna's book, *Suaimhneas agus Mishuaimneas*, offers a glimpse into the interactions that took place as Gaeilge when the language was going full tilt. A beautiful title – *Calm and Not So Calm!* In one of his stories, 'An Grá', there are a few *línte galánta* – beautiful lines: '*Ní minic a fheicimid thú na laethanta seo*' – it's not often I see you these days'; '*Tá aithne againn ar a chéile le fada an lá*' – we know each other as the day is long; '*Bhí cuma chráite air ach tháinig sé chuige féin*' – he was all broken up, but he came back to himself. Every day is a language learning day. However, you must keep it relevant to your interests. Don't box yourself in to allocating time for class, as if that's enough. *Tábhachtach cinnte* – important sure – but not on its own. Classes have their place, and if you can manage to source a course that suits you, make sure there is an informal/social aspect to it. Many marriages started out in *Oideas Gael* leading to a beautiful *Oideas scéal!*

Donegal footballer Michael Murphy learned the Gaelic football trade in his back garden. This was his environment to finetune his skills at a very young age. Choose your environment to finetune your new linguistic skills. *Cleachtadh, cleachtadh, cleachtadh* ... practise, practise, practise! *Cleachtadh a dhéanann máistreacht* – practise makes perfect.

When the going gets tough, buy a pair of runners. One of the best pieces of advice I got was to start burning road. *Uimhir a haon* to clear the head, *uimhir a dó* to get into a bit of shape and *uimhir a trí* to spend time on your own. Time on your own is key to get the language part of the brain in shape. You can have the following conversations with yourself.

Táim ag bogadh ar aghaidh – I'm moving ahead. *Tá an foirgneamh liath ar mo chlé* – the grey building is on my left. If you're running in the capital, there is a good chance it is *ar do dheis fosta* – on your right also. *Tóg an chéad chasadh ar chlé* – take the first left turn. *Fan sa lána ar chlé* – stay in the left lane. *Féach nó breathnaigh nó amharc go cúramach* – look or look or look carefully. We have three 'looks' here which demonstrates that we can say things in so many ways – so don't get bogged down trying to look for a specific word or direct translation. Gaeilge is its own language and has enough flexibility to allow you to *draoi suas* – magic up – a sentence without worrying about whether it fits in or whether in fact it's grammatically correct. We will leave that to the *saineolaithe* – experts. For years I was hearing the word '*unc*' on Raidió na Gaeltachta and hadn't a clue what it meant. It is used amongst native Irish speakers in Donegal – and it is used for *amharc* – to look – pronounced 'aurk'. Foclóir.ie went with a similar pronunciation with Ulster and Munster dialect. Interestingly, when you tune into the sound used in Conamara it is pronounced 'offurk'. I regularly hear the Gaelic word '*coitianta*'. I thought it was the name of a place. It is the Irish word for common. The point is, once you start listening to a language you start to zone in on words that are being repeated. Go after those words. They are waiting for you.

Witnessing people reinventing themselves is a joy. The human spirit takes on a life of its own once new challenges are presented. I'm certainly not the first person who has gone back learning Irish. I'm one of many. Josie Doohan went back learning Gaeilge later in life. Spending time with him in the *tSean Bheairic, An Fál Carrach*[88] was a

---

[88] I checked out *An Fál Carrach* on Logainm.ie, and I came across *Bóthar an Fháil Charraigh* – Falcarragh Road, in Dublin. Notice how it changes when preceded by *bóthar*.

good motivation for me as Josie had been there, done that, and wore the T-shirt.

For sight or view, each dialect has a different point of view.

Rather than falling into the age-old trap of saying, 'I can't understand Conamara or Ulster Irish,' instead, get under the bonnet and find out what makes this language tick. It's one engine made up of thousands of parts. *Coinnigh ag gabháil* – keep going – even if you are *tuirseach* – tired – *agus traochta* – shattered.

Think of all the traffic that goes through your head. Yes, you do talk to yourself quite a bit. To be honest, sometimes it can be far from complimentary. When you finish giving out about others you move on to yourself (or the inverse of that) – and you rarely spend much time thinking highly of yourself. Or maybe that's just me! The trick is – start talking to yourself, as Gaeilge. In your head – you don't need the neighbours talking about you! Depending on what level you're at, the extent of your conversation may be just – *Joe is ainm dom agus is maith liom sneachta* – as highlighted in one of the red tops a few years back. A big win in this transition is that it eliminates the negative self-analysis that sometimes dominates our thoughts. *Coinnigh dearfach* – stay positive. I used the following expression in some of my speeches. *Beidh an dearcadh dearfach* – the future will be bright.

DÁLA AN SCÉIL – BY THE WAY

Mar eolas – FYI – Big Neil Gallagher confirmed to me a few years ago those goal posts I mentioned earlier are still in Michael Murphy's back garden. Assuming they're still up, he won't be taking them down anytime soon!

FOCAIL NA SEACHTAINE – WORDS OF THE WEEK

1. *Cleachtadh a dhéanann máistreacht* – practise makes perfect
2. *Suaimhneas* – calm/tranquility

Caibidil 33: *While the hand is giving the tongue is praising*

3. *Bhí cuma chráite uirthi* – she was all broken up
4. *Níorbh fhada gur thosaigh sé* – it wasn't long before he started
5. *Ní minic a fheicimid thú* – it's not often I see you
6. *Beidh an dearcadh dearfach* – the future is bright
7. *Tá aithne againn ar a chéile le fada an lá* – we know each other as the day is long

DO THURAS FÉIN – YOUR JOURNEY

1. _____
2. _____
3. _____
4. _____
5. _____
6. _____
7. _____

‖ Teanglann.ie phrase:
Bhí sé ag tomhas na bhfocal – he was measuring his words ‖

Cabidil 34

Maireann croí éadrom i bhfad

A light heart lives long

Cé leis thú – *Who do you 'belong' to?* This way of asking who you are reflects a sense of family/community and tradition going back generations. Language roots us in history and brings meaning to the landscape through our expressions, our outlook and articulation. Language reflects who we are spiritually, socially and mentally. Language weaves through our essences. The learner of Gaeilge has a great opportunity to design his or her learning path. Taking on this challenge will not only result in a language competence outcome; it will also help to inspire the learner to take ownership and grow in self-confidence. Ultimately, the learner should be at the centre of designing the learning construct and should shape the learning. The teacher/educator facilitates this process. The proof is in the pudding. No need for a roth nua anseo – *new wheel here* – the Gaeltacht areas and Gaelscoileanna and Gaelcholáiste movement have shown the way.

● ● ● ● ● ● ● ●

Cabidil 34: A light heart lives long

AN CUIDIÚ – THE HELP

I have Francie Cullen to thank for his *cuidiú* – help – in the early days of July 2014. Francie focused on the flow of the language. To be clear, it wasn't all a bed of roses with Francie *ach oiread* – either. He demanded very high standards. *Sin ráite* – that being said – Francie got me moving, got me thinking and got me talking. *Fuair mé leagan amach ceachtanna ó Francie fosta* – I also got lesson plans from Francie. I insisted that these lesson plans were available publicly as part of my very public plea for people to join me on my journey. Ten years ago, I didn't really have the time to sit down and go through material as much as I would have liked. Immersion was my outlet. Depending on what learning stage you are at, don't get disheartened if the rules are overwhelming. Today, I enjoy going over his plans as they make sense *anois* – now! *Seo sampla thíos* – here is a sample below:

> *Tuiseal Ginideach Iolra*[89]
> *Bíonn i gcónaí urú san Ghinideach Iolra: 'n' ar ghuta cé acu a, e, i, o, u*
> *Dath na n-úll* – colour of the apple
> *Doirse na n-oifigí* – doors of the office
>
> *Urú ar chonsan má ghlacann an consan urú*
> *Na consain a ghlacann urú: b, c, d, f, g, p, t*
> *(m ar b)*
> *(g ar c)*
> *(n ar d)*
> *(bh ar f)*
> *(n ar g)*
> *(b ar p)*
> *(d ar t)*

---

[89] The *tuiseal ginideach*, I missed you! *Géarchaint* – sarcasm – aside, while I didn't understand you in the beginning, I now see you in a different light.

> *Mar shampla:*
> *Grága na gcág* – cry of the jackdaw
> *Luach na ndoirse* – value of the doors
> *Solas na lampaí* – light of the lamps (nothing before 'L')

Retired teacher Rosemary Bonner passed on her notes from her teaching days including her *leabhar beag dearg, graiméar na Gaeilge* – in Rosemary's words – 'a wee red grammar book'. Arriving in the post in a large brown envelope (stop it now), the notes combined with a personal handwritten letter was the tonic I needed at the time. Included in the notes were a few examples of the *gnáthchaite* which I will share with you. These couple of examples were from stories that Rosemary heard from her *máthair mhór* – grandmother – *blianta ó shin* – years ago:

- *Bhíodh earraí le díol ag na fir siúil* – goods used to be sold by travelling men
- *Bhíodh an fear déirce ag iarraidh déirce* – the begging man used to beg for alms
- *Chodlaíodh siad ins na sciobóil* – they used to sleep in the barns
- *Shuíodh siad ag an tine* – they used to sit by the fire

Thanks to Rosemary, I can associate the *gnáthchaite* (pronounced *grá* in the hills) with her timely and generous intervention. The difficulty I have with grammar books is that all the tenses are piled in together. The word 'tense' itself isn't lost on me. WordNet defines 'tense' as a 'grammatical category of verbs used to express distinction of time'. In addition, WordNet also defines 'tense' as 'in or of a state of physical or nervous tension'. A state some of us can relate to when we were up to our necks in grammar for the best part of two decades. Keep the faith though. Time is a healer. *D'fhág Rosemary teachtaireacht deas agam* – Rosemary left a nice message for me: *Maireann croí éadrom i bhfad* – A light heart lives long.

Cabidil 34: *A light heart lives long*

Dála an scéil – By the way

Fite fuaite best describes the interwoven connection of help I received over the years. There is an eager network of people who are just waiting to be asked. People like to be asked. I am conscious that I'm leaving many people out who helped me on my journey. This is not deliberate. I am grateful for every interaction. It may have been a quick chat, a brief hello, a courtesy text, a nugget of advice, a helpful email, a kindly worded letter or a chat over a warm cup of tea. I am grateful for all the help, and I am grateful that I got to meet many people whom I otherwise would never have met.

Focail na seachtaine – Words of the week

1. *Maireann croí éadrom i bhfad* – a light heart lives long
2. *Shuíodh siad ag an tine* – they used to sit by the fire
3. *Grága na gcág* – cry of the jackdaw
4. *Luach na ndoirse* – value of the doors
5. *Dath na n-úll* – colour of the apples
6. *Doirse na n-oifigí* – doors of the office
7. *Solas na lampaí* – light of the lamps

Do thuras féin – Your journey

1. _____
2. _____
3. _____
4. _____
5. _____

Beidh Tú Alright: *Maireann croí éadrom i bhfad*

6. _____

7. _____

|| Teanglann.ie phrase: *Tiontú focal* – translation of words ||

Caibidil 35

An bairille a mbíonn an fíon ann fanann cuid de sna cláir

The barrel that has the wine in it, some of it will remain in the boards

Everyone likes to back a winner. And when you're losing in public you lose big. The Irish language – yes that would be me – has been struggling in second place (maybe even third) for several decades – sorry, centuries. But in fairness, the Irish people never kicked me when the language madra *– dog – was down; some merely ignored me – probably an even bigger insult.*

I have been an officially recognised language in the EU since 2007 and the derogation was lifted in January 2021. Translation and interpretation opportunities now exist in Brussels, commanding very generous salaries.⁹⁰ Well, that should certainly take care of the 'what use is it anyway?' excuse. Mammies and daddies of Ireland take note!

● ● ● ● ● ● ●

Mícheál Mac Giolla Easbuic leaves a rich legacy in his native 'in thru'. *Rugadh agus tógadh Mícheál i gCill Charthaigh, Tír Chonaill* – Mícheál was born and raised in Kilcar, Tír Chonaill (Donegal). *Ceapadh mar Uachtarán Oireachtas na Gaeilge é in 2012* – he was appointed President of Oireachtas na Gaeilge in 2012. *Tá eagráin de scéalta a cheantair curtha le chéile aige, agus is í a aidhm an oidhreacht áitiúil a bheith ar fáil do na glúnta le teacht* – he has put together edited stories from the area and it was his aim to make this local heritage/legacy available to the coming generation. Mícheál asked me to launch two of these editions under the banner *A Thiontaigh [ag Tiontiú] go Gaeilge: Turning to Irish*.⁹¹ He was passionate about the language, and he was certainly one of the people who inspired me during the early days of my language *turas*. *Tá Mícheál ar shlí na fírinne anois mar fuair sé bás ag deireadh na bliana fiche fiche* – Mícheál is on the path of the truth now as he passed away at the end of 2020. I never got to thank him properly and, to borrow a phrase that was used in one of the stories in his *leabhar* – book – *Páidí Dubh as Tír Chonaill le Séamús Mac Mánas* – *Ach ní mar sin a bheadh sé* (p. 36) – It was not to be. *D'fhág Mícheál oidhreacht ollmhór agus beidh an tionchar le feiceáil sna laethanta agus na blianta atá le teacht* – Mícheál has left a massive legacy and this impact is visible today and will be seen in the days and years to come. Mícheál gave me a lovely expression the first time I met him, '*A mór,*

---

⁹⁰ When I was appointed to the Gaeltacht in 2014, Grace Harkin was in second year in Coláiste Ailigh. She is now in full-time employment in Brussels working as a translator.

⁹¹ The two books I launched were *Scéalta as Tír Chonaill Cnuasach a Cúig le Séamus Mac Mánas* (2017) and *Páidí Dubh as Tír Chonaill le Séamas Mac Mánas* (2013).

Caibidil 35: *The barrel that has the wine in it, some of it will remain in the boards*

B mór agus C mór' – a lovely play with both *Gaeilge agus Béarla*! I used it in many of my presentations as Minister for Education.

> *Ádh mór* – good luck
> *Bí mór* – seize the moment
> *Saoi mór* – wise one

My strong message to people who have a good command of Gaeilge and are fluent Irish speakers is this, never underestimate the *cumhacht* – power – you have when it comes to inspiring someone on their learning journey. It may be a quiet word, an encouraging word or just a gentle whisper. It's the combination of all these encounters which encourages passion and curiosity. The curiosity becomes a daily pilgrimage and one's appetite for all things historical is whetted continuously.

Get to the bottom of your own name. McHugh/Hughes is a translation/anglicisation of *Mac Aodha* – Son of Hugh. My father is Denis, just for the record! My curiosity led me to William Nolan, Liam Ronayne and Mairead Dunlevy, editors of *Donegal History and Society*. They didn't let me down:

> The most southerly territory of Tír Chonaill was known as Tír Aodha, which became anglicised to the barony-name TirHugh … it is clear from all the earlier sources already cited that Tír Aodha did not originally extend south of the Erne … Áth Seanaigh [Seanaidh], which is the basis of the name Béal Átha Seanaigh [Seanaidh] – Ballyshannon in English , was originally the name of a ford on the River Erne, which marked the southern extent of Tirhugh … Tír Aodha differs from the names of the other ancient territories of Tír Chonaill in several respects … it is the only one of the early territories not to have been named after any of the various descendants of Niall Naoighiallach – Niall of the Nine Hostages. According to tradition, the personage from

whom Tír Aodha, *'the land of Aodh'*, is named was one Aodh Ruadh Mac Badhuirn, a mythological figure, from whom also derived the placename *Eas Ruaidh,* 'the cataract of (Aodh) Rua', now Assaroe on the Erne outside Ballyshannon.[92]

I am not saying that my family name is a direct lineage to the late Mr Mac Badhuirn, nevertheless, what whets the curiosity is that if you journey through these southern parts of Donegal, you will come across the name Mac Aodha/McHugh. While my family comes from the northern side of the county in Creamhghort (Logainm.ie #1412965): '*Gort:* field/*Creamh:* wood, garlic, corruptly anglicised Cranford', the other major congregation of McHughs are in *Na Gleanntaí* – Glenties (Logainm.ie #14724), *Ard an Rátha* – Ardara (Logainm.ie #1414059) *agus Tír Eoghain* – Tyrone (Logainm.ie #100030) which wouldn't be a million miles away from Tír Hugh. You will also come across the McHughs in Galway, Mayo, Sligo and Leitrim. The two big family names in Inis Eoghain are McLaughlin and Doherty. The McHughs would be thin on the ground, in the land of Eoghain.

Regarding surnames, *féach thíos* – see below – *ó* Dr Charles Dillon, *eagarthóir* – editor – of *Foclóir Stairiúil na Gaeilge:*[93]

Sloinnte Gael – Gaelic surnames
Tá próiseas 'aistrithe' go Béarla ar siúl ar shloinnte na Gaeilge ó tháinig an Béarla chun na tíre mar theanga údaráis, riaracháin agus dlí.

---

[92] Nolan, Ronayne and Dunlevy (eds), *Donegal History and Society* (1995), Geography Publications.

[93] 2017, *Acadamh Ríoga na hÉireann*/Royal Irish Academy. I launched *Corpas Stairiúil na Gaeilge 1600–1926* in October 2017, which was a step towards the publication of *Foclóir Stairiúil na Gaeilge*. The corpas has 3,000 texts and up to 19 million words. The Royal Irish Academy in Dublin worked with their staff in Charraig, Dún na nGall to digitise the material. Minister for the Gaeltacht Seán Kyne committed further funding to the project in 2019.

Caibidil 35: *The barrel that has the wine in it, some of it will remain in the boards*

[A process of 'change' to English of Gaelic surnames is ongoing since English came to the country as a language of authority, administration, and law.]

Amanna cuireadh litriú Béarla ar shloinnte Gaeilge –
[Sometimes English spelling was applied to Gaelic surnames –]
Ó *Gnímh* – Agnew
Mag Uidhir – Maguire
Mac Aodha – McHugh
Ó *Corráin* – Curran

Amanna eile aistríodh an sloinne go dtí leagan Béarla a bhí ag teacht leis an Ghaeilge ó thaobh na céille de –
[Other times the surname was changed to an English version that was similar in meaning to the Irish –]
Mac Aodha – Hewson [son of Hugh]
Mac Gabhann – Smith [son of the (black)smith]
Mac an Easpaig – Bishop [son of the bishop]
Mac an Bhreithimh – Judge [son of the judge]

Amanna eile, agus b'fhéidir mar gheall ar easpa tuisceana nó leath-thuiscint ar bhunús sloinne (ag an duine ar leis an sloinne nó ag duine eile – ní fios) aistríodh an sloinne go dtí leagan Béarla nach raibh ag teacht leis an Ghaeilge ó thaobh na céille de
[Other times, and perhaps due to lack of understanding or misunderstanding of the original name (by the person with the name, or by someone else – we don't know) the name was changed to an English version that did not have the same meaning as the Irish version]
Mac Con Aonaigh – Bird, Rabbit (*'éan' agus 'coiníní' cloiste* [heard])
Ó *Dubháin* – Doone but also Kidney (*duán = kidney, ach sa sloinne tá dubh+an i gceist* 'little dark one')

> Ó Duibhne – Deeney but also Peoples
> Ó nIonúin – Noonan but also Darling
> Mac an tSaoir – Mason but also Freeman (son of tradesperson)

Former TD Michael Noonan and former MP Alistair Darling led the response to the financial crisis. In sharing the same surname, Ó nLonúin, this is a must for your next table quiz!

According to *Donegal History and Society*:

> The creation of the county in 1585 united for the first time the historic territories of Tír Chonaill and Inis Eoghain under the common name of Donegal. It also gave the place name Donegal a broader reference than it had previously, as, until then, the name referred exclusively to the town at the foot of the river Eske. It did not have any territorial application. Tír Chonaill, in all its various anglicised forms, had all but disappeared from official documents by the early seventeenth century. The name, seemingly, was not used even to designate the unofficial geographical area by the newly arrived English-speakers in the area …. The native Irish-speaking inhabitants of the county were much slower to adopt the new name, however. For them, the name Dún na nGall still referred exclusively to the town of Donegal while the name Tír Chonaill was adopted as the name of the county.[94]

Interestingly, the most popular baby name for boys in England in 2020 was Connell! That wheel is fairly coming around sur!

---

[94] Nolan, Ronayne and Dunlevy (eds), *Donegal History and Society* (1995), Geography Publications, pp. 158, 159.

Caibidil 35: *The barrel that has the wine in it, some of it will remain in the boards*

DÁLA AN SCÉIL – BY THE WAY

'*Bíonn*' and '*Tá*' can sometimes cause confusion. '*Tá*' is a specific moment in time, e.g. today, now or at this moment. Whereas '*bíonn*' is the habitual or on-going repeated circumstance, e.g. usually, often, or always.

FOCAIL NA SEACHTAINE – WORDS OF THE WEEK

1. *Eagarthóir* – editor
2. *An bairille* – the barrel
3. *Sloinnte Gael* – Gaelic surnames
4. *Oidhreacht* – heritage/legacy
5. *Fíon* – wine
6. *Acadamh Ríoga na hÉireann* – Royal Irish Academy
7. *Na blianta atá le teacht* – the years yet to come

DO THURAS FÉIN – YOUR JOURNEY

1. _____
2. _____
3. _____
4. _____
5. _____
6. _____
7. _____

> Teanglann.ie phrase:
> *Tá tú ag dul thar leath na bhfocal* –
> you are leaving out half the words.

Caibidil 36

Is maith an scéalaí an aimsir

Time is a good storyteller

Now is the time to honour those who have kept me alive – those who have continued to have the conversations at home, in the shops, in the pubs and on the football and GAA pitches. Roger Casements GAC Portglenone is one example of a club that is honouring the legacy of a very important individual and promote sporting and cultural traditions. Those who got on with it and don't know why mo chara – *my friend* – takes a séimhiú and don't know why ár gcara – *our friend* – takes an urú, but just know that they do. To the Gaeilgeoirí who started late in life and were never afforded the opportunity at a younger age, I salute you. Thank you ár gcairde – *our friends*. Yes, you've guessed it – three variations of friend(s), what a tremendous language I am indeed! Umhal fosta – *modest too!*

● ● ● ● ● ● ●

Caibidil 36: *Time is a good storyteller*

Logainm.ie has an explanatory note on Ros Goill (Logainm.ie #111413)– 'the promontory of Goll; Goll – personal name'. In Irish literature this place name is sometimes linked to Goll Mac Mórna, a leader of the Fianna. I had the pleasure of meeting up with the late Leaslaoi U. Lúcás (Leslie Lucas) who resided in Ros Goill in my younger days. *Acadamh Ríoga na hÉireann* – the Royal Irish Academy – produced a collection of his work, *Cnuasach Focal as Ros Goill* – Word Collection of Rosguill – *curtha in eagar ag* – edited by – Tomás de Bhaldraithe.[95] Three decades after meeting with Leaslaoi, *fuair mé cóip* – I received a copy – of *Cnuasach Focal as Ros Goill ó* Charles Dillon, *eagarthóir* – editor – of *Foclóir Stairiúil na Gaeilge*.

Here are some of the phrases used in my parish down the centuries with a focus on the verb *'beir'*. It will show how extensively this verb was used in daily communication. As I do this, I am thinking of the interactions that would have taken place in fields, shops, along the side of the road, *ag crosbhealach* – at the crossroads – in pubs, wake houses and raking[96] houses in my parish *fadó fadó* – long ago. Compliments of Leaslaoi U. Lucas – *anois ar shlí na fírinne* – now on the way of the truth – *go raibh maith agat, a Leaslaoi*.

- *Bhéarfaidh mé duit é ar an chaoi go dtabharfaidh tú ar ais é* – I would give it to you on the condition that you give it back
- *Bheir mé maol ar an ghadaí ag goid mo chuid móna* – I caught the robbers stealing my turf

---

[95] Leaslaoi U. Lúcás, *Cnuasach Focal as Ros Goill* (1986), edited by Tomás de Bhaldraithe, Acadamh Ríoga na hÉireann.

[96] Raking was a tradition whereby neighbours came together in the evening when the work was done. Stories were shared (mainly ghost stories in the month of November), people danced, and songs were shared. I often think of my former neighbour, Pat Doherty, who facilitated these evenings. It was the ultimate community service. I see there's an entry for raking in Foclóir.ie; *'ag rácáil'*. One of the few words I do remember from secondary school is another word for raking – *'Ag airneáil'* from the Séamus Ó Grianna novel *Caisleáin Óir*.

- *Is cuma c'fhad is ritheas an madadh rua béarfadh [béarfar] air sa deireadh* – it doesn't matter how long the fox runs, he will be caught in the end
- *Béarfaidh tú air nuair a chluinfeas d'athair fá dtaobh dó* – you will suffer the consequences when your father hears about it
- *Ar [A] fhad is a ritheas an gearria*[97] *béarfar sa deireadh air* – however long the hare can run, he will be caught in the end
- *Char bheir mé ar goidé a dúirt sé* – I didn't catch what he said
- *Cha rachainn fad mo chois a dh'amharc air* – I wouldn't think it worth going to see

'*Char*' and '*cha*' are used in many Donegal Gaeltacht areas for *ní*; *chan fhuil* for *níl* and *cha raibh* for *ní raibh*. *Cnuasach Focal as Ros Goill* reveals that *cha* was used extensively in everyday life.

The natives of Ros Goill down the centuries, along with other traditional Donegal Gaeltacht areas to this day, would use '*chífidh*' instead of '*feicfidh*' – will see.

Thiocfadh linn – We will give things a go – is a lovely expression which can still be heard in Ros Goill conversations *inniu* – today. *Na Dúnaibh* native Declan Mc Fadden gave a lovely descriptive explanation of '*thiocfadh linn*'. It's about having a positive mindset and giving things a 'go' and making every day count. *Ar dóigh* can still be heard in Gaeilge interactions. *Dóigh* covers quite a bit of ground, ranging from way, manner, state, condition, to hope, expectation, trust, confidence, to burn, scorch and sear. If you ever hear a native speaker from *Na Dúnaibh* responding to a '*Caidé mar atá tú ceist?*' with '*ar dóigh*', you can be sure that the spirits are in a good place. If the response is '*go measartha*', the form will be just middling. Then again maybe it's just a reflection of modesty! *Tá sé ar a sheandóigh* – This expression was used to explain a person's recovery after an illness. He is on his old way/he has recovered/he is on the mend. The following expression

---

[97] *Giorria* is the modern spelling for hare.

Caibidil 36: *Time is a good storyteller*

was also used which gives very good advice indeed. *Tionn beirt níos fhearr ná tionn duine amháin* – two people see more than one person.

Listening to a group of *Na Dúnaibh* natives (men) ribbing/rising each other was something which always fascinated me. Having read and explored many of the old sayings as Gaeilge it seems to me that much of the interaction is based on historical sayings and witty one-liners. While it's communicated *as Béarla*, the language through generations lives on. Mind you, you certainly don't want to get caught in the crossfire. Here are three examples of the type of one-liner that was used extensively in everyday conversation:

- *B'éigean duit fanacht gur rugadh thú* – you have to wait until you are born (to an impatient person).
- *Beireann an oíche achan straigléir chun an bhaile* – the night brings every straggler home.
- *Tífidh/Chífidh tú an té a thiocfas chun an tsaoil san oíche níos mó na an té a thiocfas sa lá* – You will see a person coming to life at nighttime much more than during the day

The above gives you a glimpse into the vocabulary pertaining to my own parish. This is an obvious hook for me, and I am grateful that such work went into ensuring that this rich tapestry will be protected for future generations. Having gone through the book a few times, it's interesting to note that the use of '*rug*' – the past tense of '*beir*' – was not recorded, or I certainly couldn't find it. *Bheir* was used extensively in the past tense. Francie Cullen pointed out that most of the discourse was in the *modh coinníollach* – something that might or might not happen. 'I would cut the hay if the weather would only pick up' or 'I would go home after this pint if I had any sense.' 'If I had the money, I would spend it.' The description of 'an unreliable person' was one that stood out – *Bhéarfadh sé trasna na habhann thú agus d'fhágfadh sé ina lár thú* – he would take you across the river and he would leave you in the middle!

Not every parish will have a resource as rich as this one, however there will be books written by scholars and in-depth work carried out by researchers over many years which will give you an insight into the richness of the place where you live. *Beir ar an leabhar sin* – grab that book. Dúchas.ie will lead you to *Bailiúchán na Scol*, where many surprises await you. Every parish in Ireland will have people who can be identified as a reference source for local knowledge. These sources are invaluable.

Dála an scéil – By the way

Flaithiúlacht – generosity: You may still hear this word in English conversations. If one has it, one will spend it. Not always mind you! 'Tight as tuppence' is used in *Ros Comáin*. Not sure what the Irish expression is in *Cabhán*! – '*Ní thabharfadh sé a chac don na préacháin*' is one used in Conamara I am told. In an interview with Oliver Callen on 7 August 2024, writer Donal Ryan used the word '*flahulac*' in a chat *tríd Béarla*. The Irish language continues to 'pop up' in many of our English conversations.

Focail na seachtaine – Words of the week

1. *Giorria* – hare
2. *Sa deireadh* – in the end
3. *D'fhágfadh sé ina lár thú* – he would leave you in the middle
4. *Goid* – steal
5. *Gadaí* – robber
6. *Abhainn* – river / *Sruth* – stream
7. *Beir ar an leabhar sin* – Grab that book

Caibidil 36: *Time is a good storyteller*

DO THURAS FÉIN – YOUR JOURNEY

1. _____
2. _____
3. _____
4. _____
5. _____
6. _____
7. _____

Teanglann.ie phrase:
Nach aici atá ná téarmaí – what grand words she has

Caibidil 37

Mair, a chapaill, agus gheobhaidh tú féar

Live horse and you will get grass

Enough of this playing hard to get. No more excuses. So many self-appointed experts in the field of where it all went wrong. Tá mé anseo – I am here; bhí mé i gcónaí – I always was; beidh mé i gcónaí – I always will be. I am part of your DNA. I am not just a legend. I am part of your name: Mac a' Bhaird, Ó Suilleabháin, Mac an tSaoir (son of), Ní Ógáin, Nic an Ghoill, Ní Dhomhnaill (daughter of) … I am part of where you're from: Corca Dhuibhne, Carraig Airt, An Teach Dóite, Leitir Móir … I am you. We are in this together. Surely, we can get things going again. Let's start at the very beginning. Let's dance again. I'm done with the bickering.

●●●●●●●

Caibidil 37: *Live horse and you will get grass*

Looking back

It was a lovely fresh morning for a run as I passed *Droichead na Life* – the Ha'penny Bridge.[98] The signage as Gaeilge was always there but was never on my radar until now. Remember, when you're sitting in your car and stuck in traffic along the quays have a look around you. Gaeilge is all around you. Maybe Guinness/Diageo might use some of their wall space for some nice Gaeilge signage in the future. Just a thought!

- *Cé Uiséir* – Usher's Quay
- *Oileán Uiséir* – Usher's Island
- *Droichead Phrionsias Uí Shearbháin* – Frank Sherwin Bridge
- *Cé Wolfe Tone* – Wolfe Tone Quay
- *Cé Árann* – Arran Quay
- *Cé Urumhan Uachtarach* – Ormond Quay Upper
- *Siúlán an Bhaitsiléara* – Batchelor's Walk

Jogging was my escape – and still is I suppose. I was worried about pulling the calf as it was a bit tight from the day before. I stopped at a wall to give it a stretch. A Dubliner who was helping children across the road says, 'I see you're hitting the wall!' Dublin humour is a study in itself and no doubt those quick-witted retorts have a foundation in the Irish language. Another morning, I said, 'How's it going?' to a lady selling flowers on Grafton Street to which she replied, 'How long have you got?'

At Heuston Station (named after Seán Heuston, executed leader of the 1916 Rising) a bird decided to do its business, which landed on my right index finger. I presumed it was a *faoileán* – seagull – and as it missed my head, I was happy out! I believe it brings you luck. *Ní*

---

[98] Built in 1816, the original name of the bridge was Wellington Bridge. The official name since 1836 is Liffey Bridge. It is now commonly called the Ha'penny Bridge as a toll was charged to cross it up to March 1919.

duine piseogach mé – I'm not a superstitious person – I don't buy into the seven years of bad luck after breaking a mirror or walking under ladders, because seven is my lucky number. I've just got three things: *an chéad rud* – the first thing we just talked about – the bird poo; *an dara rud* – the second thing: you go out the same door you come in when visiting a homestead; *an tríú rud* – the third thing: black cats are a good omen when *ag stocaireacht/canbhasáil* – canvassing.

Back to that morning. There was a nice feel to the day and straight after the bird poo incident the sun came out. I began reminiscing. About a difficult time. A time when doubt nearly got the better of me, at a time when I was faced with a choice. Do I face the music, or do I slip silently and gently out the back door into the night? The door I didn't come in.

Out of sight, out of mind. 1989 through to 2014 had been a quarter century of 'I know I should go back and learn Irish'. Ryan Tubridy often threatened to go back and learn – I hear you Ryan, I was that soldier, and I would still be that soldier only for Enda Kenny's intervention. *Go raibh maith agat, Enda.* How many of us do that? Threatening to go back and take lessons? Followed by excuses – don't have time, too old and past it – and sure I was never any good at languages anyway. This *seanfhocal* has relevance: *má theastaíonn uait aithne a chur orainn, mair inár dteannta* – if you want to get to know us, live with us. I met Catherine McKenna from the Department of Celtic Languages and Literatures at Harvard University during a ministerial visit. She encouraged her students to get involved with the Irish scholarship programme. She was of the belief that full Irish immersion in the Gaeltacht would be critical. Summer colleges and *mná tí* (Gaeltacht hosts), play a crucial role in ensuring full immersion is key for young people who wish to brush up on the spoken word.

For adult learners, the scope may not be there for full immersion for a prolonged period. There is no shortage of options when it comes to online and that's all good; however, the tried and tested on-site physical learning has proven to be the best way of learning a language. Whether that's going to Germany for six months for full immersion to learn German, Coláiste Lurgan to experience learning Gaeilge creatively and by having fun, or Coláiste Uisce where the focus is on water sports, and you learn Gaeilge along the way. Cill Charthaigh, Árainn Mhór, Rann na Feirste, Gaoth Dobhair, Loch an Iúir, Coláiste Uladh, Dún Lúiche, Gleann Fhinne, Na Dúnaibh *agus* Gleann Cholm Cille will always have a *fáilte mhór fosta*.

I believe that *Covid naoi déag* has heaped further pressure on the Irish language. When people didn't meet, there were less opportunities to chat as Gaeilge. Throughout this book I have detailed many areas where good practice works in both formal and informal settings. I don't have all the answers, and I couldn't hold a candle to all the leaders who have driven, nurtured and protected the language over the years. We need to embrace those individuals, listen to them, and design a policy that will foster a realistic, relevant, and fun approach to the development of our wonderful and rare jewel in the crown – so everybody can enjoy it.

DÁLA AN SCÉIL – BY THE WAY

The Irish word '*nasc*' has numerous meanings *as Béarla*; connection, bind, bridging, link, bond, tie – to name but a few. Research work carried out by the Foclóir Stairiúil na Gaeilge team found evidence that '*nasc*' was the word used for jewellery. '*Seodra*' is commonly used for jewellery *inniu*.

FOCAIL NA SEACHTAINE – WORDS OF THE WEEK

1. *Forógra* – proclamation
2. *Cascá* – Easter
3. *Olltoghchán* – general election
4. *Sínitheoirí* – signatories

Beidh Tú Alright: *Mair, a chapaill, agus gheobhaidh tú féar*

5. *Folúntas* – vacancy/void
6. *Oibrí óige* – youth worker
7. *Comórtas* – competition

Do thuras féin – Your journey

1. _____
2. _____
3. _____
4. _____
5. _____
6. _____
7. _____

> Teanglann.ie phrase:
> *Focal ar fhocal* – word for word

Caibidil 38

Teachtaireacht fá choinne an diaspóra

Message for the diaspora

We should not forget that the Irish language helped the English language on its way. And, never forget that the Irish language – mise – was a different breed, very much up there with Mandarin in terms of its descriptive nature and focus on idioms. As is said in China, when I walk with two others, there must be one whom I can learn from. As Gaeilge we have 'giorraíonn beirt bóthar' – a journey shared is a journey shorter.

● ● ● ● ● ● ● ●

I was appointed Minister in the Department of Foreign Affairs with responsibility for Irish Aid and Irish Abroad in 2016. My next-door neighbour coined the title 'Minister for Far Away' – not the best of labels if you're in the business of gathering votes locally! Still though, I enjoyed the post and I have very fond memories.

Beidh Tú Alright: *Teachtaireacht fá choinne an diaspóra*

I visited many countries in my time as a TD and minister. In 2019, I stood on the *Wanli Changcheng* – Great Wall of China – where I was introduced to an interesting Chinese proverb: 'On a journey of 10,000 miles, the first step is the most important.' I couldn't help but compare this proverb to our very own *tús maith leath na hoibre* – a good start is half the work. Cantonese and Mandarin, through their idioms, have many messages of advice and instruction passed down through the ages, very much like the Irish language. We still have this, albeit mostly through the medium of *Béarla*. We can trace our history through our respective languages. *Tiocfaidh muid le chéile lenár dteanga* – We come together with our language. Our forefathers and foremothers passed on advice, instruction, and guidance.

Advice on how to live a more enriched life, advice on how to empower the next generation: *mol an óige is tiocfaidh sí* – praise the young and they will flourish.

Arriving in *Bostún* as a newly appointed Minister for the Diaspora and being met by then Ambassador Breandán Ó Caollaí was an important time for me. Walking through Logan Airport *ag labhairt Gaeilge* with Breandán felt good. It felt right. *Mo chara* Liam McGroarty, *ina chónaí san Eilvéis* – living and working in Switzerland – shares that same feeling when we chat Gaeilge on the phone. A variety of languages can be overheard in his workplace and for Liam it's a case of identifying as Irish and being proud of this. I visited *Uganda, An Chéinia, An tSúdáin Theas, An Liobáin, An Iordáin, An Albain, Londain, agus An Albáin*[99] – Uganda, Kenya, South Sudan, Lebanon, Jordan, Scotland, London, and Albania. I met many people conversing as Gaeilge. Irish-born and American-born take the promotion of the Irish language and culture very seriously. I remember getting my knuckles wrapped for referring to Saint Patrick's Day as Paddy's Day in Philly. I was fortunate that my late aunt Mary Cannon was there to console me over a bottle of Bud.

---

[99] *An Albáin* = Albania/ *An Albain* = Scotland. The difference in a fada could mean touching down in Tirana instead of Edinburgh!

Caibidil 38: *Message for the diaspora*

I saw firsthand the great work in *Nua Eabhrac* and Milwaukee. At a political level they include the former United States Secretary of Labor and former Boston Mayor Marty Walsh, of Ros Muc and Carna extraction, and Congressman Brendan Boyle of Gleann Cholm Cille fame. Marty was a key supporter of *Ionad Cuimhneacháin na nImirceach* – The Emigrants Commemorative Centre – in Carna.[100] Ambassadors for the language in London are working hard at promoting an Irish language playgroup at the London Irish Centre.

Conradh na Gaeilge in *Glaschú* – Glasgow – do great work in promoting the language and all things cultural from music to sport. The International Muintearas *Zúm rang Gaeilge* – Zoom Irish classes – include folk from Auckland, Worchester, Boston, Biorra, Rhode Island, London and loads of other places. Many people around the world are doing incredible work in both using and spreading Gaeilge. It is *le feiceáil* – visible – *agus beo* – alive. During my time in An Roinn Oideachais I witnessed the same energy for all things Gaeilge in *An tSile, An tSin, Aontas na nÉimíríochtaí agus An Bhrasail* – Chile, China, UAE and Brazil. *Maith sibh!*

The Irish and Scottish Gaelic cultural heritage in the Canadian province of Nova Scotia is still visible. Canada is on my bucket list. Catholic Memorial High School in Canton, Massachusetts has Gaeilge on the school curriculum. I have fond memories of visiting the school with Maura Concannon, Richie Gormley[101] and Seán Ó Coistealbha. There's no shortage of great Irish people doing incredible things globally to protect, preserve and nurture our cultural and linguistic heritage. Colleen Kennedy, Chair of the Milwaukee Irish Fest Foundation has been involved for 41 years. She was formally recognised as volunteer of the year in 2021.

---

[100] It was a pleasure working with Máirtín Ó Catháin on the Emmigrants Commemorative Centre. He put his heart and soul into it and still does to this day.

[101] Lord Mayor of West Roxbury Richie Gormley does incredible work promoting Irish cultural heritage while also honouring the legacy of his great-great-grandparents, who left Lecarrow in County Roscommon before the Famine.

Beidh Tú Alright: *Teachtaireacht fá choinne an diaspóra*

The international success of Cumann Lúthchleas Gael – the GAA – is reflected in the vast global footprint of well over 400 GAA clubs abroad. Dubai Celts CLG holds very fond memories for me all the way back to its formation in 1995/96. Paul McCabe and Niall McLoughlin were at the helm in conjunction with an eclectic bunch spanning Meath, Sligo, Galway, Carlow, Kilkenny, Dublin, and Donegal – and other counties in between with a little help from an English man too! It's great to see the club *ag dul ó neart go neart* – going from strength to strength.

The recent arrival of the Donegal Dubai GAA team is testament to the growth of Gaelic football in the Emirates. Check out the incredible work Abdullah Al Jumaili is doing in the promotion of hurling in the UAE.

North America alone has over five thousand registered players. Dallas Fionn Mac Cumhaills is on my bucket list for a visit sometime. Donegal Boston, Donegal Philadelphia and Donegal New York are familiar territory for me and I know firsthand the work that goes into developing the games in these three cities. Australia and New Zealand account for sixty-four clubs, and the Angry Leprechauns in South Australia wouldn't be a team to antagonise! The GAA in the Far East continues to grow with clubs that include the Tokyo Samurai GAA, Beijing GAA, Taiwan Celts and the Jakarta Dragonflies. The GAA in Canada is growing steadily with over twenty-five clubs, and that's against a backdrop of five different time zones. Their county secretaries could teach a thing or two about match fixtures! Established in January 2016, the Prince Edward Island Celts GAA Club has quickly proven that a love of Gaelic games can be a contagious one. With the help of financial backing from the GAA's Global Games Development Fund, they've worked hard to persuade eighteen schools on the island, with an average of 400 pupils each, to include Gaelic football on their sports syllabus. Roger Casements GFC Toronto, Ontario, is another one on my bucket list! In keeping with the Irish tradition of showing respect to other cultures abroad, I really like this club's name: Les

Caibidil 38: *Message for the diaspora*

Patriotes de Québec GAA – GAA Gaélique & Hurling. Always good to see the fadas in the mix with the French accent in the title! Closer to home, there are over 90 clubs in Britain (*Bunaíodh 1927* – established in 1927). Glaschú Gaels, Hugh O'Neills (Leeds) and Tír Chonaill Gaels is a snapshot from Scotland to London. And I better not forget Wales and give a shout out to St Colmcilles Cardiff GAA. There are over one hundred in continental Europe (*Bunaíodh 1999*) – CLG Den Haag, Earls of Leuven and Munchen Colmcilles is a sample of clubs who fly the GAA flag on the continent. The GAA's world games were held in Croke Park in 2016 and it was impressive to watch the skill levels of the native French players on display on the hallowed ground. If there was ever a case to introduce a new sport to the Olympics, then this is it.

The success and value of the GAA globally has been more than just sport. The GAA family provides support in times of difficulty and a haven for many people who emigrated over the years. The contribution and role of the GAA globally was formally acknowledged by the Department of Foreign Affairs in their GAA International Report (2015). Many have left our shores and have made a home in many different parts of the world. While they have left, Irish culture and identity never left them.

Dála an scéil – By the way

Go through the White Pages listing for Beaver Island on Lake Michigan, and you'll see the names of O'Donnell, Boyle, Gallagher and Early dominating the pages. These family clans retain their strong historical ties with An tOileán, Árainn Mhór. There's even a few McHughs there too!

Beidh Tú Alright: *Teachtaireacht fá choinne an diaspóra*

FOCAIL NA SEACHTAINE – WORDS OF THE WEEK

1. *An Eilvéis* – Switzerland
2. *An Fhrainc* – France
3. *Na Stáit Aontaithe* – United States
4. *An Bhreatain Bheag* – Wales
5. *An tSín* – China
6. *An Bhrasaíl* – Brazil
7. *Sasana* – England

DO THURAS FÉIN – YOUR JOURNEY

1. _____
2. _____
3. _____
4. _____
5. _____
6. _____
7. _____

‖ Teanglann.ie phrase:
Caint réidh, phlásánta – fair words, fine words ‖

Caibidil 39

Deir siad go bhfuil an fhírinne searbh, ní searbh atá sí, ach garbh!

It is said that the truth is bitter, it's not bitter, but rough!

Whether it's the modh foshuiteach *or the* modh coinníollach, *to grasp the fundamentals of learning a language, it needs to be heard. And of course, it needs to be heard and spoken* – cloiste agus labhartha. *Simple as. No need for a new wheel to be designed. One wheel is quite sufficient. Micí Mac Gabhann's* Rotha Mór an tSaoil *– The Big Wheel of Life – the title of his book, is as good a place to start as any.*

Let's listen to one voice. A voice that has been ignored for too long. Let's listen to the language itself. The Gaeilge. Mise. Then maybe, through a collective understanding, we may as a nation begin to believe that this is not as big an undertaking as we always thought it would be. That just maybe we could approach this learning curve in an enthusiastic and fun way. And just maybe, that urge that's in us all – well most of us – to speak our native tongue, might happen after all.

My descriptive nature lends itself to so much curiosity. Deora Dé – fuchsia plant – literally 'tears of God'. As referenced earlier – Droichead na nDeor – the Bridge of Tears. Slí na fírinne – death, literally 'the way of the truth'. How about the descriptive nature of this when describing a likeness – macasamhail – the son of the image. Or in English 'the same again'. Look how more exact and descriptive I am! So, the next time you order a pint, never say 'an rud céanna arís' – same again – as the next one will never be the same. In a similar vein, níor thit an t-úll i bhfad ón gcrann – the apple didn't fall far from the tree.

I've had my knockbacks. I've listened to the debates. Some say I'm dead, others say I'm 'deed' while others will say that I'm ina chodladh – asleep. One thing that I've experienced is this: an rud nach maríonn thú, déanann sé níos láidre thú – the thing that doesn't kill you makes you stronger. Anois, táim réidh don chéad chéim eile – now I am ready for the next step.

●●●●●●●

Ag breathnú siar, ní fhaca mé bealach dearfach ag an am. Bhí mé gafa sa choirneál, agus bhraith mé an brú. Le sin ráite, ní raibh mé i m'aonar ar chor ar bith. Thosaigh Eimer agus Christine ag obair san oifig agus bhí Gaeilge líofa acu beirt. Chuidigh siad go mór liom sa dáilcheantar, agus chomh maith le sin, bhí Noeleen, Karin, Barra agus Maura i mBaile Átha Cliath ar mo thaobh nuair a tháinig an crú ar an tairne. Nuair a bhíonn daoine gafa i "schuch", tagann níos mó daoine timpeall ort. Caithfidh mé a rá go raibh ionadh orm nuair a fuair mé an oiread tacaíochta ó mo pharóiste féin, ó mo chontae féin, ó chontaethe eile agus ó thimpeall na cruinne. Creidim go bhfuil bun láidir faoin Ghaeilge, agus tá mé dóchasach maidir le todhchaí na Gaeilge.

Tchím anois an nasc idir ár n-oidhreacht agus ár dteanga. Ní hamháin córas cumarsáide agus comhrá, ach an geata chuig an am atá thart. Tá an fhreagracht ar dhaoine a bhfuil Gaeilge acu orainn uilig. Mothaím

Caibidil 39: It is said that the truth is bitter, it's not bitter, but rough!

an dualgas seo anois. Tá an teanga ag fás; tá an Ghaeilge ag dul ó neart go neart, ach tá sí ag streachailt fosta, agus sin an fáth a bhfuil plean éigeandála de dhíth mar go bhfuil sé práinneach. Tá plean idirghabhála de dhíth fá choinne páistí óga. Tumoideachas i nGaeilge ag teastáil ag leibhéal réamhscoile agus fríd na blianta tosaigh. Tá an plean sin ag obair sna ceantracha Gaeltachta agus ní bheidh mé ag iarraidh roth úr a athchruthú.

Níl mé idir dhá chomhairle ach oiread, mar ag breathnú ar mo chás féin, fuair mé deis ath-fhoghlaim fríd an tumoideachas. Níl an bealach sin ar fáil do gach duine. Ar thaobh eile, tá mé réalaíoch fosta, ní bheidh an plean seo ag tarlú inniu nó amárach. Teastaíonn oiliúint chuimsitheach agus acmhainní cuí do mhúinteoirí sa réamhscoil.

Níl aon oideachas trom agus tá achan chuar oideachais iontach luachmhar. Níl aon aiféala ormsa nuair a bhreathnaím siar. D'oscail fuinneog amháin fuinneog eile.

Go raibh maith agat as an am a ghlacadh chun an leabhar seo a léamh. Níl an freagra agamsa, ach táim fíorbhuíoch as an seans agus an deis. Leanfaidh muid ar aghaidh, le chéile.

Dála an scéil – By the way

Nuair a fuair Michael Collins bás, d'fhág Peadar Ó Cearnaigh an bealach polaitiúil agus thosaigh sé ag múineadh Gaeilge agus ina dhiaidh sin, thosaigh sé ag péinteáil tithe, a chéad phost. B'fhéidir go bhfuil teachtaireacht ansin domsa; beidh mo chéad phost eile ag péinteáil tithe – Tithe an Oireachtais fiú!

Focail na seachtaine – Words of the week

1. *Garbh* – rough (pronounced 'garu' in *Uladh*)
2. *Searbh* – bitter
3. *Ar dóigh/Thar barr* – brilliant
4. *Tithe an Oireachtais* – Houses of the Oireachtas

Beidh Tú Alright: *Deir siad go bhfuil an fhírinne searbh, ní searbh atá sí, ach garbh!*

5. *Ag múineadh* – teaching
6. *Fíorbhuíoch* – truly grateful
7. *Freagra* – answer

Do thuras féin – Your journey

1. _____
2. _____
3. _____
4. _____
5. _____
6. _____
7. _____

> Teanglann.ie phrase:
> *Chuaigh an chaint chun teasaíochta* – words ran high

Caibidil 40

Mol an lá um thráthnóna

Praise the day in the evening

Learning any language is a wonder. To learn a language that was the spoken word of your ancestors is a very special place to be. Níl sé riamh rómhall – *it's never too late.* Go on, léim isteach – *jump in;* bain sult as – *enjoy it;* déan níos mo botún – *make plenty of mistakes, but you will not regret it.*

At a young age, children are told how important our mother tongue is: that it's our first language; protected in the Constitution; and then some. Our next generation listens to the preaching at a young age – an age where children are open to new things, their minds wide open, their eyes and ears wide open. Suddenly, the sentiment turns sour. Irish becomes subject-based: defined by curriculum, defined by hours per week; segregated, isolated, separated, alone. I don't want to be on my own anymore. It's not good for me and it's not much craic to be honest.

● ● ● ● ● ● ●

My ten-year milestone is *anseo* – here. Ten years, plus eight in primary and six in secondary. That's twenty-four years in total brushing up on my Gaeilge. "If McHugh isn't able to speak it at this stage, he should try something else!". This is true, but at the same time I'm still learning new words, new expressions, and most of all being as inquisitive as ever.

My motivation for giving you an insight to our wonderful language was simply to let you know it can be done. Furthermore, I wanted to pass on my learnings in the hope that it might enable you to map out your learning journey. I never believed at the time that my initial misfortune would turn out to be the best gift a person could get.

Just the other morning, I was chatting to someone who resides in Drimnaraw not far from where I live. It stoked up memories of céilí dancing in Drimnaraw Hall where I 'cloustered' about on the dance floor to 'The Siege of Venice' and 'Show the Donkey'. Back in the day, my understanding was rather skewed in the form of 'The Siege of Ennis' and 'Shoe the Donkey!' While I'm at it I'll mention my confusion around the Kenny Rogers song 'Four Hungry Children and a Crop in the Field' which I interpreted as 'Four Hundred Children and a Crock in the Field'. I had enough problems with *Béarla*, never mind the Gaeilge! Whatever hopes and ambitions my mother had for me all those years ago, she learned very early on that it wasn't going to be on the dance floor.

When I hear a place name, all these decades later, I head straight for Logainm.ie, where I've a path worn. Drimnaraw has this entry: 'Droim na Rátha – The ridge of the ring fort' (Logainm.ie #14346). Little did I know back then that when we were involved in the 'Siege of Venice' it was taking place in such an historical and unique location. My curiosity and appetite for knowledge around place names goes hand-in-glove with my ongoing Irish language journey.

Like politics, learning a language is a marathon not a sprint. The Irish equivalent of a marathon is *turas mór fada* – a long journey. My first Irish interview was *as Béarla*. Sorcha Ní Riada from TG 4 was in

Caibidil 40: *Praise the day in the evening*

situ. I had never met her before, and she was probably more shocked than anyone when I replied to her *as Béarla*. You see, in hindsight, I could have winged it. I could have had a pre prepared speech and stuck to it. I could have spent my entire tenure as *Aire na Gaeltachta* carrying out this charade and going through the motions. It would have been wrong and would have been dishonest. Sorcha always treated me fairly which I'll always be grateful for.

Are good things happening? Incredible things are happening. Furthermore, there is a shift in respect in the form of being seen as 'cool' as is evidenced on a Saturday morning listening to many radio hosts using a mix of *Gaeilge agus Béarla*: *moladh* – praise – to all the presenters and DJs who continue to drive an incredibly positive agenda. Irish-language enthusiast and RTÉ broadcaster John Creedon has led the way by introducing Gaeilge in a relevant, fun and informing manner. John accompanied me in the car via the radio on my late-night trips from the hills to the capital back in my Senate days. His enthusiasm, curiosity and love for the Irish language is never found wanting. A quick story. I left Mary and Michael Whoriskey's house in An Cheathrú Chaol late one night en route to Dublin. I stopped off in Monaghan for a cup of tea to help me stay awake. While there, I sent a message to John acknowledging his choice of music and I let him know that he was helping to keep me awake on my journey from Kerrykeel to Dublin. I signed off as Senator Joe. John won't remember this, but he responded with the following: 'I'm after getting a lovely text from Senator Joe O'Toole travelling from Kerrykeel to Dublin. God, I wonder what he was doing in Kerrykeel?' Joe O'Toole would have been oblivious to this too at home in his bed.

If we can collectively make the language more visible and create that awareness the big shift will happen. *Ní sheachaíonn an tsúil an rud nach bfheiceann siad* – the eye avoids what it cannot see. Many organisations work hard at making our beautiful language visible. *Dia go deo libh uilig.*

Beidh Tú Alright: *Mol an lá um thráthnóna*

WHAT FOR THE FUTURE?

Ireland is a different country to the one a lot of us were brought up in. We are a confident nation, a proud member of the European Union and a culturally diverse nation. Go into any school the length and breadth of Ireland and you will meet a range of people with their unique linguistic and cultural heritage.

Can we learn lessons from our own colonial history and the suppression of our own language over the centuries? Anna Dillon looks at this area in 'An exploration of linguistic neo-colonialism through educational language policy – an Irish perspective'.

This is an excellent paper that critically examines the importance of home languages in the curriculum. If we look at the history of our own language and how *Béarla* has dominated the conversation for centuries, we should take a critical look at census figures and see how we as a nation can help protect the home languages of the many immigrants who have arrived on our shores. As a fully-fledged member of the EU, it is important to continue to promote Spanish, French, German and Italian. The range of curricular languages on the Leaving Certificate has expanded to include Japanese, Arabic, Ancient Greek, Hebrew Studies and Russian. The NCCA[102] has also introduced new specifications for the development of Leaving Certificate Lithuanian, Polish, Portuguese and Mandarin Chinese. A Leaving Certificate exam in Ukrainian has been introduced as a non-curricular language.

> It was announced in April 2019, that a three-year CLIL pilot project will begin in Ireland in September 2019. The Minister for Education, Joe McHugh, proposed that 'the project will work exclusively on promoting Irish by learning various curricular areas through our language' (Ireland, 2019). Evidently, this project is arriving at a crucial time as the latest inspectorate states that it

---

[102] National Council for Curriculum Assessment.

found 28% of Irish lessons are 'less than satisfactory', compared to just 4% of maths classes, and 7% of English classes (Ireland, 2016).[103]

Momentum is now needed for the implementation of CLIL which has been doubly trialled at primary school through the 2016 pilot and both primary and secondary in the 2019 pilot.

Áine Furlong has written a very interesting paper, *Teanga mar mhodh cumarsáide agus teanga mar iompróir an chultúir* – Language as communication and language as carrier of culture. I would recommend this read to policy makers in the Department of Education. I believe there's an enthusiasm within the Department of Education to lead on the fact that identity should be at the centre of the Gaeilge learning philosophy. I'm hoping this opportunity won't be missed.

I don't have the answers. I'm not an expert – far from it. I still struggle with grammar. I use English words when I'm stuck. But here's the thing, *Bím ag caint Gaeilge achan/chuile/gach lá* – I'm speaking Irish every day. When some people meet me, they say, 'you're the fella with the Irish' or 'you're the fella with no Irish', which I take as an enormous compliment on both counts. We all have the Irish. It's just a matter of rekindling the flame and looking at the learning in a different light. My primary motivation was to learn Irish as a means to an end for the purpose of my job. While doing this, I realised that my richest learnings were coming from things I love and like. I like my history and my place – this is the space where I do most of my learning. Speaking gives me the opportunity to practise the 'flow' and that's important. I developed a love for my language through the things that make me happy. My family, my home, and my friends, my community and my country. YOU, and only you know the things that you love. If you

---

[103] Anna M. Dillon, 'The CLIL Approach in Irish Primary Schools: A Multilingual Perspective', Faculty of Education, Mary Immaculate College University of Limerick.

start there, you won't go wrong – *tús maith leath na hoibre* – and in the words of our Irish supporters many moons ago, 'give it a lash Jack.'

Dála an scéil – By the way

If you've managed to get this far, I just want to thank you. I hope you have enjoyed the read. More importantly, I do hope that the time you have put in has helped you create an awareness around the language. Try and retain this awareness and remember, the eye avoids what it doesn't see. I wish you well on your own journey. You have taken the first step. *Ádh mór, bí mór agus saoi mór.*

Bail ó Dhia ar an obair.

Focail na seachtaine – Words of the week

1. *Ag teacht aníos* – coming up
2. *Cumarsáid* – communication
3. *Ní sheachaíonn an tsúil an rud nach bfheiceann siad* – the eye avoids what it doesn't see
4. *Cultúr* – culture
5. *Créideamh láidir* – conviction/strong belief
6. *Turas mór fada* – a long journey
7. *An todhchaí* – the future

Do thuras féin – Your journey

1. _____
2. _____
3. _____
4. _____

Caibidil 40: *Praise the day in the evening*

5. _____
6. _____
7. _____

> Teanglann.ie phrase:
> D*'fhág sé scéala* – He left word

Seven Steps to Speaking Gaeilge Fluently

Céim a haon - *Step 1*

Céim ar chéim

Step by step

MAKE THE DECISION, MAKE IT YOURS AND DON'T LOOK BACK

> *'I'd love to go back to learning Irish, but I don't have the time.'*
> *'I'd love to be able to speak Irish, but I'm no good at languages.'*
> *'We weren't taught to speak Irish properly.'*

The above reflections are from my own words pre-2014. This was before I was thrown into the cement mixer. In London, more than two decades earlier I was a close associate of the cement mixer and a fully-fledged hod carrier.[104] I filled the hod brick by brick. I got there though. We all get there in the end. The same rule applies to a language journey. Brick by brick with no pressure, no deadlines and no ganger man dishing out the orders, with as many tea breaks and extended lunches as you want. Liquid lunches if you wish. The beauty with

---

[104] A labourer who carries the materials in a hod for a plasterer, bricklayer, etc.

learning is that there's no end game, no end product and no cutting the ribbon. You are your own architect, designer and hod carrier all in one. Unlike me, nobody is monitoring you or, as my youngest often says after I impart some amazing worldly advice, 'that's interesting!'. You're in charge and you decide the rules. For all you adults, develop your own language journey, make it yours. *Imigh leat ar nós na gaoithe* – fly like the wind!

Set goals of course. If you're in transition in work or in life, setting a long-term goal is a good first step. Don't put a time frame on the long-term ambition to speak fluently. There is no end line. Believe me. Work back from your long-term goal and put a plan in place which is realistic from a monthly, weekly and daily point of view. Compartmentalise your learning. *Nuair a théim a luí san oíche ...*[105] – when I go to bed at night ... be grateful for the good things that happened that day – as Gaeilge. A few prayers as Gaeilge before you go to sleep, perchance? A chance to work on your past tense and go back over your day? Start at the beginning. *D'éirigh mé ar maidin ag a seacht a chlog* – I got up at 7 a.m. *D'ith mé mo chéad lón ag leath uair i ndiaidh/tar éis a seacht* – In the morning, it's hard to beat a song in the shower. That's where I learned 'My Donegal', *as Béarla agus as Gaeilge*, in the full knowledge nobody could hear me. The first greeting of the day can be hard work, depending on how open people are at that time of day. Communication can be on the blink. It's usually a brief engagement. *An raibh codladh sámh agat?* Did you have a peaceful sleep? To which you hope the reply will be, *Cinnte, bhí codladh sámh agam* – sure, I did have a peaceful sleep. However, there's no need for all interaction as Gaeilge to be both so formal. It can be as follows: *Codladh sámh? Bhí.* Simple as that. *Ar bhain tú sult as an scánnan aréir? Bhain mé* – Did you enjoy the pictures last night? I enjoyed it. Or simply, *'bhain'!*

---

[105] The opening line of the song 'Na Scadán'.

Most of the engagement *as Béarla* is brief and truncated, bordering on rude at times. The extent of participation from the customer when ordering fuel could be as minimal as 'twenty euro' or 'fill it up'. Whereas as Gaeilge our learnings were a lot more formal and polite.

Maybe this was a good thing. *Ar mhiste leat fiche euro a chur isteach sa charr le do thoil?* – Would you mind putting twenty euro into the car please? I'm not advocating rudeness; however, I am advocating making life easier. Another venue where it's important to dispense with the formalities is at the bar. *As Béarla*, orders continue to be abbreviated. Two stout, two GTI's, two vodkas, a coke and a 7up please. The brevity is all important on two fronts. The music may be loud, and the bar person will move to the next customer if you delay. So here goes for the formalised extended order as Gaeilge. *Gabh mo leithscéal, ba mhaith liom deochanna a ordú le do thoil, dhá Phionta Guinness, dhá Jin agus tonaic, dhá vodca, buidéal cóc agus buidéal seacht suas, go raibh maith agat,* as the server disappears. Rule of thumb: don't get caught up in formalising every sentence. Listening to the native Irish speakers communicate with each other puts pay to the formalities. In fact, when they are '*stucáilte*', like the tonic water in the gin, the odd *focal Béarla* is thrown in for good measure.

Own your language learning curve. You can deviate, reverse, fast forward, skip, rotate, delete, ignore, adapt, change, include, pause and re-shape at whatever stage you want on this journey. Or go back to the beginning as many times as you want. Own it and make it yours *agus bain sult as* – enjoy, literally, 'take enjoyment from it'. That's the different psyche that underpins the language: it's up to you to 'take' enjoyment from experiences and it's an encouragement to have an active participation in life. Aodh Ó Duibheannaigh's song 'An Tráthnóna sin Fadó' has a beautiful line, '*ag baint sórú as an dúlra …*', meaning taking enjoyment from nature or quite possibly 'paying attention to nature'. It is pronounced 'sórú' but might come from '*sonra*' – meaning detail or, in the plural, *sonraí* – particulars.

Beidh Tú Alright: *Céim ar chéim*

Make a start. Commit to making that start. Be accountable to you. You are the '*cigire*' – inspector. If you think it's going to be difficult, think of this Chinese Proverb – 'To get through the hardest journey we need take only one step at a time, but we must keep on stepping.'

Céim a dó - *Step 2*

Tiocfaidh an fhírinne amach ar deireadh

The truth comes out in the end

THINK AS GAEILGE. EVERY WAKING HOUR

Think as Gaeilge when you wake up first thing in the morning until your head hits the pillow at night. When you're on your own, keep thinking as Gaeilge. That's when you can make good ground. This is quality time for you, yourself, and your language muscle. Get talking to yourself as Gaeilge. The litmus test for when you know you're in this zone is when you sneeze. Straight after a sneeze you have nano seconds before you say excuse me. You won't hear the native speaker saying *gabh mo leithscéal*. You will hear '*Dia linn*', which is usually said by the sneezer or anyone else in the vicinity. That's your target. Next time you sneeze see what happens. If it's you who sneezes, '*Dia liom*'; if it's your friend, '*Dia leat*'; and if you want to give everyone a blessing it's '*Dia linn*'. Or in Tiny Tim's words – "God bless us, everyone."

Your daily interactions become a word pronunciation opportunity. A simple greeting: *Dia duit. Dia is Muire duit.* A simple thank you: *go raibh maith agat.* And the weather, don't forget about the weather! From rough to beautiful in a day: *lá garbh inné/lá galánta inniu.* And, of course, an odd compliment thrown into someone who is getting younger by the day: *tá tú ag iarraidh níos óige.* Lastly, a good response to *an bhfuil tú go maith* – are you well? in the middle of your work is: *tá mo dhroim briste* – my back is broke!

GRAMADACH AGUS INSCNE – GRAMMAR AND GENDER

Let's talk about the grammar! No need to overthink it, and where it all went wrong, but we do need to talk about it. Grammar and gender rules go hand in glove. On the same trajectory as tea and toast or night and day. No different to many of the European languages, some words are masculine, and others are feminine, which ultimately impacts on the grammar. There is no other way around this. You need to learn them. *Oíche fhada* – long night – takes a *séimhiú* as 'oíche' is feminine and *lá fada* – long day – does not as '*lá*' is masculine. You got that, right? Followed by *na laethanta fada* – the long days. No change with the fada, so all good in the hood. Contrary to the night following day, there is a twist. There's always a twist, but don't go beating yourself up. Teanglann.ie does a great job in explaining what happens when the definite article (*an* – the) appears before the word, i.e. the genitive case. Still with me? Don't leave me, Tayto! *lá fada* changes to *an lae fhada*. Spot the two changes? And we leave it there. Don't over complicate things. Small chunks at a time and use your inner voice to repeat. Repetition is *rí* – king – or *banríon* – queen.

The Portuguese language also differentiates between feminine and masculine but in a less cryptic way:

- *Obrigado* – thank you (masculine singular)
- *Obrigada* – thank you (feminine singular)

Obrigado to Cecelia *ó Bhrasaíl* who taught me some Portuguese during Covid-19.

The English language can cause all sorts of difficulties when it comes to gender, which is ironic as the language itself doesn't differentiate on gender grounds. You will hear inanimate objects constantly being referred to as 'her' as opposed to 'it', from cars to tractors. This doesn't tend to happen with Gaeilge. 'Keep 'er lit' is another expression that has crept in but if you go to Gaoth Dobhair you will hear the equivalent expression *coinnigh a' gabháil* – keep going.

Grammar and gender are two important cornerstones of the Irish language. Don't get too hung up on them at the beginning of your language journey. This is meant to be fun, and believe me, when you get the hang of speaking Gaeilge, you will enjoy the grammar bit too. I cannot believe I'm after saying that!

The *ciorcal comhrá* (Irish conversation group)[106] is a great concept which enable to meet on an informal basis under no pressure. The group itself takes the lead and that dictates whether it's all Irish, bilingual or otherwise. There will be a *ciorcal comhrá* in your community. If not, this is your golden moment. You could set one up?! A group of like-minded people on the language front with the added attraction of a bit of craic and a cup of tae. Remember this though, you're not part of this just to learn from others. The group setting enables you to be a contributor on the learning journey. That is education at its best.

---

[106] If you happen to be near the ATU Colab on a Wednesday morning at 10.30, Bairbre from the Leitir Ceanainn Líonra will have a *fáilte* for you.

Céim a trí - *Step 3*

An té a bhfuil builín aige gheobhaidh sé scian a ghearrfaidh é

Whoever has a loaf will get a knife to cut it

MAKE THE LANGUAGE RELEVANT TO WHAT YOU DO

If you like singing, then there's your play. If you're no good at singing, but like singing, close the bathroom door and knock yourself out. If you've a son, daughter, niece, nephew, grandchild, then sing bedtime songs. 'Óró, sé do bheatha' bhaile' is always a favourite. Or make one up, even if it's all over the shop grammatically in the beginning. 'Twinkle, twinkle little star, how I wonder how you are.' Remember, Gaeilge is not an exact translation to or from *Béarla*. Have a bit of fun with your own translation. You can keep the 'twinkle twinkle' and be sure to use the beautiful word for star – *réalta*. In Galway you'll hear *manín* or *buachailín* as terms of endearment. The same goes for *bóín* – little cow – and you may know an Irish girl called *Réiltín* – little star. '*Twinkle, twinkle réiltín beag.*' The 'how I wonder how you are?' can be a trickier space. However, in Gaoth Dobhair you'll hear '*ag wondráil*' thrown into sentences here and there. '*Twinkle, twinkle réaltín beag. Táim ag wondráil, bhfuil tú go breá?* If you want to be more accurate there's a variety of published books in this area over the past few years.

Sport and exercise is an area where Gaeilge can be introduced on a gradual basis. There's a ready-made class waiting for you to join at the Falcarragh parkrun in Dún na nGall. When? Every Saturday morning at 9.30 a.m. Run, jog or walk there's plenty of participants with plenty of Irish who would be more than willing to help you along. They have invested in a main stage and loud hailer to start the race which is like a scene out of the Michael Collins movie. While Fál Carrach is in the Gaeltacht, there are many other parkruns promoting Gaeilge outside the Gaeltacht. A shout out to Letterkenny parkrun for their endeavours.

The Pop-Up Gaeltacht phenomenon is another option to immerse yourself in the language. It was the intention of the founders that even the less confident of those speakers should have a public space in which they could converse at their ease.

Pick your spot. You know the things you enjoy and like doing. And, if you feel there's no outlet in your world that enables the learning of Gaeilge, maybe be that 'acorn' and start something novel with Gaeilge at the heart of it.

Céim a ceathair - *Step 4*

Is fanách an áit a bhaighfeá gliomach

It's rare the place you'll find lobsters

BUILD UP YOUR STÓR FOCAL – VOCABULARY

If you like gardening, start with vocabulary related to that. If you like climbing or walking, there's an abundance of amazing words you will meet on your daily travels. There's no end to the *bailiúchán* – collection – of words you can garner.

- *Ag cócaireacht* – cooking
- *Ag dreapadóireacht* – climbing
- *Ag garraíodóireacht* – gardening
- *Grianghrafadóireacht* – photography
- *Ag tumadóireacht* – diving
- *Ag taisteal* – travelling
- *Ag feirmeoireacht* – farming

- *Ag aclaíocht* – exercising
- *Ag staidéar* – studying
- *Ag damhsa/ag rince* – dancing

A couple of years back I came across an outdoor display by the Design and Crafts Council, Ireland, in Kilkenny City, celebrating fifty years of craft in Ireland. Some words that hadn't been on my radar till then: *seodra agus miotal* – jewellery and metal; *troscán* – furniture; *ceirmeacht* – ceramics; *adhmadóireacht* – woodwork. Every day is a learning day and the more opportunities where we can see both *Gaeilge* and *Béarla* side by side in equal prominence, the better.

On your springtime walks you'll pass the *lus an chromchinn* – daffodil. Finding the meaning behind the flower is an adventure in itself: herb of the crooked head! The beautifully pronounced *nóinín* – daisy – is one of my favourites. *An Fraoch Corcra* – the purple heather – graces this wee island rock of ours, on the sides of our *sléibhte agus na cnoic* – mountains and the hills. Some years you will see more *corcra* than others. Your *fón poca* will be in your – well you guessed it – your pocket. Foclóir.ie is just an *ordóg* – thumb – away when translating from *Béarla* to *Gaeilge*. Teanglann.ie and Téarma.ie are also just a touch away when translating *ó Ghaeilge* (notice how *Gaeilge* changes to *Ghaeilge* when a preposition [*ó* – from] precedes it). The access to these electronic resources is a tremendous asset on your language journey. *Ní trí thimpiste a thit sé sin amach* – that didn't happen by accident. There has been a consistent drive on the part of language groups, to provide language rights to Irish citizens. This has culminated in the provision of fingertip online resources for everyone to avail of. *Fiontar agus Scoil na Gaeilge* at DCU is internationally recognised for the quality of programmes it delivers through the medium of Irish, and for the innovative nature of the teaching, research and work of the academic staff and researchers on digital projects. *Maith sibh agus go raibh maith agaibh uilig.*

We live on an island surrounded by the sea. There's a lot happening out there. *Portáin agus gliomaigh* – crabs and lobsters; *míolta móra agus na siorcanna* – whales and sharks. This should get you started. Let your curiosity lead you to places you never knew existed. When you come across the caterpillar on the wall get the phone out and you'll be signposted to *'bolb'*.[107] Curious about the metamorphosis which will follow, key in 'butterfly' and you'll be presented with the beautiful *'féileacán'*. You're in charge of your learning journey. You decide on the vocabulary you want to learn. *Bain sult as.*

---

[107] You'll remember me combining *'tolg'* with *'bolg'* on the couch. I've a new addition now: the *bolb* crawled up on the *tolg* and jumped onto the *bolg*. A good tongue twister to help you on your way.

Céim a cúig - *Step 5*

Seachnaíonn súil ní nach bhfeiceann

The eye avoids what it doesn't see

OSCAIL DO SHÚILE — OPEN YOUR EYES

We've never had as much Gaeilge around us. From road signs to signage in/on public buildings. Familiarise yourself with these free resources. You will become so accustomed to recognising this rich arsenal of vocabulary that you will constantly seek them everywhere you go.

One place where I tried to avoid but had to face it head on was *Ospidéal Naomh Séamus* – Saint James's Hospital. I was one of the lucky ones. I'm on the *bealach mo leasa* – the road to recovery. Through my journey of recovery, the signage offered me a distraction from the worry and the boredom. I quickly ran out of signs!

Back to the road signs. They are a resource onto themselves. I know they also drive people crazy when there is no sense to the place names. I do get that. *Tuigim* – I understand. Brian Friel's *Translations* does a great job in trying to set the context and is a play worth seeing if you get a chance, even if you've seen it before. Logainm.ie is a helpful resource in finding out that little bit extra about a place, particularly the handwritten notes. It will also give you a good insight into the lack of logic that went into the translation of our place names. That translation is part of our history now and I think we have both an individual responsibility and an opportunity to find out more and delve into the real meaning behind our place names. Pollwaddyuisce off the coast of Árainn Mhór Island is a good place to start. It's a boat journey well worth taking. Jerry Earley will jump at the opportunity to bring you if he's not too busy singing songs. Michael McHugh will take you on an up and close inspection of the caves and stacks. The place name has been anglicised to one word that makes no sense. However, when the phonetically similar Gaeilge name is explained you will be enlightened. *Poll an Mhadaidh Uisce* – hole of the water dog, i.e. the otter. In fairness, the translation considered the Ulster pronunciation for dog. Not *madra* but *madadh*, which leads to the lovely sound for fox – *madadh rua*, which down the country is *sionnach*. A visit to Pilltown in *Cill Chainnigh* – Kilkenny – got my curiosity going. *Baile an Phoill*,[108] on first inspection could mean 'the town of the hole'. Not very complimentary to the good people of Pilltown! But here the word *poll* is a loanword from English 'pill' and actually refers to a tributary of the River Suir. *Baile an Phoill*/Pilltown in Waterford contains the same word, referring to a sea inlet. After speaking to one of the natives, Mark O'Doherty, it was explained that this location was the scene of the Battle of Pilltown (1462), resulting in many casualties on the Butler side. The Irish word for blood is *fuil*. It has been suggested that the translation experiment went for the phonetics, using the sound of

---

[108] *Fuar Thoill*/Cold Hollow is a mountain in the highlands of Scotland. So, here's a suggestion – I stress suggestion. Does the topography of Pilltown lend itself to the name *Baile an Thoill* – town of the hollow? Incidentally, there is a place in Cork called *Fuarchoill*/Cold Wood (Logainm #8980). Another suggestion for discussion: town of the wood.

Céim a cúig – Step 5: *The eye avoids what it doesn't see*

'ph' in *phoill* rather than 'f' in *fuil*. However, a close examination of the evidence shows that any attempt to connect the *fuil* – blood – lost in the battle to the place name Pilltown is purely down to the common tendency to reinterpret place names. The battle of 1462 is referred to in the Irish annals as 'cath(a) Baile an Phuill' (see Logainm.ie #128244). Furthermore, the town of the blood would be *Baile na Fola* in Irish, which is clearly not the name of the place. Further up the road in Dún na nGall, Cnoc Fola (Logainm.ie #14497) has a note: 'Cnoc Fola "hill of the blood" – Here the celebrated Balor was slain if tradition be a true chronicler'. Once again, a reminder that the 'n' is not pronounced in Donegal, it's 'cruck'!

The record can be set straight across the country in relation to place names. Where better to do this than in the classroom, where local knowledge and wisdom can be tapped into. Many teachers are already doing this in the education system, the perfect place to make good ground. When I experienced these moments of clarity about the proper name for places it was magical. And when I arrived at dead ends, I didn't stop. I turned around and went at it again from a different angle.

Staring at the ceiling while lying on a hospital bed wasn't on my bucket list. However, my recovery was aided and abetted by excellent care from the care team in Dublin and Letterkenny. Handwritten scribbles from my children were just the tonic. During those days and hours back in early 2021, I got stuck into writing this book. It gave me something to pass the time. 'Something to pass the time?' If time ever needed encouragement! My main motivation for writing this book was based on a call I made back in 2014, when I asked people to join me on my journey. Many did, and I still get random strangers coming up to me to this day to let me know about their own journey. Thank you random strangers for coming up to me. You kept me going. This book offered me an opportunity to reflect, which helped me during my transition from politics to a different life. We all face different transitions in our life at some stage. Health and work transitions were my two.

I believe I was prepared for these life changes as a direct consequence of the confidence I gained from my Irish language journey. I'm hoping that the words I penned over the past few years will encourage you to make the same decision and follow through on a journey of discovery and joy. What will be the title of your book? In the meantime, as you ponder, make every day count.

Céim a sé - *Step 6*

Ní hé lá na báistí, lá na bpáistí

The rainy day isn't the children's day

LEARN YOUR HISTORY

The Irish language and Irish history are inextricably linked, and one cannot survive without the other. Bonnie and Clyde, Hansel and Gretal, and Kane and Abel are stories that wouldn't exist without the other. I believe Gaeilge has been separated from the history of Ireland for too long. A reunion is badly needed: Gaeilge explained. During my short eighteen-month sojourn as Minister for Education, I advocated for a short course on the history of the Irish language as part of the Junior Cycle. I hope that one day this will be introduced with the possibility of introducing it in primary school. I'm aware that many teachers already do this to set the context in their teaching of the Irish language. My main energies at the time were focused on ensuring history was retained as a compulsory subject for Junior Cycle. Having achieved this, I started the conversation about adding this to the curriculum. I'm hopeful progress will be made. This would be an add-on to the existing curriculum and would not displace or replace the rightful core place of Gaeilge as it stands today.

Start with your name: what does it mean? Where did the name come from? Or why did it change?

Next, look at your townland. How did it get its name? What is the meaning behind the place name and how does it compare to the anglicised version? In most cases there will only be a phonetic correlation. However, while the anglicised version is a source of irritation for some, it is still part of our history. By developing a deeper understanding of this period in our history it may trigger an incentive for people to learn more and develop a deeper appreciation. Through recognising the efforts our ancestors went to, in naming our town lands appropriately, in the first place, would be a rewarding exercise for sure.

What went on in our townlands? Significant events? A battle or two? And don't forget our rich Irish mythology. Jennifer Doherty McLaughlin, from Clonmany, has worked extensively on the social history, genealogy, and place name history of Inis Eoghain and beyond. If you ever make it to Clonmany, there is a rock in a field with the handprint of Fionn Mac Cumhaill. Remember the legend of the Giant's Causeway and the story of the Salmon of Knowledge along the banks of the Boyne? And don't forget the memorable stories of Fionn's son, Oisín, from Tír na nÓg. There are stories and legends in your own backyard that are worth exploring. The one in Clonmany is the one that always intrigued me. I hope to see that handprint one day. Logainm.ie has historical name references dating back to 1302 for 'Cluain Maine (Logainm.ie #15379) in Inis Eoghain Thoir'. There are also archival records which are helpful in trying to establish the meaning behind the place name and its connection with Naomh Columba.

I met many people on my language journey, and they all had a story to tell about their place, or even my place. Born in 1971, I was raised as a Claggan man. Claggan was my home in the townland of Dún Mór.

Only recently, a fellow parishioner, Michael Cullen, reminded me that Claggan comes from the Gaeilge word *cloigeann* – head. I remember my childhood 'snow days' sliding down the crown of our field on a 5-5-10 fertilizer bags with my brothers and sisters. We started at the 'head' of the field and ended up in a 'heap' at the bottom! Now it's the turn of my children, nephews and nieces when and if the *sneachta* comes.

Discovering new facts and uncovering the meaning of words was critical in terms of the building blocks needed on my language journey to *cumasaigh* – empower – *fás* – grow and *forbairt* – develop. As you map out your own learning journey in a planned fashion, don't be shy about reaching out for help, which is out there for sure. *Ádh mór* – good luck!

Céim a seacht - *Step 7*

Bíonn súil leis an bhfarraige

There's hope with the sea [Hope springs eternal][109]

COINNIGH DEARFACH — KEEP POSITIVE

I can't thank people enough for chatting to me as Gaeilge over the past ten years. That is where the war was won for me. Former Secretary General in the Department of Education Seán Ó Foghlú engaged with me as Gaeilge during our weekly one-to-one meetings. This had a knock-on effect during my interaction with other work colleagues. Creating that language awareness in our working environment had a positive *tionchar* – impact – even if it meant helping with some of my

---

[109] *Bitesize Irish* unearthed this proverb for me. I love it. Since taking up sea swimming last January with the Splash & Dashers off Trá Mór, this proverb takes on a whole new significance.

Céim a seacht – Step 7: *There's hope with the sea [Hope springs eternal]*

colleagues' children's *obair bhaile*! It was my pleasure, Derek! There's no shortage of Gaeilge speakers in the Department of Education, which was positive when meeting colleagues casually in the canteen and corridors. My time with my colleagues in the Chief Whip's office saw me reverting to my school teaching days. *An bhfuil tú i ndáiríre* – are you serious? – was one of our expressions learned in a very busy office faced with intermittent political challenges or 'hanlin's'! Informal meetings with former Attorney General Seamus Woulfe was a weekly opportunity to engage *as Gaeilge fosta* while discussing legislative matters.

Former Secretary General in Roinn na Gaeltachta Joe Hamill was also a source of great encouragement in the early days. He had a good understanding and appreciation that the best way to approach the growth of the language was through encouragement and pragmatic policy development.

My final formal political position was chair of the EU Affairs Committee, and I used every meeting as an opportunity to bring Gaeilge to the fore. GRMA Barry agus Fiona. I've never separated the language from what I do daily. Wherever you find yourself, be it in work or non-work related, you have an opportunity to lead the way and bring Gaeilge to the fore in your environment.

The good news is this – no rote learning. Discover where the words in your life come from, the meaning behind the words and how it is relevant to the world you live in. The seven words or phrases at the end of each chapter are *ag baint amach* – coming from – my life journey. Your words will be your *carraigeacha/clocha* – rocks/stones – which will assist you in building your *cairn* on the hill or mountain to your language goal. *Cloch i do láimh agus paidir i do chroí* – is a phrase the folk used when they put a stone on the burial cairns on their funeral trek across the mountain.[110] Up in the hills of Donegal,

---

[110] That came from Tomás Mac Seáin in Oileán Acla, via Séan Ó Coistealbha as An Spidéal.

mo sheacht ndícheall is 'my seven bests', so all you can do is *do sheacht ndícheall* – 'your seven bests'. We can only do our best.

Staying positive is easier said than done. The real world of life happens when we are busy making other plans. Things can upset the apple cart. Relationships, health, family and work are the common landing zones when things go wrong. This is the real world. Doing something new and different with a sense of curiosity may help you during these tough times.

Gaeilge is incorporated into my life. It's not a pastime. It's not a hobby. It's who I am. It's where I come from. And, it has shown me the road home.

General note regarding Logainm.ie

Bunachar Náisiúnta na hÉireann/The Placenames Database of Ireland is maintained by Fiontar & Scoil na Gaeilge (DCU) in order to facilitate the research of An Brainse Logainmneacha/The Placenames Branch at the Department of Tourism, Culture, Arts, Gaeltacht, Sports and Media – the official placename researchers of the State – and to disseminate its toponymic data to the public. Each placename entry has a unique ID number, e.g. **Baile na nGallóglach**/*Millford* (#1416620). The recommended Irish forms found on Logainm.ie are labelled either '*deimhnithe*/validated' or '*neamhdheimhnithe*/non-validated'. The first label denotes placenames whose legal Irish versions have been declared in placenames orders made by the Minister under Section 5 of the Official Languages Act 2003 (see https://www.logainm.ie/en/resources/orders); the second denotes interim recommendations made based on current available evidence. (Logainm.ie also maintains a repository of the official Irish forms of street names, estate names, road names, etc., currently in use; note that the Irish and English forms of these names are solely the responsibility of the relevant local authority.) Other proposed explanations and translations, for example the suggestions made by John O'Donovan during the course of the first Ordnance Survey in the 19th century, are also found among the archival records shown on Logainm.ie. However, although these notes can be of historical interest they are frequently superseded by modern research; therefore, they should not be taken to carry the imprimatur of An Coiste Logainmneacha/Placenames Committee or An Brainse Logainmneacha/Placenames Branch. Note finally that English spellings have nothing to do with the work of the Placenames Branch, which only concerns the Irish versions of placenames.

Appendix/ *Aguisín*

My 11-a-Side Irregular Verbs Football Team

Goalkeeper	Beir [to catch]	Shay Given
Right full-back	Feic [to see]	Seamus Coleman
Left full-back	Ith [to eat]	Paolo Maldini
Sweeper	Tabhair [to give]	Franco Baresi
Centre-half	Tar [to come]	Paul McGrath
Centre defending midfielder	Faigh [to get]	Roy Keane
Centre-midfield	Abair [to say]	John Breslin
Right midfield	Déan [to do]	Jean Tigana
Left midfield	Clois [to hear]	Andy Townsend
Striker	Bí [to be]	Amber Barrett
Forward	Téigh [to go]	Tyler Toland